D0759376

THE PENTAGON'S BATTLE
FOR THE AMERICAN MIND

THE PENTAGON'S BATTLE FOR THE AMERICAN MIND

The Early Cold War

LORI LYN BOGLE

Texas A&M University Press ⚜ College Station

Bogle, Lori Lyn.
The Pentagon's battle for the American mind : the early Cold War /
Lori Lyn Bogle.—1st ed.
p. cm.—(Texas A&M University military history series ; no. 97)
Includes bibliographical references and index.
ISBN 1-58544-378-6 (cloth : alk. paper)
1. United States—Armed Forces—History—20th century.
2. United States—Armed Forces—Political activity—History—
20th century. 3. Civil-military relations—United States—History—
20th century. 4. Church and state—United States—History—20th
century. 5. United States—Religion—1945–1960. 6. Civil
religion—United States—History—20th century. 7. Cold War.
8. Evangelicalism—United States—History—20th century.
9. United States—Politics and government—1945–1989.
10. Conservatism—United States—History—20th century.
I. Title. II. Texas A&M University military history series ; 97.
UA23.B567   2004
322'.5'097309045—dc22   2004005987

This book is dedicated

to Stella (Graalfs) Johnston,

the most creative person I know.

Contents

Illustrations

Preface

The idea for *The Pentagon's Battle for the American Mind* came while I was sitting in Prof. Randall B. Woods's course on American foreign policy at the University of Arkansas. I had recently decided to concentrate on the social and cultural dimensions of diplomatic history and was intrigued by his lecture on domestic influences on early Cold War policy makers. In particular, his statement that a short-lived alliance existed between members of the radical right and some high-ranking military officers who sought to build grassroots public support for their conservative domestic and international policies through a series of anticommunism seminars struck me as odd. Why would the military, the epitome of law and order and presumably outside the mainstream of politics, align itself with political extremists? Who authorized these anticommunism seminars? Why did they end? Finally, did this alliance ever threaten civilian control of the military?

Finding the answers to these questions took me a considerable distance away from diplomacy into the field of social and cultural military history. What I discovered was something that now seems pretty obvious to me: From the foundation of the American Republic, the armed forces have played a central role in defining and shaping the ideal of the American character.

My investigation is richer as a result of the aid of a number of individuals and organizations. The Harry S. Truman and Franklin D. Roosevelt Presidential Libraries, the Mary Hudgins Dissertation Fellowship (University of Arkansas), and the U.S. Naval Academy all provided financial aid. Numerous libraries and archives provided research assistance. I especially want to thank Andrea Cantwell, Beth Juhl, and Michael Dabrishus of the Mullins Library at the University of Arkansas for their expertise and friendship. In addition, I want to express my appreciation to the staffs of the U.S. Army Military History Institute at Carlisle Barracks, Pennsylvania; the Naval Historical Center in Washington, D.C.; the Library of Congress; the Truman, Eisenhower, and Franklin D. Roosevelt libraries; the Seeley G. Mudd Library at Princeton University; Valley Forge National Park and the Freedoms Foundation Archives in Valley Forge, Pennsylvania; the Teachers College at Columbia University; the Union Theological Seminary in New York, the Moody Bible Institute in Chicago; and the Biblical Counseling Foundation in Palm Springs, California. I also wish to thank copy editor Dale Wilson for his patience and encouragement during the manuscript's final preparation for publication.

I will always be grateful to my dissertation director, Prof. Randall B. Woods, for encouraging me to venture into uncharted areas. Professors Virginia Lass and Willard B. Gatewood, who mentored me throughout the project and through some difficult personal times, will always be among my dearest friends. I owe much to Don Orso, who guided me toward completion. I also wish to thank my colleagues at the Naval Academy and my friend Elizabeth Coelho for their belief in me and in the worth of this study. A special thanks goes to my husband, Dave Patterson, my four children and their spouses—William and Liorah Bogle, Kenneth and Beth Bogle, Katie and Hans Geineder, and Rebekah and Paul Pedersen—and my three stepdaughters—Autumn, Brianna, and Casey Patterson—for their love and support throughout this process. All of you have made me so proud. Finally, I want to express my love to my parents, Richard and Stella Johnston, and my brother Richard and sister Lesa for being with me from the beginning. Thanks, Mom, for raising me to think creatively. It has really made a difference.

THE PENTAGON'S BATTLE
FOR THE AMERICAN MIND

Introduction

FORGING THE AMERICAN CHARACTER

We are at another Valley Forge.... Today there remains no doubt
that the sinister forces of Communism are intent on world domi-
nation either by psychological aggression or armed aggression or
both. Nor is there any doubt that the purpose of their psychological aggression is to destroy Freedom by creating among free
peoples confusion, disunity and frustration so as to break their
will to resist.

—Valley Forge Park Commission Report, 1951

During the anxiety-ridden years of the early Cold War, the
U.S. military looked back to George Washington, com
manding general of the Continental Army during the
American Revolution, for inspiration and guidance on
how best to teach the American people the self-sacrifice and resolute will
it believed were essential to winning an ideological battle with international communism. Washington's leadership seemed an ideal example for
those in the military and other government agencies tasked with taking
an active role in shaping national character and will.

In the fall of 1776, the general reported to the Continental Congress that the rebel forces under his command were facing a crisis of character and organization: the ragtag militias were unprincipled, the regular army's junior officers lacked gentlemanly qualities, desertions and plundering were rampant, and an overall lack of cohesion and regularity among the troops hampered military operations.[1] Yet, according to popular lore, a mere year and a half later Washington led his long-suffering citizen soldiers—who he had transformed into efficient, enthusiastic, and ideologically sound warriors—from their winter quarters at Valley Forge, Pennsylvania. By attempting to revitalize the national character with the same sense of sacrifice, patriotic spirit, and divine purpose believed exhibited by the Continental Army at Valley Forge, the Cold War military hoped to counteract the laziness and lack of purpose critics perceived in post–World War II American society, thereby fostering a unified and determined national will and character that would deter the Soviets from further advances abroad and be resistant to communist infiltration at home.

The Department of Defense (DOD) based its Cold War character education policies on the long-cherished belief that the citizen soldier was the foundation of America's national character. While the weather had been relatively mild during that legendary winter of 1777–78, the battle-hardened army, unpaid since August and without adequate clothing, had indeed endured considerable deprivations and low morale.[2] The military during the late 1940s and 1950s attributed the Continental soldier's ultimate success to General Washington's program of political and religious indoctrination at Valley Forge. With considerable insight into the workings of a modern army and the needs of a new republic, the commanding general had argued that his men required far more than basic food, clothing, and drill practice to be fully operational and eager for combat. It was imperative that they also form a unified, disciplined, and "moral" force with a clearly defined reason to fight. Washington called for soldiers who were worthy of victory. He reasoned that an army of virtuous, duty-bound, and resolute patriots would not only gain public support, but also serve as the model for a national character and will once the rebel cause prevailed. By inculcating his men with an emerging civil religion—a religious nationalism that was the combination of republican virtues and a belief in divine purpose—Washington, like the officers of later generations who emulated his example, hoped to improve the character, organization, and operation of the military.[3]

Washington considered martial discipline and political education essential building blocks for a revitalized and well-ordered Continental Army. The inspector general, Baron Friedrich Wilhelm von Steuben, standardized training with Prussian drill formations and promoted a more informed soldiery by urging officers to explain why orders were given before expecting their men to carry them out. Early in the war, Washington had petitioned Congress for a portable printing press with which to provide a steady flow of information to his men that explained why they were fighting. He had selections from the Declaration of Independence and Tom Paine's *The Crisis* read aloud and discussed with the troops. "These are the times that try men's souls," Paine had written during the previous, even harsher winter. "The summer soldier and the sunshine patriot will, in this crisis, shrink from the service of their country; but he that stands it now, deserves the love and thanks of man and woman."[4] Even a theatrical performance glorifying civic virtue, Joseph Addison's *Cato*, was staged by and for Washington's men at Valley Forge.[5]

Another important component of a republican army, according to Washington, was its "virtuous" reputation. The general attempted to foster righteousness by encouraging private morality among the troops through religious instruction and his own personal example. Washington never claimed to be a Christian, but he did believe, as did many of the founding elite, that a moral code similar to that found in the Bible was essential to the reputation of a republican gentleman. In like manner, he reasoned that organized religion could be a means to improve the character of the common soldier, thereby reconciling the high principles of the American Revolution with the army's less-than-ideal public image.[6] Washington had earlier outlawed swearing—a vice he engaged in privately. He also directed the army's chaplains to incorporate revolutionary ideology into the mandatory prayer services. Ministers not only exhorted soldiers to do their duty, their presence at Valley Forge also helped stem widespread public criticism regarding the troops' continued drunkenness and use of profanity. Chaplains gave the Continental Army "the show," Washington argued, "if we are said to want the substance of Godliness."[7] Finally, through his own self-imposed discipline, Washington—by curbing his anger, vanity, ambition for personal glory, wenching, gambling, and cursing—intentionally shaped his public persona to that of the American Cincinnatus, a model of civic and personal virtue upon which his officers and men could pattern their own behavior.[8]

How effective Washington's efforts were in forming a national will and character (if such terms are even applicable at such an early stage of nation building) are certainly debatable. Throughout the war, political education and religious instruction were haphazard at best. Moreover, there is no evidence that the army ever displayed much uniform virtue, civic or moral.[9] Although Washington had considerable success portraying the ideal of republican character to his men by his own public example, there is no reliable means to determine if soldiers replicated those characteristics in their own lives. It is more likely that the arrival of adequate supplies and the coming of spring and fresh recruits, coupled with the watershed event of the war—the alliance with France announced in May, 1778—were far more crucial to improving morale. Nonetheless, Washington found Valley Forge "imagery" useful at winter's end. While the general expressed his appreciation to those patriots who had endured the encampment with "uncomplaining patience," proving that the Continental Army possessed the "spirit of soldiers and the magnanimity of Patriots," he admonished others who had threatened mutiny during the previous months, to repent of their "unmanly behavior" and to follow the "noble example" of their virtuous comrades.[10] Regardless of the true source, historians generally agree that the Continental Army left its winter encampment six months after its arrival with a renewed spirit and will to fight that carried it through several years of hostilities and ultimately to victory.[11]

The Cold War military was little concerned with debating whether or not Washington's use of religious nationalism contributed in any significant way to America's victory. Instead, they embraced the collective memory or myth of Valley Forge because it "worked" for their purposes. By the late 1940s and 1950s, patriotism and morality had become intertwined in an American civil religion that venerated Washington as its first prophet and called for other "Valley Forge experiences" to teach people the character of the founding generation. An idealized Washington, a Washington with strong, manly passions controlled by the strength of his devotion to God and to the republican cause, became the exemplar of civic virtue for Americans facing an atheistic communist foe to emulate.

Throughout American history, but especially during times of great stress and emergency, military and national leaders have used the Valley Forge myth and other precepts of American civil religion in an attempt to strengthen national unity and to fashion a resolute public will. While various government institutions have directly and indirectly manipulated the precepts of religious nationalism for their separate and collective purposes, it was the American military that assumed a leadership role in the process by the early twentieth century. Portraying itself as the guardian of national character and the repository of the values advocated by George Washington and other heroic historical figures, the U.S. armed forces used American civil religion to promote a version of national character that stressed self-sacrifice, obedience, and conformity—characteristics its leaders believed were essential to national security.

American Civil Religion

Also called the "Democratic Faith," the "American Creed," the "Culture Religion," and the "American Shinto," American civil religion is a viable operative national faith. It can be defined as the presumptuous, if popular, belief that God established the United States, the "city upon the hill," to carry out a specific mission; that is, to spread the blessings of democracy and free enterprise around the globe. While the military and other governmental agencies wielded religious nationalism with a heavy hand following World War II, civil religion overall has played a positive role in American history as an empowering principle and organizing mechanism essential for effective nation building. A collective national memory centered on the Revolution and supported by civil religion offered a means for the American people to construct their past in a meaningful way. Whether or not Americans possessed a divine mission to spread democracy, a firm conviction nonetheless has existed that such was their charge.

A number of scholars have viewed this extraecclesiastical concept as idolatrous, as an aberration, and as contrary to the founding principles of the United States, especially when considering the nineteenth-century expressions of Manifest Destiny and imperialism. Others, however, have described it as an effective means of nation building used by all political states to perform the vital function of creating unity.[12] Civil religion, according to historian Catherine L. Albanese, became the "cement for social bonding, the lubricant for cultural processes, [and] the common terms for public discourse" regarding what it meant to be moral and virtuous in the new American republic.[13]

In 1967, sociologist Robert Bellah described American civil religion as an authentic religious expression, separate from, but often quite compatible with, traditional religious denominations. No more or less idolatrous than other faiths, according to Bellah and a number of other scholars after him, civil religion contained its own set of sacred persons (presidents and military heroes), events (the American Revolution, Civil War, World War II), documents (the Constitution and the Emancipation Proclamation), days (the Fourth of July and Washington's Birthday), creeds (the Pledge of Allegiance and Code of Conduct), anthems ("The Battle Hymn of the Republic," "The Star-Spangled Banner," and "America the Beautiful"), monuments (the Lincoln Memorial and Mount Rushmore), and symbols (the Liberty Bell and the Stars and Stripes) that deified Americanism.

Bellah recognized that religious nationalism had its negative manifestations, but he was convinced that it also had performed valuable functions by providing the nation's diverse population with a common faith and by playing an instrumental role in the creation of an American identity and mission as "God's New Israel." The mixing of religion and politics created a framework for the United States to organize its pluralism and democratic freedoms. By providing the people with a heritage that seemingly set it apart from other countries, a unity (even if only imagined) connected each generation to the founders and linked the future to the past. Legends, monuments, symbols, and creeds infused with political and religious imagery all played an important role in the building of the American nation.[14]

Civil religion is a critical component of nation building. A state would be hard pressed to operate without some form of religious nationalism to organize a public will that binds its citizens to the government. Nazi Germany and Stalinist Russia employed individualized forms of civil religion to increase the power of their dictators at the expense and suffering of the people. Civil religionists in democracies generally manipulated the phenomenon for more constructive purposes—both to improve national security and to increase the citizens' well-being, no matter how narrow or expansive the definition of citizenship was at any particular time. It must be remembered, however, that civil religion itself is neither good nor bad, but rather is a tool that possesses the potential for producing positive and negative results (as judged by future generations). For example, current American society considers the historic exclusion of blacks and women from full citizenship as disgraceful and a blot on the national character. However, it was not until the public believed equal rights strengthened rather than weakened national unity that these groups were included in the parameters of civil religion. Religious nationalism builds nations. It does not divide them. Its power and durability lies in the fact that its precepts are in constant flux as it adapts to reflect prevailing national standards.

From the earliest days of the United States, American civil religion possessed a special temperament that set it apart from expressions of religious nationalism in other nations. This special temperament developed out of conflicts regarding the proper relationship of the federal government to the American citizen, as well as evangelical and reform impulses that emerged in society during the antebellum years. According to the founding generation's eighteenth-century vision of republicanism, freedom from arbitrary rule could be prevented and peace and social order preserved only by maintaining relatively weak governmental structures, thereby protecting the individual liberties of its virtuous citizenry.[15]

At the same time, many of those in the ranks of the power elite were contemptuous of the character of the common people. In the uncertain years following the Revolution, fear of anarchy and rebellion led to calls for strong federal measures to control the passions of the masses.[16] The framers of the Constitution sought to reconcile this contradiction by designing a flexible document that would serve the individual rights of American citizens while fostering greater national unity and loyalty to the federal government. Washington, Alexander Hamilton, James Madison, John Adams, and others reasoned that the future of the United States would rely on the will of the people—a people who could *learn* to willingly set aside their personal ambitions during times of national crisis for the greater good of the nation. Coercion could be kept to a minimum if Americans were taught the virtues of sacrifice, self-restraint, love of country, justice, obedience to law, deference to civil authority, industriousness, sobriety, prudence, modesty, piety, rationality, honesty, courage, manliness, and belief in individual liberty—all of which the founders considered necessary for the maintenance of public order and the preservation of the republican experiment.[17]

The revolutionary political elite—some deist, some Unitarian, and some holding to a variety of other beliefs that were not evangelical Christian in the sense the phrase is understood today—appeared to have fully understood the mythical proportions that their generation would play in the development of what Benjamin Franklin had earlier termed "Publick Religion."[18] They preached natural rights and civic virtue and encouraged the incorporation of spiritual dimensions into political/military events during the Revolution and early national period. During the 1830s and 1840s, theological developments during the Second Great Awakening strengthened themes of repentance, regeneration, and divine mission in the American psyche. By the close of the century, the secular and spiritual meshed in the rhetoric of turn-of-the-century reformers known as Progressives—people who hoped to rationalize government and American society with a unified code of values.[19]

By blurring distinctions between Enlightenment reason and biblical revelation, civil religionists from the Progressive Era to the Cold War cast the United States as a chosen nation whose public and private character had degenerated soon after the end of the Revolution, separating it from divine protection. To regain God's favor, according to an oft-repeated refrain, the people needed to repent of their immorality and selfishness and seek redemption through the civic virtues of sacrifice, discipline, and increased manliness. When government leaders (especially those in the military) perceived that the national character and will lacked the resolve they believed was essential for national defense, they used civil-religious imagery to improve the character of the American people and to foster greater national unity.

Since the late 1960s, the concept of civil religion has been both widely criticized and praised. Bellah himself defended and recanted before returning once again to pointing to a specialized form of civic piety that shaped the national experience. More recently, Conrad Cherry, Catherine Albanese, and others have renewed the debate over the existence of religious nationalism in American history.[20] This examination, using the tools of the historian, approaches the concept of civil religion more for its utility as a historical device rather than as a methodological question in an attempt to determine the traditional role of the military in the shaping of a national character and will. Like Bellah, I argue that civil religion has played an overwhelmingly positive role in American nation building. Unlike Bellah and other scholars, however, I concentrate on the armed forces' role in interpreting and transmitting civic religious principles to the American public. Whether or not the army, navy, and air force have served this function effectively is not fully debated. Instead, I argue that the early Cold War military operated under the assumption that its role as a builder of national character and will was an important component of defense.

The Citizen Soldier as Shaper of National Character

Many avenues existed in the young nation to communicate civic virtue and personal morality to the American people. The family, church, law, press, and the political process all participated, but free public education and military service played the most prominent roles from the beginning. Other scholars have demonstrated the crucial part schools played in communicating the dictates of Americanism to the nation's youth. However, few historians have considered the fact that the armed forces also played a vital role in shaping a national character except to note that military service was a ready means for new immigrants to be assimilated into American culture. Of central importance to understanding American society and culture is the recognition that the martial life also transmitted a particular set of "military values" to the nation's youth. By promoting conformity over individualism and stressing the obligations of citizenship in a republic rather than the rights, the military more often than not propagated a specialized interpretation of democratic society—an interpretation that was a practical response to the establishment of the nation's defenses on the twin concepts of the citizen soldier and universal service.

The revolutionary generation astutely designed a military system for the new nation that maintained a delicate balance between conformity and individuality. To avoid dangers to personal liberties inherent in the maintenance of a large standing army during peacetime, the Uniform Militia Act of 1792 placed militias (which were to enlist all able-bodied white men between the ages of eighteen and forty-five) under the control of the individual states, while establishing a small professional force for frontier defense and as the nucleus for a regular army that could be expanded during times of war. Army officers, according to the citizen-soldier concept, should be egalitarian rather than elite, a corps of "professionals" skilled in the military art who would lead citizen soldiers in time of emergency and, like George Washington at Valley Forge, uplift the soldier's character through the example of gentlemanly virtue. However, the heart of the nation's security, according to advocates of the system, was its virtuous citizenry. They believed that citizens would do their duty by taking up arms during times of crisis and then gladly lay down their weapons once their services were no longer needed. Americans, who reportedly covet liberty over all else, would thus avoid the corruption of values that many believed would occur if they remained in the military for very long.[21]

The citizen-soldier concept became deeply entrenched in the mindset of the young republic's leaders, who in turn supported training that would simultaneously enable soldiers to meet their military obligation and to instill an attitude of national preparedness in the American people. From the earliest days of the nation, however, a basic (and lasting) flaw in the plan was clear: the system worked only with a civic-minded public. The first secretary of war, Henry Knox (1789–94), who along with others doubted the virtue of the masses, proposed creating "Camps of Discipline" at which all young men would receive a political education along with training in fundamental military skills. Policy makers rejected his plan because of its centralizing tendencies over state militias, but Knox's conviction that Americans needed to be taught how to be citizen soldiers remained.

While military experience was seen as an effective means of instilling the qualities considered essential for good citizenship, it did not train Americans to be independent, contributing members of the community. The creation of citizens capable of restructuring society through the democratic process was a development of the Jacksonian Era and not a concern of the armed forces during the formation of the republic—or most of American history for that matter. Instead, military citizenship education has consistently stressed the conformist aspects of such education and sought to discourage wasteful individualism in favor of cooperative values. Overall, the army and the navy hoped that by teaching recruits how to be dutiful citizens the nation's civic virtue would be strengthened and the national defense secured. The military persisted in citizenship education that emphasized conformity. Only when under considerable duress—such as when confronted with the rapid demobilization following World War II, the civil rights movement of the 1950s and 1960s, and the antiwar movement during the Vietnam conflict—was any democratization of the process, to include greater freedoms of speech and opinion, attempted.[22] While this tendency toward conformist citizenship education in the military has been evident throughout American history, it must be remembered that the armed forces have never been monolithic or possessed a singularly martial mind-set. Nor has civilian control of the military ever been seriously threatened by its emphasis on duty and conformity.

The military promoted conforming citizenship training whenever it had the time and resources to do so, but it has failed to produce a critical mass of service personnel to serve as models for the civilian population to emulate. In wartime, when the ranks of the army and navy were filled with impressionable youth, teaching men how to fight took precedence over increasing their civic virtue. At the end of hostilities, the services quickly demobilized (as the public demanded), leaving few Americans under their direction precisely at the time they had the resources to carry out extensive citizenship education. Even if given the opportunity, it is highly unlikely that the armed forces, dedicated to the preservation of democracy, would seek to fundamentally alter their relationship with the American public. The United States has never become a military state and the services have shown little interest in creating one. Yet, the American military has taken its role as guardian of national virtue seriously, thus giving the nation's civil religion a special martial/conformist temperament.

Military Religion

Although the armed forces of other nations have used religious nationalism to shape their national character and will, the concept plays a particularly important role in the United States. In general, the American military adapted civil religion to meet the special circumstances of promoting its conception of the citizen (a conformist citizen soldier) in a democratic state, legitimizing its mission and authority within the American republic, and building troop morale among a diverse and independently minded rank and file. Morale, considered by the military to be "the rational and emotional attitudes that motivate and sustain soldier[s]," was of vital importance to the development of disciplined, obedient troops.[23] Difficult to define precisely and virtually impossible to measure, the armed forces attempted to increase morale or the "will to fight" through a variety of means, including civil-military religion.

Military religion, the most powerful variant of American civil religion, is the belief that the military, as the defender of the "American Way of Life," is a holy instrument of God's will and the interpreter of national values. Converting the War for Independence into a religious epic, military religion claims that no sacrifice, material or physical, is too great a price to pay for the cause of liberty. By manipulating the precepts of this variation of religious nationalism, the armed forces not only gained public support for increased appropriations and manpower ceilings, a constant struggle for a military in a democracy, but at times even justified extending its conformist citizenship education to the public as well. Under such a concept, each branch of the service could be considered a unique expression or "denomination" of the American Way of Life, separated by mission (land, sea, and air), but sharing a common set of rituals (rituals of induction and basic training), sacred symbols (the American flag), moral code (the Uniform Code of Military Justice and Code of Conduct), and priests (military chaplains).[24]

To say that many officers at the highest levels of command have manipulated the tenets of civil-military religion is not to suggest that they were acting cynically or hypocritically. Many military personnel fully subscribe to its basic tenets. Those individuals, hereafter referred to as "true believers," answered a "calling" to martial service and, as career officers, dedicated their lives to serving their nation. The military, however, contains many more "unbelievers." They enter the service for a variety of reasons, but lack the reverence for military tradition and discipline possessed by the true believers. These individuals rarely remain beyond their initial term of enlistment, making it possible for true believers in the American civil-military religion to rise to positions of power within the military hierarchy. Therefore, while the officer corps has never possessed a master plan on how to shape American character based on religious nationalism, the armed forces have generally operated according to the precepts of military religion because a preponderance of those in power possessed, in varying degrees, such a belief system. No cabal of officers met during the Cold War to construct the precepts of a military religion. Instead, its development and prominence occurred naturally, the result of the overwhelmingly conservative nature of high-achieving military officers and the especially potent civil-military religious climate of the day.

During times of rapid modernization, when existing social structures were stressed to the limit, religious nationalism became more pronounced in the ranks of the armed forces as the American people sought a means to bring order to their lives. At these unsettling times, social critics often claimed that materialism, moral laxness, and effeminacy had weakened the American character, thereby undermining the spiritual foundations of the republic. To redeem a people believed to be corrupted by wealth and sin and unwilling to sacrifice for the common good, true believers both inside and outside the military called for the suffering and sacrifice of war. Americans fought the War of 1812, the Mexican War, the Civil War, and the two world wars for a variety of reasons, but these conflicts also represented social crusades to restore national virtue. True believers claimed that wartime service fostered a national character that was both virtuous and "manly" by teaching "greedy," "soft" Americans discipline and self-control.[25]

The coupling of virtue and manliness within the American civil-military religion presented the U.S. armed forces with a fundamental and persistent contradiction at the core of its identity. While manly behavior is a social construct that is shaped by many factors and has undergone a number of transformations over time, the military has traditionally defined itself as a bastion of masculinity that is separate from and superior to the "softness" or effeminacy of civilian society. In accordance with its masculine identity, informal military culture has indirectly encouraged hard drinking and womanizing among its members in order to transform "boys" into "real men." Many even considered such activity a rite of passage to adulthood for young males in American society. Hard drinking and sexual conquests have been important aspects of the masculine bravado of military service. "Come fill your glasses, fellows, and stand up in a row," is a phrase West Point cadets have traditionally sung since the celebrated ballad "Benny Havens Ho" first appeared in the 1830s.[26]

Ironically, the making of real men had a negative effect on the military's ability to attract quality volunteers during the nineteenth and early twentieth centuries. Middle-class parents discouraged their sons from enlisting in what they perceived as an "immoral" institution. The War Department claimed that the resulting dearth of well-qualified enlistees meant the majority of men filling the ranks were "low-level" recruits who generally came from lower-class backgrounds and had a substandard education. However, before middle-class Americans would place their faith and trust in the armed forces, they demanded that the military provide a moral and "civilized" environment for their sons.

Without the threat of a war to stir up public passion, the U.S. military experienced great difficulty in justifying its defense appropriations and manpower allocations. During these lean times, when it appeared to true believers that the nation's security was in danger because of downsizing, "revitalization" (or purification) movements occurred within the armed forces to rid the ranks of the appearance of wickedness. Such movements, designed to garner middle-class support, confronted the military with a serious dilemma: once the manpower crisis ended (usually with the advent of a war and/or conscription) many feared that measures instituted to attract quality recruits had "softened" or "feminized" the military, thereby weakening the national defense. When possible, the armed forces transformed religion into a manly pursuit and reinterpreted masculinity to include the control, but not the elimination, of male passions.

Although the military provided only one interpretation of citizenship, it never enforced absolute obedience on the American people. Instead, it constructed a framework of conformity that could be enlarged and incorporated by society when the need arose. The fundamental contradictions between conformity and individuality, masculinity and femininity, and the citizen soldier and a professional warrior have at times strained the delicate relationship between the armed forces and society. That, however, is the dilemma of maintaining a military in a democracy. The dissonance between the civilian and military worlds should not be regretted, but rather celebrated, for the nation's civil-military relations have colored the national experience in unique and intriguing ways.

Scope of this Study

While attempts to shape the national will by other government agencies will be investigated, more significant to this study is the military's role in the process; that is, the attempt by the armed forces to strengthen the national character and efforts to use such activity to transform society along lines favorable to a martial mind-set. Chapter 1 considers the historical antecedents for military character shaping during the Cold War. Although the armed forces have played a role in such activity from their earliest days, they first assumed a prominent role in the early twentieth century, when the War Department gained sufficient manpower resources and public support to pursue such activity beyond its ranks to include the American people. At that time, "military Progressives"—reformers within and without the armed forces who favored the controlled environment of the military as a means to regenerate society along "progressive" lines— incorporated political indoctrination, athletics, and religious instruction in an attempt to create physically and morally fit and mentally alert citizens. After World War I, the military failed to extend its character shaping with a program of universal military training (UMT). It did, however, incorporate these principles where it could in the 1920s and 30s with Citizens' Military Training Camps (CMTC) and the Civilian Conservation Corps (CCC). When Pearl Harbor provided the impetus (along with manpower and other material resources) to unite the home front during World War II, the War Department modernized its moral education by incorporating the latest scientific techniques advocated by civilian psychologists and social engineers for readying recruits for combat in the most time-efficient means possible. Character shaping was of secondary importance to a nation fully mobilized for war. Nonetheless, the lessons learned during World War II would be integrated into postwar military efforts that were more extensive and activist than at any other period in American history.

Chapters 2 and 3 consider postwar developments that played a role in nurturing an influential evangelical element in the hierarchy of the newly created Department of Defense and other government agencies. The threat of atheistic international communism, the rise of evangelicals within American society and the military chaplaincy, the general increase of the influence of the armed forces in society following World War II, the rise of McCarthyism, and the perception in the late 1940s and 1950s that the American people lacked the traditional civic and moral virtues necessary for an ideological battle, prompted a number of high-ranking members of the DOD to take concerted and organized steps to articulate an American ideology and to shape the national character along lines that supported a conservative military mind-set.

The final chapter investigates the later years of the Eisenhower administration, when the historic trend in the military toward active character and citizenship shaping resulted in highly controversial Cold War seminars. "Strategy for Survival," "Project Alert," and other joint military-civilian anticommunist conferences proposed by the Joint Chiefs of Staff (JCS) and sanctioned by the National Security Council (NSC) were organized under DOD's authority but exploited by ultraconservative civilians advancing their own political and religious agendas. Although their actions violated the sensibilities of many Americans concerned about the propriety of military officers being involved in such highly partisan events, it must be remembered that even during those exceptional times civilian control of the military was never seriously threatened. When it became clear that a lack of quality control had encouraged a number of individuals, both active and reserve, to radicalize anticommunism seminars, DOD ended its active participation. Cold War seminars, while certainly sensational because of the measure of cooperation between the military and the radical right, were also indicative of the military's claim that it played an important and natural role in shaping national character and will.

Missing from this study are both an investigation of the role race played in this short-lived military/ultraconservative alliance and an in-depth treatment of character-education efforts by the military after DOD ordered officers to cease affiliating with political extremists in Cold War seminars. The end of racial segregation in the military seriously limited the interaction between the goals of military personnel and members of the far right who, for the most part, considered the civil rights movement to be an attack on traditional American values. In addition, the military's morale-building and character-shaping efforts during the Vietnam War were considerably less active and would not see a revival even approaching the level of the early Cold War until the Reagan years. I consider both of these topics so complex that I have decided they deserve considerable more study and I intend to devote separate monographs to their investigation.

Increased character and citizenship education and the search for a resolute national will certainly were not the only factors the armed forces believed necessary for national security. Throughout American history there has been little doubt that a well-equipped and trained fighting force backed by popular support remained the chief goal of the defense establishment. Regardless of the need for military might, however, the evidence is compelling that as Americans became fearful the nation might in fact lose its Cold War struggle with communism, nearly all segments of society agreed that it would take an ideologically sound America to win the battle for the hearts and minds of the world for democracy.

An Explanation of Terminology

The term *national character,* or *national identity,* has defied simple definition and is commonly used as a synonym for American exceptionalism (how America differs favorably from other developed nations). Specifically, national character consists of three related but divergent components: the national personality, morale, and will. Most critics who oppose the use of the term *national character* in reality are rejecting the existence of a national personality. While the idea that nations have identifiable personalities has been dismissed (although no good alternative has been discovered to explain adequately differences in perceived temperaments between countries), studies of the national will and morale continue to receive serious attention.[27]

The concepts *national will* and *national morale* are often used interchangeably. It is clear, however, that the two differ significantly. Specifically, national morale is a state of being, a measurement of public support for the general intent of national policies. National morale can be high or low. It is quantitative, but no adequate methodology exists to measure its level accurately. The national will, or national purpose, on the other hand, is qualitative. It is a process of becoming. The national will creates the state by providing the unity that validates and sustains governments. This does not, however, deny the significant role of a power elite in starting the process, maintaining its parameters, or believing that it can take steps to shape the people's will to support its policy objectives.

According to an excellent study by political scientist Thomas Henry Bell, national will is a consensus among people on the fundamental principles that bind a nation together. The national will does not require that all concur on every issue. Everyone, for example, does not have to agree that the nation should go to war. Commonly held American principles that underlie the national will could either determine that the nation should, or should not, go to war. Americans supported or condemned the Vietnam War based on the same traditional convictions regarding freedom and civic virtue. Because of this duality, effective governments manage the national will to achieve support for their policy initiatives. If policy makers correctly comprehend the nature of the national will, they can take steps to manipulate it when needed. This has been especially important during times of war and national emergency, when unified popular support has been considered essential to the nation's security.[28]

While the national will is strongest in nations facing grave danger, fear alone does not explain public patriotism when no threat exists. If based on ecclesiastical religion, the state becomes the will of God and the citizen who obeys that will earns divine favor. Such a national will is clear, and the means to manage the will are easily understood. The process is more complex in pluralistic societies organized around the precepts of civil-military religion. In this quasi-veneration of the state, the government seeks to be creative in the management of national will through the use of imagery and rhetoric.[29]

For the purposes of this study, the term *national character* will be used because Americans have used it for most of their history as an inclusive term signifying the nation's purported personality, morale, and will. Because the American public and policy makers alike made no distinctions among these three components during the early Cold War, this term seems appropriate. In addition, rather than proving or disproving the existence of a national character, this study attempts to analyze the impact of popular belief in America of the existence of such a phenomenon and the influence of the conviction held by a number of policy makers that the state, during times of perceived degeneracy, possessed the power and obligation to recreate and/or enhance it. Such concepts figured significantly in the making of national policy and the shaping of American society during the early Cold War.

Valley Forge was not the only theater in which the drama of American freedom and special mission was played out. Sacred ground at Independence Hall in Philadelphia, Yorktown, Gettysburg, Pearl Harbor, and other legendary sites all arouse patriotic passions. I have chosen to open each chapter with a Valley Forge connection (either direct or indirect) because civil religionists during the Cold War often likened George Washington's efforts to create a virtuous army during the Revolution to America's ideological struggle with the Soviet Union following World War II. Believing that the national character had degenerated and was ill-equipped to withstand a prolonged ideological confrontation, the U.S. military and, to a lesser degree, other government agencies called on the public to repent and to once again acquire the manly, patriotic characteristics of the Continental soldier—a soldier believed to have possessed the discipline and self-sacrifice necessary for national defense in a democratic society

CHAPTER 1

Engineering Patriotism

Behind every army stands a nation. As the two, united, represent

the sum total of potential force, so too, they form a single mental

unit, each component of which is dependent on the courage, good

will and endurance of the other.

—Col. Edward Munson, Morale Branch, U.S. Army, 1918

In 1904, Theodore Roosevelt, the first sitting president to visit Valley Forge since George Washington in 1787, spoke to an overflow crowd in Rev. W. Herbert Burk's temporary chapel located on the outskirts of the Continental Army's legendary winter encampment. Roosevelt's sermon had been arranged to aid Burk in raising funds for a religious shrine to honor the Republic's first president. Valley Forge, neglected since the Revolution, had become a virtual wilderness, visited only by relic hunters and picnickers. Appalled by this irreverence toward the Republic's founding, Reverend Burk designed his Washington Memorial Chapel as a civil-religious complex to teach both new immigrants and native-born youth the patriotic faith of the revolutionary elite.[1]

The purpose of the memorial would fit well with Theodore Roosevelt's progressive ideals, which sought to counter a reported degeneracy in the national character.[2] Americans at Valley Forge, Roosevelt preached to the spellbound crowd, had "warred not against the foreign soldiery, but against themselves." He attributed their eventual triumph to their commitment "to do duty well," not just on one momentous day but every day.[3] With Roosevelt's endorsement and the help of a professional fund-raiser, Burk raised enough money to begin construction of an ornate "Perpendicular Gothic" church that reflected his civil-religious interpretation of American history, an interpretation that venerated the first president as the personification of the nation's Christian principles. Despite the fact that much of the original Valley Forge story was concocted, the myth of Valley Forge as portrayed at the Washington Memorial Chapel had struck a patriotic and popular chord with the American public.[4]

For nearly thirty years, Burke shaped his memorial into a religious shrine dedicated to American civil religion. Strapped for funds to continue construction during the Great Depression, Burk attempted to repeat his earlier public relation's success by inviting Pres. Herbert Hoover to visit his memorial complex. Members of the Valley Forge Park Commission (founded in 1893), jealous of their organization's official right to interpret the historic site, convinced the president to instead allow them to serve as his official host while he conducted an inspection of Washington's headquarters and other park restorations. Adding injury to insult, the commissioners built a speaker platform for Hoover within sight of the Washington Memorial Chapel and made it clear that Burk would not be allowed to participate in the festivities. However, Hoover's nationally broadcast radio message on Memorial Day in 1931 could only have cheered the beleaguered minister's heart. With no end to the depression in sight, the president claimed, the United States faced another Valley Forge experience. In the future, he argued, the nation must rely on "the inventiveness, the resourcefulness and the initiative of every one of us. . . . If we weaken, as Washington did not, we shall be writing the introduction to the decline of American character and the fall of American institutions. . . . Valley Forge is our American synonym for the trial of human character through privation and suffering, and it is the symbol of the triumph of the American soul. . . . God grant that we may prove worthy of George Washington and his men of Valley Forge.[5]

Burk died two years later and was buried behind the half-finished memorial that he had dedicated so much of his life to building. Without his single-minded devotion to the cause, further construction stopped and the Washington Memorial Chapel waned in importance, coming to serve largely as a wedding chapel and architectural curiosity. Valley Forge National Historical Park, however, grew in popularity and quickly developed into a first-rate tourist attraction. By World War II, millions of

Americans had visited Valley Forge. One promoter of the day, pointing to the site's enduring relevance in light of the war then raging around the world, contended that the country was in desperate need of another Valley Forge experience to defeat this "evil thing that has come upon us." By visiting that "hallowed shrine and kneel[ing] before the Divine Life" as Washington had done so many years ago, according to the Valley Forge enthusiast, Americans could rediscover the Republic's spiritual foundations and gain the strength necessary to face the nation's current trials and tribulations.[6]

Despite claims regarding the memorial's suitability as a spiritual retreat, the civil-military religious interpretation of Valley Forge fell into disuse during the so-called Good War. The armed forces, enamored with the motion-picture industry and the advice of eugenicists and psychologists, placed less emphasis on progressive ideals and civil-military religious imagery. It turned instead to new secular means to train men efficiently in the martial skills it deemed essential to an effective fighting force, to teach a national purpose beyond mere revenge, and to foster a virtuous American character. Such a departure from civil-religious imagery proved temporary, however. With the dawning of the Cold War, the military would embrace civil-religious precepts with evangelical zeal—a zeal that not only used new techniques learned during World War II, but also drew on historical antecedents first established during the Progressive Era, when "military progressives" promoted universal military training as a ready answer to reverse a perceived degeneracy in America's national character.

Military Progressives and the Citizen Soldier

The American military engaged in character shaping long before the Progressive Era. Colonial militias were largely political in nature and, with Washington's forces during the Revolution and the national army created following the war, the military played a vital and continuing nation-building function by providing a means for youth to affirm their democratic citizenship and manhood. Prior to the turn of the century, however, military political and moral indoctrination was dwarfed by the similar functions of public education. Not until the 1880s and 1890s, with the emergence of a "new" army and navy intended to overcome the negative effects of the rapid and demoralizing demobilization that followed the Civil War, did the services assume greater responsibility in this area.

The military increased its character-shaping activities at that time for two reasons. First, its leaders acted out of heartfelt concerns for the state of the national character, which many claimed had lost its masculine vitality because of industrialization and overcivilization. Second, such activities were a public relations move to attract middle-class recruits into the ranks and secure ample appropriations from Congress. Both reasons played a role not only during the Progressive Era—as the nation sought to prepare militarily, ideologically, and even spiritually for its expanded world responsibilities—they also were amazingly consistent with motives expressed during the early Cold War, when policy makers sought an effective defense against international Communism.

An organized movement within the military to improve the national character, a movement possessing both force and coherence, first coalesced at the turn of the century in the form of a group of reformers within and without the armed forces hereafter referred to as "military progressives." Fearing that the virtue of the American people had degenerated since the founding of the Republic, these reformers attempted to reverse the negative effects of modernization upon the national character and will through a number of strategies. Military progressives exposed moral corruption through reform journalism or "muckraking." They also incorporated religious instruction, recreation, and political indoctrination into military morale education hoping to purify the armed forces without compromising the services' masculine identity. The regeneration of society along civil-military religious precepts was to occur, these progressives claimed, when soldiers returned to civilian life, taking what they had learned in the armed forces with them. The projected result would be the creation of a patriotic, unified American character—a character that was both manly and virtuous and based on a conformist citizenship model. Whether through the preparedness movement of 1913–17, the War Department's World War I Morale Branch, the Citizens' Military Training Camps of the interwar period, or the Civilian Conservation Corps during the depression, military progressives worked to revitalize the American people by creating physically, mentally, and morally "fit" Americans who possessed the "manly" and patriotic characteristics of the idealized Continental soldier at Valley Forge.

The precise identity of early twentieth-century reformers popularly known as progressives continues to be a source of historical debate. Although no simple explanation exists, scholars have reached a measure of agreement on certain characteristics common to this diverse group.

Among these were an emphasis on individual duty, efficiency (both in government and society), and an effort to identify and eliminate the sources of social disorder and disharmony accompanying the Industrial Revolution. Progressives supported an activist, regulatory government powerful enough to rescue the individual from the grip of impersonal forces exemplified by giant corporations. They generally were optimistic about human rationality and believed that with ample education society would correct the mistakes of the past in ways that conformed to progressive ideas. Inclined to condemn materialism and to invoke democratic and highly moralistic rhetoric, progressives generally subscribed to the tenets of the nineteenth-century philosophies of Muscular Christianity (manly religion) and the Strenuous Life (Spartan living to counter "overcivilization"). They envisioned an efficient and rational society, steeped in Protestant Christian tenets. Whether calling for social justice for the masses or social control to impose their own white, Protestant, middle-class standards on the nation, progressives were cultural nationalists who promoted the precepts of American civil religion in their attempt to mobilize patriotism and establish a unified code of values by which all Americans should live.[7]

Not all progressives were supportive of military solutions to national ills, but both social-justice and social-control progressives were represented in the armed forces. A number of the progressives serving in the military urged a system of less-rigid discipline as they sought the "democratization" of the services. However, during America's involvement in World War I, when nearly unlimited government power prevailed, the conservative, more coercive side of progressivism became dominant, alienating its liberal wing, which feared militarism. Those labeled here as "military progressives"—that is, those who valued the dedication to duty, efficiency, and discipline of the armed forces and promoted character and citizenship education within military ranks—fit most comfortably in the category of this conservative, coercive side. Military progressives included both active-duty personnel and civilians who viewed the military as a useful institution for implementing their reforms for the nation at large.

At the turn of the century, widespread interest in using military training to shape the character of American citizens, coupled with the close association of martial skills with Christianity, athleticism, and progressivism, revived passions for the citizen-soldier concept as the foundation of American society—an ideal that had been waning since the beginning of the Civil War. Military progressives embraced the professionalism of the armed forces (that is, the process of acquiring specialized knowledge, developing a specified responsibility to society, and forming a group identity exemplified by a code of ethics—all of which are characteristics of a modern professional military force) while maintaining the importance of the citizen soldier and universal service for national security.[8] Secretary of War Elihu Root (1899–1904) successfully championed the creation of a general staff to replace the War Department's inefficient management system. Root's call for a larger professional force and a well-trained reserve to reduce the nation's dependence on the citizen soldier during times of crisis alarmed many progressives, including Maj. Gen. Leonard Wood, Grenville Clark, and Theodore Roosevelt Jr. They believed that the citizen-soldier concept was the cornerstone of American freedom and defense. The so-called Root reforms resulted in a seventy-five-thousand-man regular force, well-equipped and well-trained, but without the large reserve base of quality men many believed was necessary for waging a world war.[9] To solve America's pressing manpower needs and to preserve the citizen-soldier concept within the professional armed forces, military progressives sought to pass legislation for a UMT program.

Universal Military Training and the Preparedness Movement

Traditionally, the American public has feared that the adoption of a policy of mandatory military training for all males would "Prussianize" American society. New circumstances at the turn of the century, however, convinced military progressives that UMT offered the nation many benefits. First, without compulsion it was unlikely that enough civilians would have the necessary skills to defend America's expanded world role. Second, nativists like pioneer sociologist Frances Kellor touted UMT as an effective means to Americanize the recent influx of new immigrants from southern and southeastern Europe, whom she claimed were destroying the nation's racial and political homogeneity. Finally, proponents argued that UMT could create the long-desired virtuous and obedient citizen that the founding elite had considered essential for the nation's security.[10]

In 1913, the army first demonstrated the various military and social benefits of UMT with Student Military Training Camps (SMTC). Selected college students willing to pay a fee for enrolling in the SMTC were attached to the regular army for a four- to five-week training course with no obligation to join the military at its conclusion. Proponents claimed that the SMTC experience would produce a trained reserve. Graduates could also serve as a pool of publicity agents, something long coveted by a military dependent on Congress for appropriations. They reasoned that the most effective way to achieve both goals—a trained reserve and publicity agents—would be for the army not to replicate basic training, but rather to present young SMTC enrollees with a friendlier, more enjoyable military experience.[11] The SMTC program was a resounding success. Enthusiastic enrollees, inspired by positive encouragement rather than badgered with boot-camp harassment, arose at 5:15 A.M. for calisthenics and breakfast. They then spent several hours at hard drill, followed by classroom instruction and more hours of physical conditioning with sports in the afternoon. War games, written tests, and a seven-day, sixty-five-mile-long hike with thirty-pound packs rounded out the students' military training.[12]

Although many SMTC graduates joined the reserves, the camps did little to create the large base of virtuous citizenry that Maj. Gen. Leonard Wood wanted held in reserve for the nation's defenses. The SMTC cantonments were a poor demonstration of UMT because all but those wealthy enough to afford the four weeks of training were excluded. Furthermore, many critics questioned just how well prepared for war graduates would be if they drilled because officers had appealed to their better nature rather than because they had been ordered to do so. The fact that the most severe punishments imposed at SMTC cantonments were verbal reprimands and dismissals, and that officers fraternized with their men during meals and recreation, led many to claim that the real purpose of the cantonments was public relations, not military training. The SMTC program laid the groundwork for military progressives to launch a more extensive effort—the Preparedness Movement that preceded World War I—to convince the public of the character-shaping benefits of a mandatory UMT plan.[13]

In May, 1915, when Grenville Clark, Elihu Root, and Theodore Roosevelt Jr., heard the news that a German U-boat had sunk the *Lusitania,* they canceled a scheduled round of golf and began planning an aggressive preparedness campaign. Clark, a rich New York lawyer who advocated UMT as a means to reduce class and racial tensions, recommended adapting the successful SMTC program for use with older men. After consulting with General Wood, who agreed to secure War Department authorization for the officers and equipment necessary for such an operation, Clark spearheaded a businessman's camp at Plattsburg Barracks, New York. During the summer of 1916, not only did twelve hundred men (many of whom were millionaires) pay for a demanding five-week course of military training and preparedness propaganda at Plattsburg, but hundreds of other businessmen on army bases at Monterey, California; American Lake, Washington; and Fort Sheridan, Illinois, also volunteered to prepare for the possibility of war.[14]

Military progressives argued that preparedness offered considerably more than the mere preparation of warriors for combat. It also was an opportunity to demonstrate the positive benefits of UMT. Historian John Finnegan claimed that Plattsburg was a type of "secular retreat." Under the influence of their martial surroundings, the well-to-do Plattsburgers underwent a "conversion experience of patriotism, individual responsibility, and collective action." By giving the upper class an opportunity to prove American masculinity, the Plattsburgers found "psychological solidarity" and military camp life became "a paradigm for the good life in America." Grenville Clark explained that the camp "was not conceived merely as a means of obtaining security against external enemies but of strengthening the nation internally against internal forces making for weakness and lack of national unity."[15]

By the end of 1916, the martial spirit had spread so thoroughly that not only had hundreds of thousands reportedly participated in military drill at official and quasi-official Plattsburg camps, but as many as 1.5 million people had also been inspired by the movement to begin rifle practice.[16] In the end, however, there was little public support for the mandatory UMT system desired by many military progressives. Critics of the armed forces charged that Plattsburgers were using war fears to force the enactment of a UMT program that would militarize the nation. To keep the momentum for preparedness moving forward, Grenville Clark founded the civilian-based Military Training Camp Association (MTCA) on February 14, 1916.[17] The MTCA launched a national advertising campaign encouraging Americans to "give your vacation to your country and still have the best vacation you ever had." However, most preparedness propaganda was disseminated on a more personal basis as Plattsburg alumni joined the MTCA and distributed camp literature to likely candidates.[18] Using these and other attempts, military progressives hoped to overcome the traditional middle-class bias against serving in the military.

Many middle-class parents discouraged their sons from enlisting in the armed forces because of the reputation basic-training camps had of being dens of iniquity. To counter this charge, military progressives adopted techniques used by early twentieth-century journalists known as muckrakers, who stimulated reform by exposing corruption. Old-school officers feared that the scandal these revelations were likely to foster would further damage the services' reputation. Yet, military progressives, secure in the stability of the armed forces as an integral component of American society, welcomed the public exposure of sordidness within the ranks as a means of forcing the War Department to adopt the training innovations of the Plattsburg Movement. A type of revitalization movement, military muckraking gave reformers a means to purify the armed forces and to provide an example of discipline, morality, and conformist citizenship for all of society to follow.

The problem that confronted military progressives was how to convey the image of the services' purity and suitability for middle-class youth without compromising their image of masculinity. The problem was all the more complex because purity had been traditionally identified as a feminine attribute. Using techniques honed by the muckrakers, military progressives employed the philosophy of Muscular Christianity in an attempt to demonstrate that a willingness to confront immorality in the ranks was an act of manliness. Further evidence of the military's "manhood" was its insistence that discipline and order could restrain men's base instincts. Such a strategy by the true believers in the officer corps assumed the character of admitting "sin" and was consistent with their religious orientation. The use of the muckraking technique persisted in the American military until the early Cold War, when reformers once again attempted to impose Progressive Era ideals on Americans by exposing alleged corruption in the ranks.

Conditions at regular army cantonments on the nation's southern border during the Mexican crisis of 1916 provided just the opportunity that military progressives needed for their first muckraking campaign. Alarmed by a rapid rise in the venereal disease (VD) rate among new recruits, Secretary of War Newton D. Baker (1916–21)—a lawyer who had played an instrumental part in ridding Cleveland, Ohio, of its dancehalls—appointed Raymond B. Fosdick, the progressive commissioner of accounts for New York City, to head an on-site investigation. Fosdick reported that officers had ignored excessive drinking and even "tolerated" the presence of prostitutes within the camps and surrounding areas. Baker threatened officers with the loss of their commands if a policy of "moral sanitation" was not immediately instituted. In a widely publicized move, the secretary of war closed red-light districts along the border and allowed only a limited number of bars to operate under the strictest scrutiny. The army also enlisted the aid of private organizations such as the Young Men's Christian Association (YMCA) and the Salvation Army to supplement the War Department's troop welfare efforts that included increased camp athletic and religious activities as a means of distracting men from immoral activity. Crediting such measures for success, the military reported a dramatic drop in VD rates along the Mexican border.[19] The popularity of the Plattsburg Movement, along with Secretary Baker's program of "moral sanitation," gave the appearance that a military base was a safe place to send the nation's impressionable middle-class youth.

President Woodrow Wilson gave the public little opportunity to demonstrate confidence in the new image of the armed forces, however. Instead, shortly after America declared war on Germany, the president instituted a comprehensive draft. Wilson agreed with Leonard Wood and other military leaders that reliance on the traditional volunteer citizen-soldier system alone for manpower was inefficient and impractical in a total war. If the nation's most virtuous and talented young men enlisted and served overseas, few gifted individuals would be left behind to mobilize the agricultural and industrial resources needed for the war effort. The Selective Service Act of 1917 avoided many of the inequities of Civil War conscription by prohibiting substitutions and levying strict penalties on anyone refusing to register with local draft boards. The title of the act also provided a means for the government to imply that the nation's entire manpower base had volunteered for service while allowing the military, in good progressive fashion, to efficiently select those who would serve without disrupting industry and agriculture. Military progressives welcomed the World War I draft as an unexpected opportunity to continue their fight for UMT by demonstrating its character-shaping benefits on a massive scale and under ideal conditions.[20] Because the armed forces could maintain strict discipline over wartime inductees (unlike the tenuous control the army had over Plattsburg volunteers), basic training seemed a perfect proving ground for progressive reforms.

World War I and Psychological Stimulation

Military progressives hoped that the suffering and sacrifice that would accompany a long war (which they preferred to one of short duration) would restore the nation's traditional values believed lost during the Industrial Revolution. Once reformed, proponents claimed, society could maintain its civic virtue by adopting a UMT program. It was not clear which was the most compelling reason behind the social-purity movement during the Great War: to make a more efficient fighting force or to establish a code of Victorian morality capable of winning the world over for democracy. Both motives no doubt came into play during the moral crusades that swept the nation following America's entry into the conflict.[21]

The diversity of the nation's draftees and volunteers presented certain challenges for military progressives. Instead of the enthusiastic college students and businessmen of the Plattsburg Movement, a true cross section of the country filled the ranks during the war. According to the army, the average inductee was twenty-two years old, uncertain of his role in the war, and often innocent as to the ways of the world. More troubling were reports that as many as a third of the men were illiterate, or nearly so, and in such poor health that the War Department classified them as physically defective. To make matters worse, the small decrease in VD rates after the publicity surrounding the Mexican border camps spurred reforms was reversed as young men poured into hastily constructed training camps throughout the nation and overwhelmed the programs put in place by moral-sanitation reformers. Secretary of War Baker actively and patriotically pursued coercive methods to counter these developments and provide servicemen with an "invisible armor" of morality. Such armor, Baker argued, would build a unified, effective, and morally disciplined army that would be worthy of victory and serve as the standard for other nations to follow after the war ended.[22]

To begin the promised reformation of society, the War Department created the Commission on Training Camp Activities (CTCA) and made Raymond Fosdick, fresh from his investigation of training camps on the Mexican border, its director. The CTCA was a scientific morality crusade (both rational and idealistic at the same time) bent on refashioning the training camp environment as the first step in remaking American society by transforming America's youth into crusaders imbued with middle-class values and worthy of the redemption offered by war. Using the authority given to the military by the 1917 draft legislation, the armed forces regulated vice in and around training camps by establishing "moral zones" in which the twin evils of alcohol and prostitution were absolutely forbidden. The CTCA preached continence (abstinence) in the camps, distributed an explicit pamphlet titled *Keeping Fighters Fit*, and filled jails and detention centers with prostitutes and unescorted "charity girls" (often the wives and girlfriends of servicemen) captured in and around military bases and held without bail until they were tested for sexually transmitted diseases.[23]

In addition to moral purification, military progressives claimed that the World War I training camp experience would be an effective means of Americanizing non-English speaking draftees. Bolstered by an Americanization movement then occurring in society, Maj. Gen. Leonard Wood argued that the army should accept the responsibility of teaching the foreign born to "speak American and think American."[24] Theodore Roosevelt predicted that "the military tent, where all sleep side by side, [would] . . . rank next to the public school among the great agents of democratization."[25] However, cultural differences and the immigrant's inability to understand orders clearly often led to abuse by officers and fellow servicemen intolerant of the alien's differences. While the War Department established some "development battalions" in which foreign-born recruits received language instruction and citizenship education, not every immigrant had the opportunity to benefit from such considerations during World War I. Many high-ranking officers preferred mainstreaming foreigners into regular fighting units to placing them in separate battalions. These officers claimed that even without specialized instruction the military experience effectively Americanized the immigrant.[26]

Finally, military progressives hoped that the average recruit, whether foreign born or American bred, would acquire the patriotic inspiration that previously had been available only to those able to afford a Plattsburg summer training camp. From the beginning of the war, the army expressed interest in politically indoctrinating its troops. However, with the service doubling in size every three months, it was all the War Department could do to train and equip recruits before shipping them overseas. For the most part, the armed forces relied on private agencies, supervised by the CTCA, to handle the bulk of morale education until the War Department could bring mobilization under control. Reformers within the military and civilian organizations such as the YMCA, the Knights of Columbus, and the Salvation Army held singing festivals, theatrical performances, and screenings of the newly invented motion picture, which stressed America's role in spreading democracy around the world.[27]

Early in the war, several officers submitted proposals for in-service morale education. Raymond Fosdick, chairman of the CTCA, along with representatives from the Military Intelligence Branch and the surgeon general's office, joined forces with the most influential voice in morale education, Col. Edward Munson, in lobbying for a Morale Branch within the War Department. Munson, a Medical Corps officer, claimed that an effective soldier must possess a "motive" or ideal for which he was willing to die. This ideal was needed, according to Munson, in order to overcome each man's sense of self-preservation to the point that "the victory of the Army of which he is a part becomes the supreme object of his desire."[28]

In 1918, Munson experimented with the "psychological stimulation" of inductees at Camp Greenleaf, Georgia. Employing a systematic program of indoctrination that included patriotic singing, athletic events, other diverse forms of entertainment, and—most important—citizenship lectures, Camp Greenleaf attempted "to develop a wholesome mental attitude toward the service and to make induction to it as pleasant and profitable as possible."[29] Along with developing the recruit's will to survive the "rifle and shell fire, mud, gas, [and] lice" waiting for him in France, Munson hoped that lessons from the War Issues Course (also known as the War Aims Course) would make the soldier a better American when he returned home.[30]

Along with its application during basic training, the War Department also incorporated the War Issues Course into the Student Army Training Corps (SATC). The SATC, a program on the nation's campuses in which enlisted men stayed in school but lived their daily lives under strict military discipline, supplemented material from the War Issues Course with literature from the controversial Committee on Public Information (Creel Committee), which created propaganda for the war effort. The SATC's instructors, overwhelmed by the number and diversity of their students, relied heavily on propaganda and often simplified and slanted materials in their effort to create an efficient, unified American ideology.[31]

Encouraged by the results of its morale and political indoctrination/propaganda efforts, the army finalized its plans for a formal Morale Branch in July, 1918. Individual officers, volunteer associations, and the CTCA coordinated their formerly separate character-education efforts through the new agency. The Morale Branch instructed service personnel on why the nation was at war and included, under the guise of good citizenship, additional training in conforming values that supported the nation's existing economic, political, and social institutions.[32] When the war ended, the agency changed its message from "Will to Win" to "Will to See the Thing Through," hosted the Interallied Games in Paris to showcase the athletic superiority of American servicemen, and instructed returning soldiers on "their future work as citizens."[33]

Military progressives continued to lobby for UMT and social purity, political indoctrination, and psychological stimulation programs after the war. At the same time, a reinvigorated character-building effort was developing within the civilian sector. During World War I, educators had used behavioral psychology to stimulate young minds to support the war effort. Once hostilities ceased, the emotional nationalism associated with the war assumed new directions. Moral instruction, however, still very much a part of citizenship education, continued to admonish students to do the right thing, withstand temptations, and form good habits and a strong will.[34] Many public schools promulgated a "Children's Morality Code" that specified the essential qualities of a good citizen: "self-control, good health, kindness, sportsmanship, self-reliance, duty, reliability, truth, good workmanship, and teamwork."[35] Despite John Dewey's progressive pedagogy that emphasized creativity and open-mindedness in the classroom, most public schools retained conventional definitions of citizenship and morality rather than adopt what many considered to be the "soft" and "permissive" ideas of liberal educators.[36]

Private efforts to shape the character of American youth augmented the public schools' attempt to promote conformist citizenship. During the 1920s and 1930s, organizations such as the Boy Scouts, Girl Reserves Clubs, Hi-Y, and the Uncle Sam's Club, used peer pressure to emphasize codes of conduct based on middle-class values. The Boy Scouts, the most noteworthy of these private organizations, incorporated much of the military's stress upon conformity and virtuous manliness as the answer to a perceived national degeneracy. Unlike his British counterpart, the American Boy Scout swore an oath—"the code of red-blooded, moral, manly men"—to be "physically strong, mentally awake, and morally straight."[37] By promoting the tenets of the American civil-military religion, Boy Scouts and other private organizations (often along with the nation's public schools) unofficially joined forces with the War Department to fashion a revitalized national character.

Although the armed forces welcomed civilian citizenship education efforts, such attempts to shape the national character were uncoordinated and seen as only partial solutions to social degeneracy and national disunity. More effective, according to the War Department, would be a mandatory UMT program. Universal military training, according to true believers of the American civil-military religion, not only would ensure a large reserve of pretrained men for future wars, it would also inculcate proper civic values in American youth and foster the public support necessary to fund a large defense establishment. There was, however, little chance that UMT legislation would pass in a nation celebrating the end of a war. The fight for UMT continued well into the 1950s, but Congress never enacted compulsory service. Because it was unpopular to talk about military training while the nation celebrated an armistice, policy makers only discussed UMT seriously during times of worsening international tension. Once war seemed imminent, however, many regarded the draft as the quicker and more efficient answer to the nation's manpower needs. Congress delayed debate on UMT until peacetime, when the nation would again be concerned only with demobilization.[38]

Unaware of the futility of their efforts, army leaders fought hard to have UMT included in the 1920 National Defense Act. When it became clear that Congress would not fund the costly venture, the War Department countered with two proposals for postwar manpower. The first called for a standing army of 500,000 men. The second and more popular measure reduced the size of the regular force to 250,000, supplemented by a well-financed and well-trained reserve. The final 1920 National Defense Act increased the size of the regular army to 280,000 and greatly expanded the nation's citizen reserve by strengthening the National Guard and Reserve Officers Training Corps (ROTC), and by creating an additional large reserve of enlisted men.[39]

Despite the fact that Congress approved no provision for mandatory service in the 1920 National Defense Act, President Wilson appeased military progressives by authorizing voluntary, free-of-charge Citizens' Military Training Camps for the nation's youth. During the 1920s and 1930s, the War Department operated the CMTC program as a means to advertise to the American public the social benefits of military character shaping. Military progressives hoped that CMTC graduates (estimated at 650,000 a year from nearly fifty camps) would not only join the reserves, but that they would also spread "the health and fitness gospel" to their hometowns, thus helping to convince the public to support future UMT legislation. To obtain the congressional appropriations and private contributions needed to keep the camps operating and to promote the program's civic virtue message across the nation, the MTCA launched an aggressive advertising campaign that portrayed the camps as the "least military form of military training" and a "moral tonic" for the nation's youth.[40]

A typical CMTC enrollee was between the ages of seventeen and twenty-four and possessed good moral character, as attested by his local religious leader or school officials. Each summer, those young men who made it through the competitive selection process would be assigned to one of four separate thirty-day courses. Designated basic, red, white, and blue, the CMTC courses progressed from simple military instruction to specialized skill training. However, the goal of camp leaders was not to turn out a host of officers for the reserves, as the original legislation stated, but to process as many young men as possible through the first two courses, in which most of the citizenship and character education took place. Officials admitted that a CMTC graduate's ability to remember much of the technical military instruction he received was of little concern to them. Even if a student forgot how to drill or operate a machine gun, camp enthusiasts claimed that he would "not forget that obedience to orders . . . is a fundamental military precept, that respect for higher authority is basic."[41] Fort Meade, Maryland, alumnus Aubrey Patterson Jr., who remembered his CMTC days fondly, said, "It was a wonderful way to get away from home."[42]

Aubrey Patterson, a Citizens' Military Training Camp enrollee assigned to Machine Gun Company H, poses at Fort Meade, Maryland, in 1935. Courtesy Aubrey Patterson.

One of the most effective ways that the CMTC promoted its citizenship message to the American public was through the publication of a series of official manuals titled *Studies in Citizenship*. The War Department distributed these manuals to officers on duty with the CMTC and the ROTC and to men in the reserves and the National Guard. Many public schools even incorporated the manual's precepts into their curriculum. By combining English language instruction with American history and political science, the authors of the military handbook taught students that "cooperation is the normal and the profitable thing" and that "competitive bargaining" only harmed the national economy. The worker who "skimps his job or loafs when the foreman is not looking" weakened the national security, according to the manual, for "the fundamental requirements for industrial development and for military strength are the same, namely, sound physique, intelligence, skill, loyalty, and solid character."[43]

The 1928 edition of the citizenship manual became so controversial that public pressure finally forced the military to suppress it. Prepared under the direction of the chief of staff, the handbook pronounced democracy to be "mobocracy," condemned pacifism and internationalism, and called for the "assimilation and amalgamation of the bloods of all nations into the virile life stream of America." The problem with the character of American youth, the chauvinistic manual concluded, was the nation's emphasis on materialism over spiritualism. "[I]t is the mission of this course to specially emphasize the moral aspects of citizenship— to build up home discipline, reverence for religion, and respect for constituted authority. Education and training in citizenship form a vital part of national defense."[44]

Despite its public relations success with the CMTC program, the military struggled throughout the decade to convince the public to provide adequate funding to maintain the regular army at twelve thousand commissioned officers and 125,000 enlisted men, far below its authorized strength. Because military theory of the day postulated that men and not machines was the decisive element in battle, the army vehemently protested further manpower cuts in either the regular or reserve forces, fearing that such reductions would destroy its ability to mobilize quickly in the event of war. By opting to rely on World War I supplies and weaponry instead of investing in modern matériel and technology, the War Department kept most of its expensive summer training programs for the ROTC, National Guard, and CMTC intact, but in the process reduced its regular operations to the point that the army was materially and technically unprepared for another world war.[45]

The military faced additional severe manpower cuts during the Great Depression. When Pres. Herbert Hoover urged the War Department to keep its expenditures to "the barest necessity," it reduced costs by canceling construction projects and eliminating all but the most basic maintenance on military bases. Chief of Staff Douglas MacArthur openly opposed Hoover's plans to reduce the army's manpower base further. He also rejected the idea that the army should be used for relief work, believing such activity would weaken its war-fighting capabilities. MacArthur eventually reversed his position on support for Pres. Franklin D. Roosevelt's youth work program, the Civilian Conservation Corps, after realizing that participation in the president's so-called Tree Army would provide leadership opportunities for his regular officers and employment for reservists in economic distress.[46]

While fortifying its manpower resources figured foremost in the War Department's mind-set, the army also believed that the CCC, like the CMTC, offered an excellent opportunity to instill proper military values in American youth. Theodore Roosevelt Jr., Robert McCormick, Grenville Clark, and other military progressives agreed with MacArthur's recommendation that the CCC add a mandatory military training component to teach "manly self respect and wholesome citizenship" to American youth. A number of officers—including Chief of Staff MacArthur and Maj. Gen. George Van Horn Moseley, the deputy chief of staff—wanted to completely militarize the agency for the sake of efficiency. To calm the ensuing public outcry, FDR issued a statement emphasizing the absence of military drill in the camps. Despite that fact, there was little doubt that the War Department used CCC camps to instruct campers in military discipline.[47]

The War Department used the CCC in its attempt to create individuals who conformed to its conception of good citizenship through literacy education, instruction in manners and morals, and political indoctrination. The chief agents of character education in the CCC were the army's chaplains, who hoped to reach disadvantaged youth by combining religious and patriotic themes into their weekly character-education lectures. Camp health facilities controlled the VD rate by providing prophylactic stations. In addition, the army relied on sports and religion to distract campers from impure thoughts and to replicate the same "invisible armor" Newton Baker had advised was needed to protect the virtue of World War I soldiers.

Along with religious and moral instruction, character-education lectures and civics classes in the CCC also included political indoctrination. The army, believing that dissent was wasteful, attempted to make each enrollee conform to the military's code of ethics.[48] This conformist citizenship education was in direct opposition to the efforts of liberal educators (employed with the CCC) who viewed the CCC as an opportunity to incorporate their contributing version of citizenship (educating individuals to actively restructure society through the democratic process) into American society. With no provisions made for education in the original CCC legislation, the army and the Department of Education (DOE) fought for control of this important aspect of the operation. The army maintained its final authority by threatening to pull out of the CCC but the DOE forced a compromise to allow civilian advisers into the camps. To the military's dismay, the DOE published a manual to help advisers answer campers' questions on historical, social, and political issues—including those regarding the New Deal, which the manual clearly supported. Many commanders claimed that the men under their direction were not sophisticated enough to discuss these controversial issues and moved to censor the material at the local level. When liberal educators sought to create participant councils empowered to establish their own camp rules, the army refused to cooperate.[49]

After the Japanese bombed Pearl Harbor, the War Department quietly introduced drill in the CCC camps. Few criticized this addition, however, as war fever calmed public fears regarding the dangers of militarization. In 1942, having achieved all its goals, the army asked to be released from its CCC duties so it could fully devote itself to the war effort. Congress considered reorganizing the CCC under the leadership of other government agencies, but without the army's support, the CCC was forced to cease operations that same year, never to be reinstated. Meanwhile, the CMTC had ceased operations two years earlier with little opposition.[50] While the prewar mobilization effort diverted military progressives' attention away from UMT, the need for in-service political indoctrination to teach men why they fought remained strong and became a source of contention within the ranks. Older line officers feared that Chief of Staff George C. Marshall's efforts to "democratize" the military as it mobilized for World War II would weaken discipline and good order and ultimately leave the nation vulnerable to attack.

As the army began dusting off its mobilization plans in 1939, many in the War Department believed that the service's experiences with the CMTC and CCC programs had prepared it well for maintaining troop morale. Confidence plummeted, however, after Congress raised enlistment ceilings and large numbers of reportedly "low-quality" men overflowed training camps, replicating conditions at cantonments on the Mexican border in 1916.[51] The army reactivated its morale education functions in July, 1940, with the creation of the Morale Division. Although established under the direction of the adjutant general's office to deal with the complete range of morale activities, including information and education, the division had little time for Colonel Munson's "psychological stimulation" as millions of raw recruits poured into hastily constructed training camps.[52]

Believing that its manpower resources were virtually unlimited, the army sought the most time-efficient way to identify mentally competent recruits without physical defects that might impede the training process. The most precious commodity during mobilization was time, and to economize in this one area, the army was willing to process forty thousand men to find twenty thousand first-rate recruits. Healthy "interchangeable" and "reconvertible" men reportedly could perform any job in the army with minimal additional instruction beyond the standard basic training. Using General Classification Test scores and the results of a brief psychological examination performed at one of the nation's 108 induction centers as a yardstick, the army rejected more than a million men out of a pool of 9 million recruits because of alleged emotional and mental defects.[53] Despite psychologists' dubious ability to predict a man's fitness for combat based on a simple three-minute interview in which a naked recruit responded to a series of questions such as "How do you feel?" and "Do you like girls?" the War Department embraced the principles of behavioral psychology in its wartime management of men.[54]

Chief of Staff Marshall tried to improve morale by furnishing each soldier with abundant and "improved" material goods and by incorporating some of the spirit of the Plattsburg Movement into basic training.[55] Instead of "monotonous drilling," which he believed "achieved obedience at the expense of initiative," Marshall encouraged a "new discipline" based on "respect rather than fear; on the effect of good example given by officers; on the intelligent comprehension by all ranks of why an order has to be and why it must be carried out; on a sense of duty, on *esprit de corps.*"[56] Veteran career officers, who viewed service personnel as interchangeable parts in the military machine, saw little value in psychological motivation. Instead, they called for more military drill and discipline to reverse the declining moral and morale conditions seen developing in training camps around the nation.

In 1940, soldiers angered by the extension of their service obligation, which they had originally been told would be only one year, launched the "Over the Hill in October" (OHIO) protest movement. *Life* magazine reported in 1941 that National Guardsmen serving with an unidentified division (later revealed to be the 27th Infantry Division at Fort McClellan, Alabama) had declared that they would desert in October, when their terms of service originally had been scheduled to expire. A protest by a few disgruntled draftees was understandable in light of the unexpected extension, but when the *Life* article charged that up to 95 percent of the men in the division believed the president's "national emergency" was a sham, the War Department became alarmed.[57]

General Marshall, who refused to discuss the *Life* article publicly, privately recruited *New York Times* publisher Arthur Hay Sulzberger to investigate the charges. However, instead of vindicating the military as Marshall had hoped, the two-hundred page, confidential "Railey Report"—submitted to the chief of staff by *Times* staff member Hilton Howell Railey in September, 1941—made the *Life* article, in Sulzberger's words, look like a "Sunday School version."[58] Railey graphically depicted the low morale and lax discipline that permeated the army's training camps. Along with a general carelessness in dress and military courtesy, *Life* had reported that enlisted men openly challenged their superiors when off duty. When Railey asked an officer if he feared his men, the officer replied, "We are scared to death of them and most of us feel that the sooner we get out of this mess the better we will like it." One general, who called for demobilizing the National Guard immediately, claimed that the widespread disloyalty could be blamed on a lack of discipline in the nation's homes and schools and on "communist agitators" believed to have infiltrated the camps.[59]

Railey, as had the *Life* reporter before him, blamed the sorry state of affairs on poor leadership, inadequate training, and insufficient equipment. He recommended to Marshall that in the future the army should de-emphasize "entertainment and amusement" and devote more attention to teaching men about why they were fighting and the "revolutionary nature" of the current international crisis.[60] While the army might not be able to go directly to the American public with this vital information, Railey believed the service had a "magnificent opportunity to teach ... intellectual, though perhaps largely uneducated young Americans what war is all about."[61]

Acting on Railey's recommendation, Marshall discharged all soldiers over the age of twenty-eight and instituted an indoctrination program on foreign policy during basic training's weekly army orientation program.[62] The program, which did not begin in earnest until shortly after the Japanese attacked Pearl Harbor, consisted of fifteen lectures prepared by experts at West Point, to be delivered by selected officers followed by open discussions on current war developments. This orientation, the War Department claimed, assured that "the American soldier ... [would not] be just the best trained soldier in the world, not just the best equipped soldier in the world, but the best informed soldier in the world."[63]

Marshall hoped that by giving the individual soldier the plain facts and letting him draw his own conclusions, charges of propaganda could be avoided. To further this idea, the chief of staff fully supported camp newspapers and periodicals that allowed servicemen to practice "limited" free speech.[64] Convinced that open discussion periods and camp newspapers represented efforts to democratize the army, some officers argued that such activity would lead to disobedience and disrespect and could inadvertently promote fascist and Communist ideology. In addition, these officers were disturbed by Marshall's reliance on a research branch headed by Samuel Stouffer that conducted troop surveys throughout the war to assess GIs' opinions and attitudes. They believed that if the upper echelons of the War Department listened to such opinions, authority had ceased to flow from the top down. These officers participated in the orientation program without enthusiasm, often quickly reading lectures to their men word for word, and in some cases disobeying Marshall's orders altogether by refusing to hold open discussions.[65] Marshall steadfastly supported camp newspapers, open discussions, and opinion polls in the belief that if the army showed little interest in the welfare of its men and refused to better their condition and keep them informed, they would become embittered veterans, unsupportive of a strong peacetime army.[66] He did, however, acknowledge that orientation lectures for "soldiers bone tired from their initial encounter with basic training ... proved baffling, bewildering, or just boring."[67]

After December 7, 1941, America entered the war fully committed to defeating the tripartite powers, but with no consensus regarding the nation's postwar goals. Organized religion had declined in importance as a force in military morale education after leading clergymen rejected war as sin, condemned propaganda in all forms, and claimed that the draft sentenced the nation's youth to "syphilis and slavery."[68] Because few leaders were interested in incorporating religious tenets into army orientation lectures, organized religion instead concentrated its efforts on maintaining morality in and around the nation's training camps. However, Pearl Harbor convinced church leaders, along with the majority of Americans, that the war was truly a moral crusade. Because troop education policies were already in place by the time of the Japanese attack, organized religion was left out of the indoctrination formula. This is not to imply that no one attempted to incorporate the tenets of the American civil-military religion into the Troop Information and Education (TI&E) program, just that efforts to do so after the war were considerably more concerted and evangelical.

Instead, the War Department experimented with new psychological and social engineering techniques (rather than religion and recreation) to instill in the fighting man initiative and self-reliance, characteristics believed to have been eroded by the technological advancements of the Industrial Revolution.[69] World War I enhanced the image of psychologists as civilian experts on morale, but their popularity declined after the war ended. In 1938, when the possibility of another major war became clear to many, psychologists attempted to join the defense effort by advocating the creation of a national will—a will in which each citizen would be willing to sacrifice himself for the good of the whole. The September, 1942, issue of the *American Journal of Psychiatry* said there was "a new emphasis on will to fight rather than simply on ability to fight" and recommended that Americans be taught why they were fighting, along with steps to increase hatred for the enemy.[70]

Frederick Osborn, the head of Special Services, agreed with General Marshall's views on morale and encouraged full freedom of expression in all organized discussions, including the sensitive area of military policy, in order to create a "mentally alert soldier."[71] Osborn, who surrounded himself with social-science experts, was a leading spokesman for a reform movement within the science of eugenics. Before the war, reform eugenicists had associated with Nazi scientists and their concept of "selective breeding," but openly criticized the Third Reich's anti-Semitism and "forced" sterilization of "inferiors." Even so, Osborn had praised Nazi eugenics in 1937 as the "most important experiment . . . ever tried." Under his direction, the Morale Branch/Special Services Division experimented with social engineering.[72] Convinced that environment played as important a role as heredity in the development of human character, Osborn called for the government to saturate the recruit's environment with particular ideas and information to bring about the desired patriotism. He claimed that the numerous cases of shell shock during World War I were the result of soldiers being ignorant of why they were risking their lives. During World War II in England, where the population endured nightly bombing raids, mental hospitals remained empty, because, according to Osborn, the British government had articulated a clear national purpose. Although he personally stressed psychological indoctrination in his morale education plans, Osborn's reform eugenics ideas were never fully implemented by the army.[73]

In 1942, a year after the completion of the Railey Report, the army concluded that troops still had an inadequate understanding of America's role in the war effort. Hoping to remedy this situation, the Roosevelt administration extended its own efforts at morale education. The Office of War Information (OWI), created by Roosevelt in June, 1942, struggled to "influence public opinion at home and abroad" with a "strategy of truth."[74] Although the OWI avoided lying directly to the American public, it did shape "facts." Elmer Davis, the head of the OWI, said "the easiest way to inject a propaganda idea into most people's minds is to let it go in through the medium of an entertainment [motion] picture when they do not realize that they are being propagandized."[75] To accomplish this goal, Davis issued a manual for moviemakers and threatened to revoke their export licenses if they did not submit screenplays for review and allow the agency to rewrite some of the dialogue.[76]

The seven films that made up the highly acclaimed *Why We Fight* series, produced by the Morale Branch/Special Services Division and directed by Frank Capra, was an effort to win the minds of the nation's recruits and to defeat any spirit of isolationism still lingering in the American public. The series, which was aimed at both civilians and new recruits, was shown in public movie theaters across America. Each film relentlessly presented the danger to the homeland posed by the Nazis and Japanese. While claiming to portray only the facts of the war, Capra's team, inspired by a private screening of a captured copy of Hitler's *Triumph of the Will* (1935) molded "facts" into a particular version of foreign policy. According to this version, the tripartite powers, beginning in 1930, had developed a master plan to control the globe. The most important step in this plan was the conquest of America. Adolph Hitler, Benito Mussolini, and Emperor Hirohito, visually and ideologically, became indistinguishable in this one-war theme. The Axis powers were portrayed as predators, efficient and cunning, who softened up their victims with promises of peace before destroying them. Americans hated war, according to the series, but would fight when war was thrust upon them.[77]

A few months after the debut of the first film in the series, *Prelude to War,* the army's Special Services Division held a series of conferences to sell commanders on the value of the information and education functions of morale education. Speaking in Baltimore, Maj. S. L. A. Marshall proclaimed: "it is our task in Special Services to harden the resolve of soldiers so that they will be better prepared to destroy the enemies of our country. It is our task, likewise to shape their thinking so that this thing will not happen again. . . . Not only . . . [will] they have unlimited resolve to get on with it but they . . . [will] return home looking at old problems with new eyes. It is our task to make them see."[78]

Another name change and refinement of focus occurred on September 5, 1944, when the army, again unhappy with the term *morale,* changed the name of Osborn's division to Information and Education (I&E). Commencing at the end of the war, weekly I&E discussions concentrated on issues relating to demobilization, such as postwar employment, veterans rights, the GI Bill, and—the army's cure-all for its postwar troubles—UMT. Overall, programs late in the war and shortly after its conclusion stressed a positive attitude toward a strong defense establishment, especially the need to maintain adequate manpower levels for the nation's expanded world responsibilities. Soon, however, the I&E Division began to disintegrate, just as the World War I Morale Branch had. This setback proved to be only temporary, however, for the domestic and international events of the Cold War guaranteed there would be a future role for in-service political indoctrination.[79]

Before Pearl Harbor, morale education stressed conformist citizenship and included a variety of recreation and welfare activities. However, over the course of four eventful years of war, information and education functions moved out of obscurity into the forefront of morale education. Trying to maintain a citizen army in a democracy was a problem for the U.S. armed forces. War necessitated an understanding of the principles of democracy in order to convince soldiers that their sacrifices were legitimate. However, for an army to be an effective force in wartime, its men need to be disciplined to obey orders without debate. Chief of Staff George Marshall tried to balance the two opposing requirements for a citizen army by preserving as much freedom of expression as possible during World War II. However, this "democratizing" of the army remained within clearly defined limits. Marshall, who expected prompt obedience throughout the ranks, feared that a repetition of the conditions described in the 1941 Railey Report would weaken the public's confidence in the nation's defenses. Nevertheless, he introduced "liberal" ideas concerning troop morale that many veteran officers found disturbing. After the war ended, the peacetime army would seek an effective way to preserve the traditional American values of initiative and self-discipline while maintaining the military discipline needed for an efficient armed force. The answer, according to such leaders as Marshall, Harry S. Truman, and Dwight D. Eisenhower, would be through a system of UMT that fostered unity rather than diversity of opinion. According to its proponents, UMT would instill in American youth the "spiritual" and "patriotic" values deemed necessary to maintain a strong national defense and to preserve national historic values.

The claim at the beginning of the Cold War that the nation lacked a resolute national will offered a ready explanation for a number of policy setbacks and provided ample justification for new initiatives in psychological warfare during the Truman and Eisenhower administrations. Initially with Truman's plan for universal military training and later with Eisenhower's psychological warfare programs promulgating an evangelical democracy, civil-military religion was used as an organizing mechanism to achieve the desired national will. Because it was popularly believed that the nation's homes, schools, and churches had failed to teach the values necessary for defense, "Cold Warriors" sought to reclaim the nation's moral heritage by inculcating the American people with the civic virtues of the revolutionary generation. Using religious nationalism with unprecedented zeal, the military attempted to fortify the national character for a climactic battle with the Soviet Union—an enemy that was militarily strong, atheistic, and ideologically alien to democracy, capitalism, and other concepts held dear by Americans.

CHAPTER 2

The American Civil-Military Religion and the Cold War

Throughout the history of mankind, symbols have exerted an im-

pelling influence upon the lives of men. The cross and flag are em-

bodiments of our ideals and teach us not only how to live but how

to die.

—Douglas MacArthur

The stained glass windows gracing the entrance of the Washington Memorial Chapel at Valley Forge are icons of American civil religion. Depicting episodes from the life of the nation's first president, the most venerated panel portrays George Washington at prayer, somewhat reminiscent of the biblical account of Jesus Christ in the garden of Gethsemane. Nicola D'Ascenzo's inspirational rendition is based on an oft-told story first published in 1804 by Mason Locke "Parson" Weems. According to Parson Weems, Issac Potts, a Pennsylvania Quaker and Tory, unexpectedly discovered the commander of the Continental forces secluded in the Valley Forge woods, kneeling in the snow and in earnest prayer for his new country. Rushing home, Potts announced to his wife that he could now support the revolution with a clear conscience. "Thee knows that I always thought the sword and the gospel utterly inconsistent; and that no man could be a soldier and a

Christian at the same time. But George Washington has this day convinced me of my mistake," the former pacifist reportedly testified. "If George Washington be not a man of God, I am greatly deceived—and still more shall I be deceived if God do [sic] not, through him, work out a great salvation for America."[1]

Although widely accepted, the Weems story is without historical basis. Parson Weems fabricated the tale, along with the "cherry tree incident" and other Washington myths, in order to sell his series of character-shaping books to the nation's youth. Despite the fact that there was no evidence supporting the prayer story, popular biographers and even many historians of the nineteenth century accepted the Weems narrative. Unconcerned about its authenticity, they were convinced that George Washington, as the exemplar of America's civic-religious foundations, most likely did utter such a prayer. The legend's popularity continued throughout the nineteenth and early twentieth centuries as the nation embraced a developing civil religion that gave meaning and mission to the American experience.

After falling into disuse during the Second World War, Washington iconography revived as the nation sought to "return" to the "faith" of its founding fathers during the uncertain years of the early Cold War. Along with other military-religious imagery of American civil religion, the U.S. government and a host of private patriotic organizations enshrined the Washington prayer story, and it became one of the tenets of America's national faith and defense. It mattered little that historian Paul F. Boller Jr. furthered the work of previous scholars and irrefutably discredited the Weems account in 1963; the public perception that the fanciful parson had told the truth persisted and became reality for disciples of American civil religion.[2]

More than any other segment of society, the U.S. armed forces embraced the correlation between military defense and God's will epitomized by the Valley Forge prayer story. During the early Cold War, the military attempted to communicate to the Soviet Union that the American people possessed a resolute national will and prepared for combat by incorporating a religious mission into its traditions and culture. According to its proponents, a religious military would also demonstrate to the public the value of a peacetime army as a character-building institution, attract high-quality middle-class volunteers into its ranks, and, in the hands of the individual services, provide a means to preserve each distinct version of national security (land, sea, and air) from rival branches of the armed forces seeking greater appropriations.

The military's use of religion during the early Cold War had additional, less obvious implications as well. First, by playing a central role in American civil religion, the military became identified in the public mind as the instrument of God's will. Once this divine role for the armed forces was fully incorporated into the developing Cold War consensus, it became difficult for "patriotic" Americans to criticize aggressive measures. "Good Americans" (those who were true believers in the American civil-military religion) would support war as a solution to the nation's security needs, whereas pacifism became associated with disloyalty in the minds of many. Second, certain high-ranking individuals within the Department of Defense, encouraged by the widespread dissemination of religious nationalism and empowered by a growing military influence in American society, for a short period of time strained the limits of civil-military relations by joining forces with ultraconservatives in conducting highly politicized anticommunism seminars for the American public during the late 1950s and early 1960s. Unaware of the potential dangers in these trends, the postwar military establishment engaged in religiously oriented citizenship indoctrination during Troop Information and Education (TI&E) programs in its continuing efforts to fulfill its constitutional and "God-given" duty to provide for the common defense. Its character-shaping duty seemed especially important in light of a reported collapse of American civic and moral character following World War II.

Demobilization and the State of the National Character

As World War II came to a close, the U.S. armed forces, the mightiest military machine in the world, prepared for greatly expanded global responsibilities. Within two years following V-J Day, however, army manpower had dropped by nearly 7 million to a mere 630,000 men, making it difficult for the service to fulfill its occupation duties. A highly effective letter-writing campaign, promoted by more than two hundred "Bring Back Daddy" clubs, featuring pictures of GIs' children and an avalanche of baby shoes, convinced many politicians to support accelerated demobilization rates despite security needs to the contrary. A particularly disturbing factor in the rapid manpower reduction was a series of soldier protests on U.S. military bases around the world that gave the appearance that the American character and will lacked the discipline and resolve needed for a protracted conflict with the Soviet Union.

In January, 1946, after Army Chief of Staff George C. Marshall ordered demobilization slowed down to keep the army from literally "running out of Army," twenty thousand soldiers stationed in Manila "rioted." Their chief complaint was of improprieties in the point system that determined each man's place in the demobilization schedule.[3] While little actual violence occurred, uniformed protestors carried signs proclaiming "Service yes, but Serfdom never!" and "We're Tired of False Promises." Others wrote letters to their congressmen. One warned, "either demobilize us or, when given the next shot at the ballot box we will demobilize you."[4] Additional protests soon erupted in Guam, Japan, France, England, Germany, Korea, India, Austria, and even on some bases in the continental United States (including Andrews Air Force Base outside Washington D.C.). Lieutenant General Matthew B. Ridgway, who observed demonstrations in London, expressed "anger and disgust" at the "disgraceful exhibition" of American soldiers protesting against their government.[5]

Marshall responded to the "demobilization riots" with further democratic reforms and an increased emphasis on religion during troop information training periods. The army's Doolittle Board, named for its chairman, Lt. Gen. James H. Doolittle of the Army Air Forces, advertised its open-mindedness by soliciting letters ("Tell it to Doolittle") from soldiers on how best to reform the service and attempted to improve the army's public image through internal reform. Because the board gave the appearance that the services had been fully "democratized," it became a scapegoat for alleged disciplinary problems during the Korean War. "The postwar 'Doolittle Board,'" according to *New York Times* columnist Hanson Baldwin in 1953, "caused severe damage to service effectiveness by recommendations intended to 'democratize' the army—a concept that is self-contradictory." Whether or not that was true, the board's psychological effects were profound, especially through its suggestion that the military should improve the "character, knowledge, and the competency of those serving."[6]

The War Department, alarmed by the demobilization riots, immediately increased its efforts to build up the morale of its troops. Convinced that recreation, entertainment, and political indoctrination no longer sufficed, a number of high-ranking officers advocated a greater focus on religion in the ranks. The use of religion to imbue soldiers with a fighting spirit was fraught with obvious contradictions that were readily pointed out by pacifist organizations across the nation. The postwar U.S. armed forces, however, believed it to be an effective and efficient vehicle for improving the civic virtue presumed to be lacking in young recruits. According to General Marshall, "spiritual morale" was what won wars, "and that type of morale can only come out of the religious nature of a soldier who knows God and who had the spirit of religious fervor in his soul." The general added, "I count heavily on that type of man and that kind of Army."[7]

Marshall typified postwar military thought in that he sought the most effective and efficient means both to foster discipline within the ranks and to improve the army's public image. Along with these practical goals, Marshall also advocated incorporating religion into TI&E programs to counter what he considered a deplorable lack of traditional patriotism and morality within American society. Marshall and others operated from the belief that national security rested on the civic virtue of its citizens—a virtue that had always implied an informed citizenry and personal moral code beyond mere obedience to duty. During the early Cold War, the armed forces, in much the same fashion as turn-of-the-century military progressives, attempted to strengthen national defense and to revitalize the American spirit by inculcating recruits with the core values thought lacking in modern society. Not only would a moral soldier be an obedient soldier, according to the "military mind," but a "civilized" and "sanitized" training camp experience would also convince middle-class parents that their sons would not be corrupted by military service.

Middle-class soldiers dutifully served during World War II, but after the end of hostilities, parents preferred other vocations for their children and demanded that their sons not enlist in or be drafted into what they often considered to be an immoral environment. Wartime accounts had suggested to the public that a rapid decline in morality occurred once youth entered the armed services. Removed from the restraints of family and church, GIs reportedly engaged in sexually aggressive behavior—often with the knowledge, and sometimes even the approval, of their superior officers. "[Soldiers] cannot, they must not, be mollycoddled," a senior navy officer claimed in 1941. "[S]exual aggression . . . makes them the stern, dynamic type we associate with men of the armed force. . . . Imagine, if you can, an army of impotent men."[8]

Despite the War Department's best efforts to improve morality within the ranks, an informal military society rejected "feminine" characteristics and encouraged its members not only to be aggressive on the battlefield but also in their relations with women. After the war, the military's reputation declined even further because bored and bitter veterans awaiting overdue discharges and "low-quality" recruits, as the military classified those of lesser education and financial resources, lacked a clear sense of mission and sought worldly "diversions." The War Department was especially alarmed at GI behavior in occupied Germany. When absence without leave (AWOL) and VD rates skyrocketed, chaplains condemned the "cheap, tawdry and bawdy entertainment" provided to the occupation forces by the United Service Organizations (USO), and pleaded for "restraining influences" to prevent "complete moral chaos."[9]

Postwar Revivalism

Along with the reported immorality within the ranks, social critics also pointed to an alleged corresponding decline in domestic virtue following the war. Church membership and enrollment in college religious studies had increased, but this renewed interest in theology apparently had little impact on public mores.[10] A nearly equal increase in materialism, alcohol and cigarette consumption, promiscuity, and violent crime, especially among the nation's youth, convinced many that America faced a postwar morality crisis. In 1945, Henry L. Stimson, making his final remarks as secretary of war, predicted this perceived degeneration of the national character. Stimson feared that the American people, who were courageous and resolute during wars, would (as he claimed they had traditionally) become self-indulgent and apathetic to their peacetime civic responsibilities. Immediate action must be taken to reverse this trend, Stimson warned, otherwise foreign powers would "not only regard us as unprepared, which will be true, but they will also regard us as too irresponsible ever to take the trouble to prepare or to defend ourselves."[11] National security planners generally agreed with Stimson. Drunkenness and debauchery indicated vulnerability, according to the Cold Warriors. They called for the revitalization of America's "traditional" democratic and moral core values through patriotic, evangelical Christian revival.

At the end of the war, neoevangelical theologian Carl F. H. Henry called for conservative Christianity to save civilization from "the ruins of its dying culture."[12] Henry hoped that a mass revival would be the agent of America's salvation, but most historians, sociologists, and liberal theologians disagreed. According to these critics, revivalism, considered dead since the days of Billy Sunday and Aimee Semple McPherson, contained too many "emotional dangers" to be considered as a solution for the national malady. However, there emerged during the war a new generation of evangelicals who used modern mass-communications techniques to reach the public with an old-fashioned gospel message infused with patriotic appeals. These neoevangelicals, moderates who in 1942 organized as the National Association of Evangelicals (NAE), differed significantly from their evangelical predecessors, the separatist and often intolerant American Council of Christian Churches (ACCC). By adopting a reformist stance and tapping into the dominant youth culture, the NAE effectively spread its salvation message across the nation.[13]

Modern evangelicalism comprised a wide variety of conservative Protestant sects with differing degrees of adherence to the infallibility of the Holy Bible and need for separation from the "corrupting influences" of the world. Evangelicals generally believed in Arminianism (free will), adventism (a focus on the immediacy of the second coming of Jesus Christ), and millennialism (a coming thousand-year reign of Christ on the earth). They additionally divided human history into numerous "dispensations" (time periods) and called for converts to be "born again" by inviting Jesus Christ into their hearts, thereby accepting the baptism of the Holy Spirit. Fundamentalists (ultraconservative evangelicals), who attempted to separate from the world politically and culturally, enjoyed their greatest support among the rural, small-town lower classes. In contrast, neoevangelicals were more attractive to the middle class because they were willing to engage the world in order to save it. Both varieties of evangelicals were anticommunist during the Cold War, but it was the separatist fundamentalists who ironically played a pivotal role in the formation of the politically oriented radical right of the 1960s (as will be discussed in detail later).[14]

During World War II, neoevangelicals co-opted wartime patriotism and, to the dismay of fundamentalists who had yet to be politicized, co-operated with liberal Protestants and secular political conservatives in their effort to assert an emotionally fervent moral authority over the nation. The Youth for Christ ministry, the foremost neoevangelical association of its day, popularized religion with crusades that "saved" people by celebrating patriotic themes and American purity along with calling the sinner to repentance. Through the personal testimonies of Hollywood stars, sports idols, and war heroes and by providing entertaining "swing-tempo" gospel music and dynamic sermonettes that concentrated on current events, the Youth for Christ movement gained thousands of converts. Military bases were popular sites for Youth for Christ crusades. After being converted at one such rally, a born-again sailor claimed, "ever since

I left the protection of my home, I have felt almost adrift, with no sense of security. I don't want to get caught in the current of vice. I needed something to stabilize me and in my new faith in Christ, I have found it."[15]

Both the Truman and Eisenhower administrations attempted to harness the stabilizing forces of the emerging revival movement in order to forge a unified national character during an era of increasing domestic and international tensions. The combination of wartime nationalism along with the missionary impulses expressed by the Youth for Christ and other postwar revival ministries had renewed the public's interest in America's role as the "redeemer nation." Policy makers capitalized on this growing religious nationalism to gain support for the policies they believed essential to the maintenance of national security. Sharing middle-class concerns regarding the current state of public virtue, the federal government attempted to dedicate America to an "evangelical democracy" by taking steps to reform the national character with military discipline.

The image of a militant, anticommunist, evangelical democracy became increasingly important to policy makers as the Soviet Union advanced militarily and politically throughout the world after the end of World War II. National security planners worried that America's rapid demobilization and the lack of an identifiable, resolute American character had encouraged communist aggression. By 1947, the Soviets were entrenched in Eastern Europe, parts of the Far East, and had even managed to win political victories in some Western democracies. Preoccupied with rebuilding their war-torn nations, the Western democracies were unable to mount an effective challenge to the Russian threat. Moreover, the United States could do little to aid Europe beyond offering economic assistance. Rapid demobilization had reduced American troop strength to a mere 554,000 by 1948 and, in an effort to prevent another depression, Pres. Harry S. Truman enacted his "Fair Deal" programs and expanded foreign trade rather than increase the defense budget. Even after announcing what became known as the "Truman Doctrine" in 1947, greatly extending the military's worldwide responsibilities, the president, to the disbelief of the armed services, continued to call for defense reductions.[16]

Unification and the Growing Influence of the Military

Plagued by a lack of national determination to mount aggressive and costly measures against the Red Army's nearly 5-million-man force, the White House instead relied on economic diplomacy (reconstruction loans and the Marshall Plan), a plan for universal military training (to provide the nation with a massive reserve of trained manpower in the event of war), and, most importantly, the nation's unrivaled nuclear arsenal to provide Europe with the security that the U.S. military was unable to supply with conventional forces. In this increasingly anxious atmosphere, a revitalization movement developed within the War Department to reorganize the armed forces into a more efficient and effective fighting force. The first step in the reorganization process was to "unify" the armed forces.[17] Unification did create a more efficient military establishment. It also unleashed passions for evangelical democracy already present in the hierarchy of the officer corps by inadvertently increasing the armed forces' influence in American society at a time when evangelicals had finally achieved greater representation within the military chaplaincy.

Inadvertently, the battle between the army and navy plans for unification gave the military a greater voice in domestic matters concerning national will and character. Congress finalized unification in the National Security Act of 1947 by striking a compromise between separate proposals for a postwar military establishment put forward by the army (highly centralized) and the navy (loosely coordinated). The navy, which had never supported unification, was forced to accept a single cabinet-level department, the National Military Establishment (NME), with a civilian secretary and a separate air force, although the army and navy retained some air capabilities. Along with a "chairless" Joint Chiefs of Staff that managed but did not command the unified services, Congress established a host of cabinet-level defense agencies called for by the navy (such as the Central Intelligence Agency [CIA] and the National Security Council [NSC]) in order to link and integrate economic, military, and diplomatic resources into a modern corporatist body. Finally, the Office of the Secretary of Defense (OSD; not yet a cabinet-level position) possessed little real authority. The president named former Navy Secretary James V. Forrestal, who had worked tirelessly to prevent unification, as the NME's first secretary. Forrestal was frustrated by the fact that he could confer with but not command the true powers in the military establishment: the three service secretaries. By combining the army and navy plans, Congress, in effect, emasculated the nation's defenses, which had become, according to one knowledgeable observer, "little more than a weak federation of sovereign military units."[18]

Under the highly decentralized and diversified defense system, conflict between the three services was inevitable, especially with regard to defense appropriations and the much-coveted air capabilities of the army and the navy. The young, dynamic air force, heady with its newly won independence, secured increasing percentages of the budget—to the detriment of the other military branches—and moved to consolidate all military aircraft under its authority. It gained support by insisting that only land-based bombers carrying atomic weapons could adequately protect American interests. In 1948, the president's Air Policy Commission issued a report that supported the air force's request to increase its fifty-five-group force to seventy groups. In response to bitter opposition from the army and the navy, Forrestal called for a meeting of the JCS to iron out differences between the branches concerning their individual roles and missions. Instead of the cooperation he expected, the meeting in Key West, Florida, deteriorated into an open battle for the nation's nuclear capabilities. Forrestal mediated a compromise after convincing the navy to withdraw its demand for land-based bombers in exchange for preserving its ability to wage atomic war with carrier-borne aircraft.

In 1949, however, Louis A. Johnson, the new defense secretary, convinced the JCS to cancel the navy's CVA-58 "Super Carrier" program as a cost-reduction measure. A number of prominent admirals, including Arthur W. Radford, feared that this was an attempt to undermine the navy and retaliated by appealing directly to Congress. Radford denounced the air force's B-36 bombers as "a billion-dollar blunder" that performed badly under combat conditions. Others insinuated that the plane and had been contracted by "irregular" procedures. Chief of Naval Operations Louis Denfeld publicly criticized Secretary Johnson, the president, and the air force hierarchy in what he called a covert attempt to eliminate naval aviation. This so-called Revolt of the Admirals was such an embarrassment to the White House that the president ordered Denfeld's relief and Congress promptly amended the National Security Act in 1949 to prevent future acts of insubordination.[19]

Much to the navy's dismay, its role in unification and the subsequent Revolt of the Admirals foiled its original desire for a loosely organized military establishment. Under the reformed National Security Act, the individual services lost much of their former independence, while the defense secretary gained cabinet ranking, a larger staff, and the authority to truly command the newly named Department of Defense. In addition, the JCS added a chairman to act as its presiding officer, and, most importantly, to establish its agenda and serve as the principal military adviser to the defense secretary and the president. Finally, the NSC and other agencies created to diffuse power continued to operate, but under tightened authority. Despite chronic manpower shortages and inadequate appropriations, the armed forces emerged in 1949 as a powerful centralized institution with new and undetermined influences at the top levels of government by means of the new agencies created by the National Security Act of 1947 and strengthened in the final revised legislation of 1949.[20]

In a sense, the National Security Act only legitimized the growing influence of the armed services already under way in American life. After the war, this influence became increasingly evident in science, industry, and education as respected military men accepted leadership positions in these areas and a military-industrial complex began to emerge. Furthermore, the army, navy, and air force adopted new advertising techniques to improve their public image and to attract quality recruits into their ranks, while professional lobbyists advanced the interests of the services they represented by obtaining increased budget allocations and new weapons systems. To some critics, these changes represented a dangerous militarization of American society. Nonetheless, there was little doubt that a conservative "military mind" (a mind that valued efficiency, patriotism, and obedience, but differed on how best to achieve American foreign and domestic objectives) commanded great respect during a time of disturbing international crises.

As the military's new prominence became institutionalized in the National Security Act and a conservative military mind grew in importance throughout American society, the armed forces were in a particularly strong position to attempt the active shaping of a national character. First, the creation of the interdepartmental NSC had greatly facilitated this trend by formally giving the military a voice in foreign and domestic policy making. Secondly, a strong evangelical movement developing within the armed forces' chaplaincy placed some of the most vocal proponents of American civil-military religion in positions of power and paved the way for the infusion of evangelical Christianity into in-service character education. Finally, the White House, with DOD support, formulated plans to improve the national character and fulfill its chronic manpower needs by attempting to legislate a plan for universal military training that contained a strong religious component. While UMT failed to receive congressional approval, it provided the blueprint for a mandatory character-education program enacted throughout the services in 1948. By incorporating religion into the very core of military life, a life that had become increasingly influential, DOD and the Truman and

Eisenhower administrations hoped to foster a spiritual reawakening intended not only to strengthen the character of the men and women of the armed services, but to spread its reportedly redemptive powers to the rest of the nation as well.[21]

An Evangelical Chaplaincy

The coveted spiritual regeneration of the American people by the armed forces began with the campaign for a reorganized and professional military chaplaincy. Officially recognized in July, 1775, the chaplaincy remained an unorganized auxiliary to the armed forces until the National Defense Act of 1920. In accordance with that act, a chief of chaplains was appointed to provide a measure of coordination for the decentralized spiritual activities of the various services. Considerable controversy regarding the constitutionality of the chaplaincy retarded its professionalization, but by 1947, after the rapid mobilization associated with World War II convinced the military of the need for further centralization, the U.S. Chaplain Corps became an integral component of the Cold War defense establishment. Most Americans supported religious activities within the military, but they had qualms about certain breaches of the principle calling for the separation of church and state. Some questioned the appropriateness of mandatory worship; others looked askance at chaplains being paid by the government and being responsible to superior officers rather than religious authorities. Critics also claimed that, instead of being spiritual advisers for recruits, the priests, ministers, and rabbis in the chaplaincy's ranks would merely provide a cover for the armed forces to "Prussianize" American youth.[22]

Although the initial selection of chaplain candidates was left to the churches, the military, which administered its own fitness tests, determined which men would actually serve. After being commissioned, chaplains came under the same military chain of command as any other soldier. The churches retained a semblance of control by having the right to withdraw their endorsement at any point. Once in the military, however, most clergymen became "orphaned" from their home denominations and were forced to look to the Chaplain Corps for support and guidance. The officer's rank insignia and the insignia of the Chaplain Corps represented the chaplain's purported dual accountability. Thus, the chaplain, addressed as "sir" and saluted by those of lesser rank, was fully incorporated into the military machine and mind-set.[23]

The particular branch of the service to which a chaplain belonged, as well as his individual assignment, largely dictated his duties. As a rule, he was expected to hold a general Protestant service in addition to worship services for his own denomination or faith (Catholic or Jewish). In reality, however, chaplains became universal ministers. Chronic understaffing made it impossible for the services to assign recruits to bases serviced by chaplains of their particular faith groups. By necessity, a type of ecumenical or common denominator religion was developed to meet the spiritual needs of the one thousand or more men typically assigned to each clergyman's supervision. While chaplains received instruction on how to conduct ceremonies in each of the three major faith groups, for the sake of efficiency religious services often evolved into a homogenized liturgy that stressed the Old Testament, the only writings held sacred by all three major faiths and that were, not coincidentally, supportive of military solutions to political problems.[24]

Finding themselves under military orders and often isolated from their home churches, newly commissioned chaplains either adapted to this amalgamation of religious faiths or quickly left the service. Many reportedly experienced what psychologists have termed "cognitive dissonance," the anxiety resulting from the holding of two disparate views (religious calling and military duty) at the same time, and rationalized an ecumenicalism most had found abhorrent before enlistment. The chaplaincy, in short, became an adherent of America's civil-military religion.[25]

According to the precepts of civil-military religion, each branch of the service could be considered a unique expression or "denomination" of the American way of life, separated by mission but sharing a common set of rituals (for example, induction and basic training), sacred symbols (the American flag), moral code (the Uniform Code of Justice), and priests (military chaplains). The air force religion, for example, has been described as "consisting of a unified system of sanctioned beliefs and practices aimed at the legitimization of aerospace power (speed, range, flexibility, precision and lethality)." While air force religion postulated that "air power" was needed to save the nation from destruction, the same could be claimed by the other denominations of national defense (land forces for the army and sea power for the navy). The air force rhetoric was certainly the most evangelical of the military religions. Ministers of "the gospel of air power" had championed the creation of a separate service since the 1930s and, after its creation, continued their devotion to the primacy of aviation technology. The army, believing itself to be the bedrock of national defense, preached the citizen-soldier concept as the basis of America's salvation. The navy religion, messianic at the turn of the century about battleship based sea power, faced difficulty justifying its raison d'être during the Cold War. Perhaps, for this reason, the navy, more than the other two branches, sought innovative, bold solutions to the Cold War. The navy—to strengthen national security, but also to justify its existence in a rapidly changing military establishment—promoted a civil-military religion considerably more militant in tone than the religious nationalism preached by the army and air force during the early Cold War.[26]

In January, 1957, Rev. Engebret O. Midboe issued "The Report of the Bureau of Service to Military Persons," in which he claimed that during the Cold War, the military had drifted away from "denominational moorings" and moved toward the creation of a "military church"—as evidenced by the armed forces' increasing emphasis on the general Protestant service over regular denominational services. Midboe charged that commanders criticized chaplains who insisted on conducting services in their own faith rather then preaching the "Navy Religion" or "Army Religion." In 1957, journalist Drew Pearson claimed that the Midboe report proved that the armed forces were "trying to mold all Protestant churches into one all-embracing religion for American soldiers . . . 'a great GI church.'"[27]

Pragmatic to the end, the armed forces manipulated religious nationalism to legitimate their mission and authority. To the dismay of a number of historians and diplomats, civil-military religion, in all its denominational variety, provided a "moral claim" (bureaucratically strengthened through the National Security Act of 1947) by which the armed forces were injected into domestic and foreign policy decisions. The armed forces (each branch in particular), as the "guardian" of the national interest, claimed the right and duty to speak out at the highest levels of government in defense of their version of the American way of life.[28]

The wide acceptance of civil-military religion by American society during the early Cold War was quite remarkable when compared to the climate that prevailed immediately after World War II, a climate in which most faith groups had denounced any effort to militarize society. Both liberal mainline denominations and evangelical sects warned that the government's call for UMT was a ploy to shape the nation along Old World patterns. Liberal churchmen overwhelmingly continued to reject any expansion of the military into American life, but after the Cold War began, many evangelicals reconsidered their position and supported a peacetime draft in order to ensure the military had sufficient manpower "to cope with the enemies of the American way of life."[29]

This change of heart by the nation's evangelicals occurred first at the grass roots level. Evangelicals, who no doubt truly feared the communist threat, discovered that support for the military also provided a means to counter both Catholic and liberal Protestant influences on the nation's youth. Although they had previously shunned the chaplaincy because of

Cover of a 1957 pamphlet promoting "The American Way of Life."

these same influences, in the late 1940s and 1950s, when evangelical denominations grew rapidly in numbers and power, the National Association of Evangelicals embraced the opportunity provided by the chaplaincy to advance its particular messianic vision and to counter the "ungodly" influences of its rival churchmen with the armed services.

During World War I, the War Department had established a quota system in the hopes that the number of clergy from each faith group would be representative of the number of personnel of that faith serving in the military. Catholics, who at that time filled only their fair share of positions, had maneuvered themselves into seats of authority within the Chaplain Corps. They were able to do this, according to liberals and evangelicals alike, because disunited Protestant chaplains had been ineffective in frustrating the plans of the better-organized priests.[30]

Evangelicals also despised the influence of liberal Protestants on the chaplaincy, especially the Federal Council of Churches (FCC), which, through its General Commission on Army and Navy Chaplains, controlled most of the Protestant clergy appointments. The War Department recognized only three major faith groups (Catholics, Protestants, and Jews) in the endorsement process, and the FCC, as the oldest representative of the Protestant churches, was given the greatest discretion in appointing candidates from that faith group. In 1944, the NAE succeeded in obtaining government sanction for its own Commission on Chaplains in order to secure more appointments for evangelical chaplains. Simultaneously, the rapid growth of evangelical men and women in the military ranks gave the NAE expanding quotas as the Defense Department altered the endorsement process to include more "minority" religions. Evangelicals also took advantage of openings left vacant by faith groups unable to meet their quotas by offering their own candidates for selection. In this manner, a dramatic increase in the number of evangelical chaplains (although still a minority) occurred. In addition, evangelicals maximized their influence by charging that liberal ministers who opposed the draft had communist sympathies. Some even claimed that liberal denominations were a fifth column for the Soviets and "should be opposed by 'all who love America.'" These enthusiasts were ready and willing to use the military, the last untapped mission field, to evangelize the world.[31]

Evangelicals, liberal Protestants, and Catholics all coveted the chaplaincy for the opportunities it presented as a total institution. Sociologist Erving Goffman claimed that the armed forces as a "total institution" (in the same fashion as other total institutions, such as prisons and monastic religious orders) removed young, impressionable recruits from normal life, stripped them of their individuality and privacy, and brought them to a moment of crisis. In basic training, according to Goffman, recruits suffered endless and often irrational harassment by drill sergeants attempting to break their will and make them receptive to socialization along military lines.[32] The chaplain, who lived alongside the trainees in a ministry of presence, was accorded numerous opportunities for evangelism during this reshaping process, when, according to a promotional video, "hearts [were] soft and eager to receive the message of God's love and salvation."[33] Critics would later label the chaplain's work at training camps during the Cold War as "ecclesiastical brain-washing" because the "homesick and confused adolescents, already undergoing indoctrination in the basic military creed of 'Believe what you're told, do what you're told, ask no questions'" were susceptible to their psychological manipulations.[34] Once "Christianized," according to evangelicals, service personnel stationed at military bases throughout the world could serve as missionaries of American civil-military religion. Earl Parvin claims that the American soldier, "garbed in the uniform of a peace-loving nation, armed with the tools of war but required to use those tools only as a last resort" was more than a warrior. He was "an ambassador of understanding and service rather than a harbinger of hate, the Christian in uniform stands strong in his conviction and declares with truth: 'peace is my profession.'"[35]

As evangelicals gained power within the chaplaincy and came to appreciate the worldwide possibilities provided by military service, many came to consider the total institution of the armed services training camps as an ideal opportunity for their missionary work and in some cases even supported the draft. It is interesting to note that although proponents of national service legislation claimed that UMT would create a means for the government to instill spiritual values in all American males, most evangelicals (and liberal churchmen) generally opposed such proposals. This apparent contradiction in evangelical thinking is not easily explained, but part of the answer may be that because they were still a minority in the military, they could not insulate American youth from what they considered to be the "contaminating" influences of the Catholics and liberal Protestants who still dominated the chaplaincy. Whatever their reasons, evangelicals acted like traditional Republicans in that they, like Thomas Jefferson, opposed militarism while supporting a national defense proportional to national need.

The War Department had hoped to get Congress to approve a UMT program during World War II, when it was believed that the public would be most receptive to this unprecedented measure, but had failed to do so. As a result, when the draft expired on March 31, 1947, the military needed a new source of trained manpower. Despite its best efforts, the army was unable to attract enough volunteers to fill its ranks to authorized strength. Along with this practical motivation for UMT, many proponents of the plan, including President Truman, emphasized its spiritual benefits. Truman, a World War I veteran who served as a reserve officer during the 1920s and 1930s, repeatedly expressed appreciation for the values military service could instill in American youth. In the summer of 1933, the future president had gained firsthand experience by training young men at a Civilian Military Training Camp at Camp Pike (now Fort Robinson) near Little Rock, Arkansas, where he commanded a group of teenagers and taught them military skills, citizenship, and morality.[36]

Truman, along with many other proponents of military preparedness, also supported the evangelical Oxford or Moral Re-Armament (MRA) movement during the 1930s. Founded by Frank Buchman of Cambridge, England, the MRA called for a "spiritual world war" that would result in politicians forsaking expediency and asking "God rather than their constituents what they ought to do." Buchman used military slogans and psychology to attract "men of the Plattsburg type, who [were] willing to train for Moral Re-Armament, and take this message to every city, village and farm, for America to be up and to arm."[37] Critics have claimed that fascists and anti-Semites infiltrated this movement, but it is clear the MRA's similarity to the Plattsburg movement and its emphasis on "revitalized Christianity," military preparedness, and group obedience attracted Truman. One MRA pamphlet claimed that joining the organization was like "joining the army. You decide there's something worth fighting for. You enlist. You put yourself under orders. Then you are given new equipment. You find new comradeship. Your way of living changes and your whole outlook on life." Moral Re-Armament supporters, who taught a course on "ideals of the Founding Fathers and the moral and spiritual principles of democracy" advocated UMT and urged Truman to emphasize the citizenship and character benefits of the concept to overcome middle-class opposition to the plan. As president, Truman incorporated his training camp experiences and the MRA's "regeneration of the people" concept into his UMT plan.[38]

On October 23, 1945, Truman sent an urgent message to Congress calling for the immediate adoption of a bill requiring a full year of military training for every eighteen-year-old American male. Because "modern war is fought by experts," Truman explained, there would not be enough time in future conflicts to train draftees in the skills necessary for America's survival. He believed that UMT offered a cost-efficient answer to the military's pressing manpower needs. With the adoption of a national service program, the president claimed, America would confine its military spending to the maintenance of a small professional corps with the capability of quickly expanding with millions of pretrained citizens in the event of war. While UMT's practical benefits were obvious, according to Truman, of no less importance to the nation's security would be the plan's "moral and spiritual benefits."[39] Training would indeed teach military skills, but the president envisioned "a program that would at the same time provide ample opportunity . . . to raise the physical standard of the nation's manpower, to lower the illiteracy rate, to develop citizenship responsibilities and to foster the moral and spiritual welfare of our young people."[40] Some historians have claimed that Truman's emphasis on UMT's social values doomed the concept to failure. It appears, however, that Truman was cognizant of the growing interest in religious matters and adopted the most effective argument available for building a large and economical national defense to prove to the Soviets that Americans possessed a resolute national will.

In January, 1947, the army, which fully supported Truman's call for UMT, established an "experimental unit" at Fort Knox, Kentucky, to demonstrate the moral and spiritual benefits of national service to the American public. This experiment would have considerable influence on character-shaping efforts in the years to come. Claiming that the primary purpose of the Fort Knox unit was to work out the logistics of operating a national service program if enacted, the army also designed the UMT experiment to counteract negative public opinion that at times viewed the military as an immoral institution.[41] The Fort Knox commander, Brig. Gen. John M. Devine, informed the 664 volunteers in the first training cycle (altogether there were three consecutive six-month cycles) that it was their "mission to demonstrate that military training as proposed by the War Department, [was] beneficial to the youth of the nation, as well as necessary to the security of the country."[42]

The camp was a public relations success. Fort Knox, like the pre–World War I preparedness movement and the interwar CMTC and CCC, promoted a more personal relationship between instructors and trainees and provided, according to UMT enthusiasts, a more wholesome environment than many of the young men would find in their own homes. Devine staffed the camp with 482 enlisted men and seventy-five officers (a 6:1 ratio), housed the teenagers in posh quarters (complete with single-layered bunks and study rooms), and provided an extensive athletic program. Profanity was forbidden at Fort Knox, meals were served "family style," officials bused in local girls for supervised dances, and officers handled discipline quietly with a demerit system and peer court that prevented the browbeating traditionally employed by the regular army.[43]

Devine justified the experiment's "soft" approach by claiming that there was little point "in training a man in [military] techniques unless first he himself acquires the standards of civilized living."[44] Even though Devine outlawed "dirty fighting drills, bayonet training, [and] other exercises designed to instill in the heart of a trainee . . . hatred for the enemy and a desire to kill," he believed that UMT still offered the army a valuable opportunity for martial training by introducing trainees to military courtesy, sanitation, and obedience to orders considered essential to national security. "An officer will bark a command at you," an experimental unit chaplain wrote in April, 1947, "and you, as mechanically and as promptly as any robot, will execute it—you have learned one of the hardest lessons for any man to learn—you have learned to obey. . . . If you are to be a Christian man, you must be superbly controlled, and rigidly disciplined."[45]

The most important aspect of the experiment, according to Devine, was the new chaplains' program. The War Department claimed that with UMT, the chaplain would become "as important as the quarterback on a [football] team using the T-formation." One of the two full-time and one part-time chaplains assigned to the unit supervised each youth.[46] During the first week of camp, the chaplain interviewed each enrollee and inquired about his spiritual life. He then directed the UMTee (as UMT enrollees at Fort Knox were called) to support the unit's mandatory religious program covering the first four weeks of training.[47] "In UMT," according to Chaplain Maury Hundley Jr., "you are more than a body to be bayoneted or bulleted. . . . You are first, last and always a religious animal; and UMT will not let you forget it."[48]

Starting with the fifth week of camp, each man began attending a series of thirty-three mandatory lectures on citizenship and morality written and delivered by the chaplains.[49] Because Devine and the chaplains believed that "films, posters, forced issue of prophylactics, and other measures in common use [in fighting VD] are as apt to increase the venereal rate as to reduce it," no prophylactic station operated at Fort Knox and adult literature was eliminated from the PX newsstand and service club library.[50] Divine joyfully reported to the War Department that by providing a wholesome environment and establishing rapport between officers and men, 137 of the 650 men in the first cycle had asked to be baptized or confirmed in the faith of their choice.[51] UMTee Henry J. Rill Jr. of Chicago, Illinois, was thankful for the confirmation instruction provided by the camp, for he had learned his prayers and the ten commandments. "I really learn [sic] a lot and I certainly am grateful for what Father Murphy is doing," Rill claimed. "It is really too bad so many civilians get the wrong impression of the attitude of peace-time soldiers toward morals and religion."[52]

Devine touted the chaplains' program as only the "beginning of an evolutionary process out of which may be expected to come a program which will profoundly affect the moral fiber of the American people."[53] One of the Fort Knox chaplains, who claimed that he knew of "no similar situation where so much can be done spiritually in so short a time," advertised the program as a "rescue agency" for America's neglected youth. Devine, however, cautioned that UMT would be unable to completely "undo the results of poor home conditions during the trainee's preceding eighteen years," but by emphasizing the principles of moral training, it would elevate "those individuals with low moral standards" and maintain "the high standards of those trainees who already [had] them."[54]

While the Fort Knox experiment was under way, President Truman appointed a presidential advisory commission (the Compton Commission) to conduct further studies on UMT. Truman personally instructed the commission members at a White House meeting in December, 1946, to design a program for compulsory training that would mold the thinking of young Americans along patriotic lines and teach them "what it means to take care of this Temple which God gave us."[55] In May, 1947, after five months of closed hearings, the commission concluded that the "principal justification" for UMT must remain military security, but additional "social benefits," while secondary in nature, could be beneficial to the country. The commission claimed that a program patterned after the Fort Knox experiment for the regular armed forces would "provide a moral environment . . . far superior to the kind of environment in which many boys would otherwise be living." To accomplish this goal, it recommended, among other things, the appointment of officers of high character, more chaplains at each base, strict suppression of prostitution and alcoholic beverages in areas surrounding training camps, and an antivenereal disease campaign reminiscent of Newton Baker's pre–World War I moral sanitation that stressed "continence" rather than prophylactics.[56]

After spending considerable amounts of time, money, and manpower on the experiment, few were surprised when the War Department declared the Fort Knox UMT trial a success. However, opponents of compulsory service charged that "the new evangelism of Johnnie Devine," the expense, and the softness of the program, proved that UMT was unrealistic nationwide and that UMTees would be unable to stand up to traditional military training. In 1948, a congressional subcommittee (the Harness subcommittee) charged with investigating military propaganda regarding UMT not only proved that the War Department had illegally used public funds to lobby for the president's plan, it also forced the army to admit that a large-scale compulsory national service program based on the Fort Knox model would be impractical.[57]

Despite Truman's hopes and the War Department's activities, Congress never enacted a working plan for compulsory national service. While a reported 60 percent of the public supported Truman's UMT concept, the measure came under spirited attack by virtually every religious, labor, and educational organization in the country. Caught between public pressures and special interest groups, Congress compromised on the president's proposal by rejecting UMT but extending the Selective Service Act twice. It was finally allowed to expire in March, 1947. However, this proved to be only a temporary setback for proponents of military preparedness and national character shaping. Congress reinstated the draft for the army a year later in response to the communist coup in Czechoslovakia and the Berlin blockade. Even with the resumption of conscription, Truman continued to promote UMT as a necessity for America's national security and spiritual well-being.[58]

Truman lamented the fact that Congress had refused his request for UMT eight times in five years. He later claimed that if America had adopted UMT in 1945, "there would have been no Cold War."[59] The administration had proceeded with a get-tough policy toward the Soviets and had used the draft to meet its military manpower needs, but in Truman's view, the nation had failed to develop the patriotism and moral character essential to winning the battle of "isms."[60] While Truman and others utilized the rhetoric of civil-military religion in an attempt to sell UMT to the American public and to a parsimonious Congress, it was also true that as communism advanced militarily and politically across Europe, individuals throughout society truly came to fear that the nation's homes, schools, and churches were failing to teach the traditional values of patriotism and moral leadership—to develop a resolute, national will. Perhaps the rationale for UMT—the regeneration of the people—assumed a life of its own beyond its practical goals as a frustrated president and nation searched for a means to forge a national resolve against an inscrutable communist menace.

Despite its failure to get Congress to adopt UMT, the Truman administration stepped-up its efforts to evangelize the regular armed forces in order to improve the military's public image and to improve the overall moral character of the men and women in uniform.[61] Shortly after the Selective Service Act of 1948 reinstated the draft, Truman requested that the Compton Commission submit recommendations on moral safeguards for the new inductees. In a report dated September 13, 1948, the commission called on the military to adopt "as much of the Fort Knox . . . program as is practicable." The commission warned that if the military returned to its former ways in order to save time and money, "the whole future of our country, which is no stronger than the morals of the people, would be jeopardized."[62]

The Weil Committee and Character Guidance

On October 27, 1948, Truman announced the creation of the President's Committee on Religion and Welfare in the Armed Forces (Weil Committee), which would continue the Compton Commission's work of demonstrating that the nation's security depended on the military's spiritual health and a "universal understanding of the principles of citizenship and American democracy."[63] The ten-member Weil Committee, consisting of leaders in religious and social service organizations, inspected twenty-two military installations across the country and overseas and conducting hearings with leading military and civilian experts in information and education, before reporting in 1950: "this is a time of unparalleled struggle for the minds and souls of men. On one side are the dark forces of the spiritually barren ideologies which attack the religious and ethical foundations of our society. On the other are the cherished spiritual concepts and religious values which give our society the moral force without which it would soon disintegrate."[64]

The Weil Committee recommended that the armed forces take immediate action to improve TI&E programs and vaguely referred to a need for such instruction to be extended to the civilian population. The committee claimed that "the mind of the individual fighting man will become of supreme importance in developing and utilizing the weapons of an advanced technology, but also in the use of ideas as weapons. . . . The so-called 'Cold War' in which we are presently engaged is already, in substance, a war of ideas."[65]

Military leaders took seriously the Weil Committee's recommendation on improving TI&E programs in the armed forces. The same month that the Fort Knox experiment began, Secretary of War Robert Patterson, alarmed by the highest VD rates in thirty years, ordered commanding officers to begin morality training. Chaplain Martin H. Scharlemann produced eighty-eight citizenship and morality outlines to be used during the army's "Chaplain's Hour," held once a month as part of the regular TI&E program. Each outline contained reference readings and a quiz "to teach the American soldier the necessity and value of clean living, his rights as a citizen, and his responsibility to his country."[66] The army formally adopted the Fort Knox plan in July, 1948, as the Character Guidance Program. It was officially designated as a command responsibility, but it also fell under the direction of the post chaplain. Stressing a civil-military religious theme—with titles such as "Man is a Moral Being," "Worship in Life," "The Nation we Serve," and "Religion in Our Way of Life"—lessons instructed recruits to worship God, "the source of our way of life," in order to effectively serve America, his "covenant nation."[67]

In 1951, Secretary of Defense George C. Marshall extended the army's Character Guidance Program to the other services, ordering commanding officers to increase their efforts to improve the spiritual morale of their personnel. The navy aggressively implemented the directive—not merely for recruits at naval training camps, but for all its personnel, officers and men, in its cradle-to-grave (boot camp to retirement) Character Education Program. As in the army's basic training, a chaplain interviewed each new navy recruit to determine his spiritual status and to inform him of the religious activities available in the navy. If the recruit had not been baptized before he enlisted, the chaplain "strongly" encouraged the man to enroll in religious instruction classes held in the evenings or on Sunday afternoons to help him complete this Christian sacrament.[68] The navy's Character Education Program consisted of four separate courses of religious and citizenship instruction ("Our Moral and Spiritual Growth Here and Now," "Because of You," "My Life in the Far East," and "This is my Life"). Each course consisted of a succession of "guided discussions" conducted by a trained moderator (often the chaplain) who emphasized civil-military religious concepts.[69] The 1953 "Moral Leadership" program built pride in the navy and got "at the core of the threat of Communism through the exposure of our own weaknesses in the moral and spiritual area." Under the direction of navy chaplains, Adm. Arthur W. Radford's pet project taught sailors "Americanism" along with instruction on personal finances and the dangers of illicit sex and marriage counseling.[70]

The air force boasted its own Character Guidance Program, nicknamed "Carpenter's round-up" after Maj. Gen. Charles I. Carpenter, the service's evangelical chief of chaplains. When Carpenter, a strong supporter of UMT and religious adviser to Truman, heard reports that one out of every four airmen claimed no church affiliation, he instituted an aggressive civil-military religious indoctrination program for the newly independent air force. The chaplain interviewed each recruit, asked him to specify a faith, and told him "to straighten out your thinking in relationship to God."[71] In September, 1955, *Church and State* reported that chaplains listed men who refused to designate a religious preference as atheists, which in the thinking of the day was often equated with being a communist. Carpenter denied this connection, which may indeed have been exaggerated, but there was evidence that the air force subjected "unchurched" recruits to considerable pressure to adopt a faith.[72]

In his efforts to evangelize air force personnel, Carpenter turned to the Moody Bible Institute's *Sermons from Science* lectures and films. The air force, and the other services to a lesser extent, incorporated this series of Christian scientific lectures into its character-shaping attempts during the late 1940s and early 1950s. *Sermons from Science* exemplified the symbiotic relationship between the U.S. armed services and evangelical Christianity during the Cold War. The Reverend Irwin A. Moon, an independent evangelist and amateur physicist, created the *Sermons from Science* series in 1937 to demonstrate the compatibility of science and religion through public "lectures" that illustrated God's creation with scientific demonstrations.[73] After affiliating with Moody Bible Institute in 1940, Moon volunteered his services to the USO and presented his lectures to troops around the world. Called "gadget evangelism" by critics, the "optical, electrical, sound, and chemical demonstrations" entertained and amazed thousands of soldiers, sailors, and flyers during the war. The powerful finale to the four-night series of lectures featured Moon atop a large transformer in a darkened room. At his signal, over a million volts of electricity surged up from his stocking feet and through his body until six-foot-long sparks shot from his outstretched metal-capped fingertips. When Moon brought the lights back up, he preached the plan of salvation to his stunned and receptive audience.[74]

"The Million Volt Preacher," as Moon advertised himself, was not satisfied with the thousands of service personnel that his live appearances reached during the *Sermons from Science* demonstrations. While visiting training camps during the war, Moon had been impressed by the military's ability to transform raw recruits into skilled soldiers through the use of training films and decided to adapt his message to motion pictures. By 1945, the innovative minister (with financial aid from MBI) formed the Moody Bible Institute of Science and began producing a number of films.[75]

The first film in the *Sermons from Science* series, "God of Creation," opened with Moon sitting at his desk with a Bible. "We are going to explore various realms of God's creation," he calmly explained, and "before we close we will agree that He is a wonderful God." The state-of-the-art motion picture, featuring Moon's own time-lapse photography, surveyed the whole scope of God's creation from the vast expanding universe to the microscopic world of the paramecium. In the film's conclusion, Moon challenged viewers to consider their relationship to God. "Is this wonderful God a total stranger?" Moon asked. "If so, then your life is empty and pointless even though it be filled with all the knowledge and the wisdom of this world." Hope need not be lost, according to the evangelist, for "God's work as creator is not over. He stands ready today to perform for you his greatest creative miracle."[76]

Whatever the original motivations of Moon and MBI in producing the *Sermons from Science* film series and presenting live scientific demonstrations, the program was no doubt attractive to schools, industry, and especially the military because of its emphasis on obedience and good order. An MBI representative promoted the films to companies by promising that "employees seeing them would have more wholesome attitudes and could be expected to be more subject to direction and control on the job." The Fisher Body Corporation credited the motion pictures with creating "proper attitudes" among its workers.[77]

In 1947, the air force began requiring its personnel (officers and enlisted men) to view the series during its Character Guidance and TI&E programs. The chief of chaplains became interested in incorporating the *Sermons from Science* films and demonstrations into air force Cold War information programs after an MBI representative convinced a few chaplains to host a trial screening. Chaplains the world over valued *Sermons from Science* because they were nondenominational and fit well with the military's common-denominator liturgy, while at the same time fulfilling the emotional needs of American civil-military religion by inspiring troops much like an old-time revival. The air force claimed that the MBI materials gave the chaplains "a tremendous advantage in molding the desired degree of receptivity for the over-all program of character guidance."[78]

Because DOD made viewing the films mandatory during TI&E programs, it forbade altar calls. Individual chaplains found it difficult to resist, however, and reported, to the delight of evangelists at MBI, that thousands of servicemen and women around the world had accepted Christ as their personal savior after coming "forward" during one of Moon's films or lectures. In October, 1953, Chaplain Paul C. McCandless, claimed that the MBI materials had led many officers and men "from the valley of doubt and darkness to light, understanding and faith." "It is our fervent hope," said McCandless, "that this splendid ministry will continue to fortify and reinforce the religious life of the United States Air Force.... Our nation needs such a message."[79] The fact that the military encountered no serious opposition regarding its evangelicalism until the mid-1960s, suggests that either the air force kept such activity below the radar of public opinion or was operating well within the accepted norms of American society.[80]

To gain further support for its character-education efforts during the Korean War, the Pentagon held a conference in 1952 for seventy-eight clergymen of various faiths. At the conference, the military brass and civilian service secretaries delivered twenty-three addresses recommending greater cooperation between the church and the federal government in "handling the moral and religious problems involved in expanding military obligations."[81] Shortly after the Pentagon conference, the navy held its own one-day indoctrination meeting for four hundred clergymen at the Great Lakes Naval Training Center to apprise the religious community of what it was accomplishing with its Character Education Program. One speaker informed the conference participants that it was their duty to "prepare young people morally for military service." Admiral Francis F. Olds concluded: "Men with good morals are better fighting men."[82]

The armed forces conducted the two indoctrination conferences because, despite the military's best efforts to incorporate a civil-military religion into its ranks, the *New York Times* had revealed that new recruits filling training camps during the Korean conflict still lacked the civic virtue considered essential for the nation's defense needs. The *Times* articles, by education editor Benjamin Fine, not only blamed the service's TI&E program for conditions reminiscent of the lack of discipline and rampant immorality reported during demobilization after World War II, but also pointed to the general apathy of the American public as the sources of this national disgrace.[83] By 1950 it appeared to the military that its efforts to reshape the American character had failed because such efforts had been too limited in scope. If the nation was to remain secure in the face of an increasing communist threat, many believed that the armed forces needed to adopt a more sweeping, multi-faceted, character-shaping agenda. Following the Korean War, an opportunity for such an expansion became possible when twenty-one American prisoners of war held by the enemy refused repatriation, giving at least the appearance that America was indeed facing a crisis in character that demanded a military response.

Conclusion

Determining the motivations of all parties involved in military morality education is fraught with difficulties. Although the military was pragmatic in that it used civil-military religion in an effort to create efficient and effective warriors and to improve its public image, it was also true that the services were acting altruistically in attempting to revitalize the nation through its contact with enlisted personnel. Religious groups no doubt wanted a strong defense, but they differed on how best to achieve that goal. Liberal churchmen feared the militarization of society that might result from a program of UMT and a peacetime draft, whereas evangelicals, who opposed UMT for the same reason, embraced the opportunities the military provided for domestic and international revival. While military and religious interests hoped to promote their own denominational interests and theological points of view, they did so out of a conviction that they each, as the defenders and interpreters of God's will, knew best regarding the nation's spiritual welfare. Calls for moral regeneration could and did cover narrower interests to advance specific agendas, but it should not be forgotten that nearly all segments of society during the early Cold War were in agreement that there was a real need for national spiritual revitalization. Regardless of the motivations that underlay this drive, once religious nationalism had captivated the public mind, it became difficult, if not impossible, to effectively criticize military and governmental attempts to implement character education without appearing disloyal or perhaps even blasphemous.

The ascendancy of American civil-military religion during the early Cold War ensured that the reorganized and revitalized U.S. armed forces would attempt to assume the role of moral conscience for the nation. While the failure to successfully promote UMT denied the military an opportunity to directly reach all young American males with its message, the principles behind the character-shaping concept were replicated in the services' TI&E programs throughout the world. Perhaps significant is the fact that these developments occurred at the very same time the Truman administration was searching for its own means to create a resolute national will to contain communism ideologically at home and abroad. Evangelical democracy, the means promoted by a number of influential national-security planners during the early Cold War, refashioned the American civil-military religion into an aggressive ideological weapon.

CHAPTER 3

Ideological and Spiritual Mobilization

I have not done my duty unless, in all my conduct, in my examples

with my fellow citizens, I am living this democracy, indeed this

religion, the tenets of this religion. Until I have done that I am not

doing my best.

—Dwight D. Eisenhower, 1952

During the early Cold War, the U.S. armed services joined forces with a number of private political associations promoting civil religion as a means to fortify the American character and will against international and domestic communism. One such organization that worked very closely with the armed forces was the Freedoms Foundation of Valley Forge, Pennsylvania, located eighteen miles west of Philadelphia on the edge of George Washington's historic winter encampment. In 1949, Don Belding and Kenneth Wells, the president and vice-president of Foote, Cone, and Belding Advertising Agency of Los Angeles, founded the patriotic organization to educate the public about the dangers of communism and to call the nation back to its "Christian heritage." Just as the Continental Army entered Valley Forge unformed in character and vulnerable to attack, so too, the foundation charged, Americans during the Cold War lacked the inner fortitude necessary for victory. The nation was in the midst of "a psychological warfare battle for the minds of men," according to the two executives, who hoped to fashion a revitalized national character and a unified American will through modern advertising techniques.[1]

Belding and Wells worked closely with the Defense Department's Office of Armed Forces Information and Education (AFIE) and Armed Forces Radio and Television Service (AFRTS) to disseminate anticommunist and conservative economic and political views among service personnel and civilians. They encapsulated their views in the Freedoms Foundation's "American Credo." First drafted in a moment of inspiration on Ruth Wells's tablecloth, this statement of the nation's historic values combined the Bill of Rights with conservative economic policies such as private property rights, work unhindered by labor unions, the sanctity of the profit motive and a free market, and freedom "from arbitrary government regulation and control." With the written endorsement of more than 250 chief and associate justices of state supreme courts and the generous financial backing of anti–New Dealers Edward F. Hutton and Dewitt Wallace, the foundation distributed its credo to the nation's homes, schools, churches, and military bases throughout the 1950s and 1960s.[2]

Along with other active and retired military leaders alarmed by the state of the national character, retired general Dwight D. Eisenhower, president of Columbia University, lent his name and prestige to the Freedoms Foundation. In 1946, the general had declared that he was a "fanatical devotee" of an American system that consisted of "a deep and abiding religious faith among the people and a system of freedoms and rights for the individual that generally would be called 'free enterprise.'"[3] In 1949 the future president presided over the foundation's first annual awards ceremony, at which tens of thousands of dollars in prizes were presented to those individuals and organizations, both civilian and military, that the foundation believed exemplified the spirit of its American Credo. Among the recipients were former president Herbert Hoover, who was recognized for issuing a warning against excessive government spending; baseball star Jackie Robinson, who was lauded for criticizing statements by the leftist African-American Paul Robeson regarding civil rights; cartoonist Harold Craig, creator of the *Little Orphan Annie* comic-strip character "Daddy" Warbucks, whom the awards committee claimed epitomized "the promise of the American way of life"; and Mrs. Ruth Miles of Merion, Pennsylvania, for her "Credo Freedom Cookie Cutters" and "Recipes for Americans." The ceremony also honored several ultraconservatives—including Billy James Hargis of the Christian Crusade in Tulsa, Oklahoma, and George Benson of the National Education Program, headquartered in Searcy, Arkansas—which led one critic to claim that a Freedoms Foundation medal was equivalent to a *Good Housekeeping* seal of approval for political extremists seeking legitimacy.[4]

Eisenhower gave the Freedoms Foundation his full support despite occasional charges that it served as a front for the radical right and that Belding's and Wells's real goal was to indoctrinate the public in their conservative politics. By affiliating with an organization that combined patriotic and religious imagery, the general identified himself with the legacy of George Washington and reinforced his reputation as an emerging

The "Credo" of the Freedoms Foundation at Valley Forge.
Courtesy University of Arkansas Libraries.

President Eisenhower (left) chats with Kenneth D. Wells of the Freedoms Foundation at Valley Forge. Courtesy University of Arkansas Libraries.

spokesman of the American civil-military religion. Unlike Pres. Harry S. Truman, who had failed to take advantage of the religious milieu of the day, Eisenhower used its precepts as an organizing mechanism to create national unity as a bulwark against communism. Shortly after the 1952 election, on the occasion of his appointment as honorary chair of the Freedoms Foundation at Valley Forge, Eisenhower affirmed the importance of civil-military religion to the nation's future. "Our form of government," the president-elect told the directors gathered at the Waldorf-Astoria Hotel, "has no sense unless it is founded in a deeply felt religious [Judeo-Christian] faith, and I don't care what it is."[5]

During the early Cold War, the military's traditional interest in the promotion of civic virtue reached unprecedented levels after a number of factors coalesced to propel the armed forces into asserting the role of moral conscience and architect of an American will. The passage of the National Security Act of 1947 (and its subsequent revision in 1949), the growth in influence of the "military mind" in American society and culture, the increase of evangelical influence within the military chaplaincy, and the incorporation of American civil-military religious imagery into troop information provided both the means and the will for the armed services to participate in the powerful anticommunist movement then gaining strength within American society. This religious-political consensus, with Eisenhower as its high priest, ultimately presented opportunities for evangelical elements within DOD to take more aggressive steps to shape the national character and to create an American will—a process many believed was begun by George Washington nearly two centuries before during the legendary winter at Valley Forge.

Calls for Ideological and Spiritual Mobilization

As the Red Army expanded across Eastern Europe and communists were even elected to local offices in Western Europe following World War II, policy makers searched for an ideological means to contain communism. Diplomat George F. Kennan, who first articulated America's containment policy of measured responses to Soviet aggression, called for an ideological mobilization of the nation's resources to counter Russian psychological warfare. Heavily influenced by the writings of anticommunist theologian Reinhold Niebuhr, Kennan called on the administration to create the necessary will for victory.[6] In his now-famous "Long Telegram," sent from Moscow in 1946, Kennan wrote that the American people lacked the discipline and resolute character required to fight the Cold War. The federal government must therefore take responsibility for "informing" the people about the realities of the Cold War and for reforming the national character. "I cannot over-emphasize importance of this," he stressed. The government, rather than the free press, should assume this responsibility because it was, he claimed, "more experienced and better informed on practical problems involved." Kennan, who ironically later rejected "moralism" in diplomacy, argued that success depended on the "health and vigor of our own society" because communism, like a "malignant parasite," fed only on the "diseased tissue" of degenerate societies. "This is [the] point at which domestic and foreign policies meet," he observed. "Every courageous and incisive measure to solve internal problems of our own society, to improve self-confidence, discipline, morale and community spirit of our own people, is a diplomatic victory over Moscow worth a thousand diplomatic notes and joint communiqués. If we cannot abandon fatalism and indifference in face of deficiencies of our own society, Moscow will profit."[7]

In 1948, Truman responded to Kennan's call for ideological containment with a religiously oriented and cost-efficient foreign policy that identified the president with a visionary international ecumenical movement—a movement at great odds with the prevailing American civil-military consensus. During the early Cold War, national security advisers became interested in a plan to bolster European Christianity as a bulwark against communism. They reasoned that an international coalition of Catholics and Protestants could unite the Western democracies and effectively deter the Red Army. Difficulties immediately surfaced, however, when the administration began discussing the idea with European Protestants, the British cabinet and Foreign Office, and Myron C. Taylor, the president's personal envoy to the Vatican. Official recognition of the Vatican would be difficult if not impossible in view of the American Protestant community's opposition to any acknowledgment of papal authority. When the Vatican expressed its own misgivings about working with Protestants, the innovative plan quickly unraveled. It became increasingly clear to the White House that ideologically based foreign policies could not win the nation's support if they contained a Catholic element. To be acceptable within the American civil-military consensus, it was imperative that these policies be grounded in "traditional" American or Protestant principles.[8] Truman, however, by repeatedly insisting on appointing an ambassador to the Vatican, had separated himself from this consensus. Such an appointment "would produce consequences both far reaching and disastrous to the national unity of the American people," the National Council of Churches of Christ warned. The *Boston Herald* spoke for many when it claimed that "the hurt he [Truman] has done to national unity detracts from the good he has done for the world's defense against communism."[9]

Truman failed to unify the American people with civil-religious rhetoric that included calling them the "leaders of the moral forces of the world" and defenders of the "God-given" laws of "Moses at Sinai and Jesus on the Mount" because he was unwilling (and perhaps unable) to adapt his public image and world vision to reflect that of the spiritual leader of the "New Israel," God's reportedly chosen, and Protestant, nation. However, by incorporating religion—albeit a liberal, ecumenical religion—into his foreign policy pronouncements, Truman did contribute to the reduction of diplomacy to black and white, good vs. evil, American vs. anti-American decisions. With few gray areas left in the public mind, policy makers possessed considerably fewer options. Limited wars were the antithesis of God's will in the American civil-military religion, as Truman would soon discover in Korea. No matter how correct his action has been judged by historians, the firing of Gen. Douglas MacArthur, a man at the center of the civil-military religious revival, cast Truman in the role of the Devil. Limited wars were unsatisfactory to a nation that fought on the side of the Almighty.[10]

Despite Truman's attempts to contain communism militarily, politically, and spiritually, the nation was hit by devastating foreign policy disasters in 1949. Not only was America's trust in its atomic monopoly shattered when the Soviets exploded their own nuclear device, but Washington was also unable to respond adequately to the crisis. By 1950, the United States still had only two working atomic bombs in its arsenal (although many others were unassembled) and had yet to develop effective delivery systems. The worst blows to the national psyche, however, were that the Chinese communists had defeated the American-backed Nationalist forces on the China mainland and the continuing accusations that Alger Hiss and others had sold vital information to the Kremlin. News that the most populous nation in the world had gone communist, coupled with allegations that communist sympathizers had infiltrated the U.S. government, sent shock waves across the nation. The American people, who traditionally had viewed themselves as citizens of the New Israel, found it inexplicable that the Truman administration had failed to prevent these catastrophes. To many, the only explanation possible was that the current administration was corrupt, soft on communism, and out of harmony with God's will. Conservative Republicans found considerable evidence, some real and some imagined, to condemn the Democratic Party. Under increasing public pressure to reverse its "shameful" record, the White House sought radical changes in diplomacy and attempted to build the national will believed necessary to support these new policy departures and deter the Soviets from attack.

Creating a Unified National Will

In 1950, after being criticized for making diplomatic decisions in a confused, piecemeal fashion, President Truman ordered the State Department to reexamine the nation's foreign policy assumptions and to recommend an overarching plan for his consideration. The final document, NSC-68, drafted by Paul Nitze and the State-Defense Policy Review Group, not only represented the militarization of the Cold War but also heralded a unprecedented spiritual mobilization of the American people. Nitze, along with his chief State Department ally, Dean Acheson, supported drastic and immediate increases in military expenditures in opposition to Kennan's, Defense Secretary Louis A. Johnson's, and Truman's wishes. While cleverly wording the policy paper in a manner that would hit hard at the select few officials who would actually be allowed to read it and at the same time including provocative key phrases that could be leaked to the press as needed, Nitze and Acheson used the NSC-68 draft in their campaign for more aggressive foreign policies and to frighten Americans into supporting those policy initiatives.[11]

Using the rhetoric of American civil-military religion, NSC-68 argued that America faced defeat if it continued to wage the Cold War as it had in the past. The Cold War was a battle between American values and Soviet ideology. The communists were more effective in meeting their goals, according to Nitze, because unlike Americans, who possessed no unifying philosophy, the Russian people shared a set of common beliefs. The Soviet Union had a psychological advantage, he claimed, because, "in its pretensions to being (a) the source of a new universal faith and (b) the model 'scientific' society, the Kremlin cynically identifies itself with the genuine aspirations of large numbers of people, and places itself at the head of an international crusade with all the benefits which derive there from."[12]

If America hoped to compete, the federal government needed to minimize dissent and to develop a rival American ideology to counter communism. According to Nitze and his supporters, the unified national will that would replace the nation's diffuse pluralism would enable America to deter the enemy from further expansion militarily, politically, and spiritually.

At the same time, NSC-68 acknowledged that there would be difficulties involved with creating a resolute national will. Not only would such an action require a "large measure of sacrifice and discipline" as the people were "asked to give up some of the benefits which they have come to associate with their freedoms," America's security could also be jeopardized by a demonstration of its new determined character. "At any point in the process of demonstrating our will to make good our fundamental purpose," the authors warned, "the Kremlin may decide to precipitate a general war, or in testing us, may go too far." While this risk was serious, according to NSC-68, failure to demonstrate a resolute national will would be exceedingly more dangerous. "Our fundamental purpose is more likely to be defeated from lack of the will to maintain it, than from any mistakes we may make or assault we may undergo because of asserting that will."[13]

Cold Warriors defined national will or national morale as the degree of determination with which the American people supported the nation's foreign policy during peace and war. Traditionally, whenever the United States had been attacked or insulted, the national resolve (or lack thereof) was readily apparent. During peacetime, however, the will of the people (especially a democratic people) was either nonexistent or not easily identifiable. Totalitarian governments could use strong-arm tactics to dictate the national will, but in the United States—a pluralistic democratic republic—elected officials attempted to reflect it, or at least appear to do so.[14]

Since the national will varied over time and between different segments of the population, policy makers measured the people's resolve when possible before formulating policy. Studying public-opinion polls, letters to editors, voting patterns, and even enlistment rates proved inadequate, however, in designing foreign policies because the public was uninformed regarding many sensitive, complex, and rapidly changing international issues. Because of that fact, U.S. officials first determined diplomatic measures, then attempted to build support for those measures thereafter. Many reasoned that it would be necessary to impose on the nation's diverse society a single reformed "national character" in order to achieve the public support needed to fund their policy initiatives. It was hoped that this unified character would overcome the greed and irresponsibility popularly believed rampant in American society and thereby minimize economic and social conflict. Ironically, the rhetoric employed in NSC-68 generally agreed with the Soviet critique of American society that despised U.S. materialism and doubted that the people of a capitalist nation would be willing to accept the sacrifices that would be demanded of them during the Cold War struggle.[15] As the new decade unfolded and the religious longings of the American people became evident, however, policy makers recognized the possibility of using the American civil-military religion as an organizing principle for the much-coveted national will—a national will that would unify the nation around "traditional core values" in support of changing and often shifting, if not conflicting, foreign policies.

When NSC-68 went to Truman for approval on April 7, 1950, the president, who still hoped to limit defense spending, forbade any publicity of its contents without his express approval. However, Acheson and Nitze had already leaked key phrases to the press and had been successful in gaining support within the administration, making it politically dangerous for

Truman to reject the plan outright. While the president considered his options, the North Korean army invaded South Korea. Convinced that Soviet premier Joseph Stalin had orchestrated the attack to test American resolve, Truman approved NSC-68, "the most famous unread paper of its era" (meaning that while it remained classified the general public was familiar only with its basic principles), as the U.S. government's policy in September, 1950.[16]

The question of whether or not the terminology of NSC-68 was merely rhetorical and did not reflect the actual beliefs of American policy makers continues to be hotly debated by historians. It was true that the document contained religious metaphors and emotional hyperbole that its authors knew could not be modified without antagonizing the growing anticommunist sentiment. It was also true that general thinking within the State Department typically reflected a realistic rather than an idealistic approach to diplomacy. To gain support for increased defense spending, Nitze and his supporters had appropriated Kennan's idealistic language about the world struggle. Furthermore, there is also little doubt that many senior government leaders, both civilian and military, had become so frustrated and anxious over continuing Soviet advancements that they came, in time, to believe their own rhetoric and formulated policies accordingly.

Nonmilitary Efforts to Create a National Will

Along with the federal government's interest in creating a unified American will, similar attempts by privately funded and government-supported nonprofit foundations were already under way. To encourage the development of a resolute national will, these civic organizations used modern advertising techniques to extol the free enterprise system and to present an idealized version of the American Way of Life. In addition to the Freedoms Foundation at Valley Forge, the American Heritage Foundation sponsored a number of patriotic events. On the 160th anniversary of the signing of the U.S. Constitution, its much-heralded "Freedom Train," a seven-car traveling display of 133 historic documents and memorabilia, arrived in Philadelphia in 1947 for the beginning of its thirty-seven-thousand-mile, 322-city, two-year journey across the nation.[17] Clearly designed to foster patriotism and minimize dissent (evidence of racial and labor unrest was lacking), organizers encouraged the public to gather and recite a "Freedom Pledge" and to sign a "Freedom Scroll" before boarding the red, white, and blue train pulled by the "Spirit of 1776" locomotive.[18] "Indoctrination in democracy is the essential catalytic agent needed to blend our various groups into one American family," a project promoter claimed. "[W]ithout it, we could not sustain the continuity of our way of life. In its largest sense, preaching Americanism is an affirmative declaration of our faith in ourselves."[19] Stressing homogeneity over division, the American Heritage Foundation and other early Cold War patriotic organizations encouraged each citizen's civic responsibility in order "to safeguard our freedoms, preserve the liberties from which all these advantages flow, and continue to demonstrate to ourselves—and to the whole world—that the way of free men is best."[20]

While the Freedom Train and similar efforts remained popular with the public, policy makers attempted their own federally directed programs intended to foster a unified will. Deterrence, according to national security planners, required a determined, courageous American people, a people willing to engage in nuclear warfare if necessary. To achieve that level of determination, the Truman administration, through its civil defense program, taught Americans that they could, if properly trained, survive an atomic attack—a tricky task when it is remembered that the administration was also committed to scaring the public into financing containment.

In 1948, DOD established the Office of Civil Defense Planning under the direction of Russell J. Hopley. Soon afterward, Hopley—building on earlier work by the War Department—issued a report that recommended a national information campaign to ameliorate the public's growing panic regarding nuclear war. "Panic arises from fear," the Hopley report claimed, "but knowledge and understanding help to dispel fear. This enables the individual to meet the situation calmly." That same year, the National Security Resources Board (NSRB) issued a statement on civil defense that recommended national defense drills to give local police the opportunity to practice panic control. Two years later Congress passed the Federal Civil Defense Act of 1950, which included establishment of the Federal Civil Defense Administration (FCDA) as a cabinet-level agency with a director appointed by the president.[21]

The FCDA operated on the assumption that public morale, which it defined as the ability to resist panic, could be maintained by withholding information that indicated the futility of self-defense during an atomic attack. The public must be convinced that the existing social order would remain intact even if certain U.S. cities vaporized in a nuclear war. Civil defense planners believed that the discipline and self-control resulting from effective management of the public's emotions would infuse the American people with the toughness popularly believed to be lacking in the national character. Although the White House fully recognized that self-protection was virtually impossible in the event of a nuclear war, national civil defense policy nevertheless was aimed at convincing the Kremlin that the American people had the necessary resolve to endure such an attack.

The FCDA based its policy on the findings of a top-secret study by Associated Universities. Its mammoth final report, "Project East River," concluded that "(a)n attack with modern [nuclear] weapons would be much more damaging to our population, our property, our way of life, and to our democratic institutions generally than is realized by the public or even by many responsible government officials." To sustain public morale during the Cold War when the possibility of nuclear war weighed on the public mind, the Project East River study reasoned that not only would panic need to be controlled by using emotion management, but any feelings of overconfidence and complacency within the American public would also need to be dispelled by a psychological offensive.[22]

While the Project East River study was under way, the FCDA hired the Freedoms Foundation at Valley Forge to build and operate a traveling exhibit to implement its emotion management strategy. The FCDA designed the "Alert America" project, conducted in 1952–53, to "awaken our millions of apathetic patriots" to the dangers of communism and nuclear attack, while avoiding "at all costs the creation of any feeling of helplessness or resignation on the part of the people once they are made to understand the gravity of the situation." Kenneth Wells, president of the Freedoms Foundation, insisted that each exhibit also include his American Credo pyramid. For eight months, three separate Alert America convoys traveled to more than eighty cities, vividly demonstrating the horrors of germ warfare and nuclear attack to an estimated audience of over a million people. In Providence, Rhode Island, the numbers waiting to view the exhibit were so great that local officials threatened to call out the state police to stop the trucks from leaving their community.[23]

Despite its heavy-handed scare tactics and right-wing politics, Alert America convoys operated with the express approval of President Truman, who publicized the exhibits by having his picture taken accepting a metal name tag that would identify his body in the event of an atomic attack. In addition, the U.S. military donated both money and manpower to the endeavor.[24] Finally, the FCDA, faced with the daunting task of both reassuring and scaring the American public about the communist threat, sought federal experts in psychological warfare operations to teach its project designers the latest emotion management strategies.[25]

The Changing Focus of Psychological Warfare

During demobilization, the State Department had preserved a remnant of the military's wartime psychological warfare operations (psyops) structure when its Office of Information and Cultural Affairs absorbed the Voice of America (VOA) and parts of the Office of War Industries (OWI). The passage of the Smith-Mundt Act in 1948 authorized the establishment of a new peacetime propaganda agency, the U.S. Information Service (USIS). The USIS attempted to win friends abroad by advertising the material benefits of the American Way of Life. Both DOD and the CIA urged more aggressive measures be used to counter Soviet propaganda, but the State Department, which in general rejected propaganda as an instrument of foreign policy, vetoed all activist measures. Programs that went beyond mere reflections of American life, according to the majority of the diplomatic corps, were contrary to U.S. national interests and would antagonize rather than contain the Soviets. Meanwhile, the military, with its wartime psyops structure intact, was able and willing to consider such operations during the early Cold War.

The USIS, hoping to preserve its meager funding, remained conservative and cautious and fashioned itself into a "specialized press service" that informed its audience without attempting to persuade. State Department proponents of aggressive psyops efforts found it difficult to initiate more adventuresome proposals because congressional appropriations proved insufficient for the information programs already in existence.[26] George Kennan secured approval for the use of some covert psychological operations in support of his strategy of liberation (including the training of Soviet bloc refugees for indigenous freedom movements), but most State Department officials, whether because of philosophical convictions or financial restraints, remained skeptical of ideological programs. Critics claimed that the State Department had failed the American people because while it was willing to contain the communists militarily and politically, the agency was not willing to do so ideologically. Ironically, instead of winning friends as hoped, USIS information programs tended to offend their target audiences by glorifying American materialism.[27]

In 1949, after coming under attack for the loss of China and for harboring communist sympathizers, the State Department tilted slightly toward Kennan's position on psychological warfare by engaging in operations that were designed to weaken the Soviet hold over its satellite nations and to strengthen resistance to communist ideology among the Western democracies. In May of that year, the Policy Planning Staff claimed that, "to attempt evasion of an obvious ideological issue is (1) objectively, to yield much of the field of conflict to our adversaries and (2) subjectively, to subvert our own ideological integrity—that is, deny subconsciously heritage and philosophic concepts which are inner reasons that we are, for all our shortcomings, not only great but good, and therefore a dynamic force in the mind of the world."[28]

Furthermore, it appeared in January, 1950, that the Kremlin had seized the psyops initiative. Its "Hate America" campaign portrayed the United States as a warmongering, imperialist nation that maintained its excessive lifestyle at the expense of the rest of the world.[29] Two months before NSC-68 became official policy, the State Department responded by departing from its rigid antipropaganda stance and launching an innovative psychological operation known as the "Campaign of Truth" (1950–53).

It is not clear where the concept for the Campaign of Truth (also known as the "Marshall Plan in the Field of Ideas") originated, but its planners appeared well versed in NSC-68's background papers. Edward W. Barrett, the assistant secretary of state for public affairs and a former OWI official, headed the program and continued State's insistence on presenting factual information only. However, unlike State's previous ad hoc efforts, the Campaign of Truth focused on ideology. This departure was necessary, according to Dean Acheson, to "counteract the vicious lies about this nation and its objectives as perpetrated by communists and to build a positive psychological force around which the free world and freedom loving peoples everywhere can rally." The Campaign of Truth's four chief objectives were: "(1) Exposing to the world . . . the truly reactionary vicious and phony nature of Kremlin Communism. (2) Building up a spirit of unity, . . . determination and confidence in all nations of the free world. (3) Inculcating in other peoples . . . a desire to cooperate with America— by disproving Soviet lies about us and by making clear that we are a *resolute, strong and honest nation, whose moral . . . and physical strength can be counted on.* (4) Building behind the Iron Curtain psychological obstacles to further Soviet aggression."[30]

"We must make ourselves heard round the world," Truman told the American Society of Newspaper Editors in April, 1950, as he inaugurated the program, "in a great campaign of truth. This task is not separate and distinct from other elements of our foreign policy. It is a necessary part of all we are doing ... as important as armed strength or economic aid."[31] Following the president's remarks, Acheson claimed that the United States would "demonstrate that our own faith in freedom is a burning and a fighting faith. . . . [It is] the most revolutionary and dynamic concept in human history and one which properly strikes terror into every dictator."[32] By portraying the international situation as a wartime crisis, the State Department doubled its total congressional appropriations for its fledgling psyops efforts to $111.7 million for fiscal year 1951, although these appropriations would shortly be cut.[33]

Although the foreign policy elite engaged in some psychological warfare activities after 1950, its members were still uncomfortable with fostering covert action through the spread of Kennan's ideology of liberation. Unconvinced that the United States possessed the means—physically or ideologically—to support indigenous revolutions within the Soviet bloc without provoking a third world war, and divided internally over whether or not the two superpowers could safely coexist in the nuclear world, the State Department, by default rather than design, allowed much of the psyops initiative to fall to private groups and other government agencies. In the end, as political scientist Gary Rawnsley has so astutely pointed out, the State Department never took the well-financed Campaign of Truth very seriously and made no effort to measure its level of success.[34]

Despite the State Department's ideological conservatism, with the beginning of the Korean War and the official adoption of NSC-68, the Campaign of Truth became considerably more idealistic and aggressive (perhaps independently so). Edward Barrett, who made no pretense at presenting balanced truths through the Campaign of Truth, now justified any tactic. "We simply [must do] everything possible to influence the minds of men to understand our cause for which we are fighting."[35] The Korean War infused the psyops community with new vitality, for within twenty-four hours of the president's announcement that American troops would be deployed in the UN action, military psyops agents dropped leaflets over South Korea and aired propaganda broadcasts.

Hundreds of private groups, often with government support, jumped on the international psyops bandwagon. The Common Council for American Unity began a "Letters from America" campaign in 1950 to foster greater international understanding. The American Committee for Liberation, created in 1951, bombarded the Soviet Union twenty-four hours a day with its "Radio Liberation" from transmitters in Europe and the Far East. Radio Free Europe and Radio Free Asia, operating with CIA assistance, broadcast items that the State Department found "impolitic to put on the air." Furthermore, the Committee for a Free Europe sent "Winds of Freedom" balloons with pro-American leaflets into Czechoslovakia and Poland, while American popular magazines such as *Reader's Digest, Time,* and *Life* endeavored to present a positive picture of American life to their international readers. The Truman and Eisenhower administrations encouraged these private and semiprivate organizations and corporations in their efforts to convince Eastern Europeans that the United States would support revolts against the Red Army. In reality, however, America was ill prepared for such an event in areas considered vital to Soviet interests. Beyond offering sympathy for the captive nations' plight, the White House proved unwilling to roll back the iron curtain as it had promised.[36]

In 1951, the Truman administration created the Psychological Strategy Board (PSB) to organize the numerous uncoordinated and overlapping psyops efforts of both private organizations and government agencies such as the Economic Cooperation Administration, the CIA, DOD, and the FCDA. Although the State Department hoped that the PSB would be subordinate to its authority, Truman granted the propaganda agency considerable autonomy by placing it outside the formal structure. Although it was an adjunct to the NSC, the PSB possessed an independent director appointed by the president, and an interdepartmental board consisting of top policy-making officials from State, DOD, and the CIA. According to its charter, the PSB's overall mission was to plan long-range psychological strategy, to present plans for the NSC to consider, to implement approved NSC proposals by coordinating efforts between agencies and departments that retained day-to-day responsibility for psychological operations, and to report back to the council on the effectiveness of those efforts.[37]

Unlike State's earlier attempts, psyops conducted under the PSB were all-inclusive and exceedingly activist. The first PSB director, former army secretary Gordon Gray, claimed that his agency would be concerned with "those activities of the US in peace and in war through which all elements of national power are systematically brought to bear on other nations for the attainment of US foreign policy objectives."[38] By April,

1952, the PSB was fully operational and ready to take the psyops initiative quite beyond what the State Department had originally envisioned. Assistant Director for Plans George Morgan wrote: "though it seems to be widely believed inside the Government as well as by the public that our policy is simply containment, it may be doubted whether it is or had been, except for public consumption." The PSB used the VOA, Radio Free Europe, the mass media, and a variety of unorthodox methods such as traveling exhibits, folk songs, and even comic books to "export" to peoples everywhere an evangelical democracy that consisted of the very precepts of the developing American civil-military religion.[39] However, the State Department, which opposed such a move, attempted to minimize the PSB's activism by overwhelming it with small tasks and endless paperwork.

In 1953, Barrett reflected on the future needs of American propaganda in his history of the Campaign of Truth, *Truth Is Our Weapon*. Americans had been handicapped in psyops, according to Barrett, because they lacked a formula that would "fire men's imaginations with a zeal and fervor approaching that of the Communists." The formula needed, according to Barrett and others, was one firmly grounded in the American civil-military religion. Barrett took seriously a suggestion a friend humorously had once written him: "Of course, we can always fall back on the recently proclaimed formula of acquiring a sense of mission and purpose which will unloose such moral and spiritual forces that the edifice of despotism will crumble into dust, without anybody having to work at it. Lovely work if you can get it, though some of our fellow citizens might find that building up their spiritual natures was about as painful as paying war taxes." As the Cold War dragged on, Barrett and a growing number of policy makers became advocates of "the great appeal of godliness versus godlessness, the spiritual appeal against the solely materialistic" and infused the Campaign of Truth with religious pronouncements.[40]

Psychological warfare techniques that incorporated the principles of the American civil-military religion fit well with the administration's attempt to formulate a unified national will and were more palatable to the public than international Christian coalitions. Evangelical democracy presented a model for third world nations to follow—the American civil-military religious model—and increasingly became the subject of discussion among national security planners interested in revamping international information programs. Most important, the Truman administration's attempt at psyops set the stage for the next administration. Under Eisenhower, psychological warfare was in greater harmony with the prevailing religious ethos of the American people and attempted aggressive, radical, and more extensive steps to shape a national will and character. There is no doubt, however, that the Truman administration created the possibility for such actions by its attempts to get tough on communism ideologically, especially through the rhetoric of NSC-68. The most active proponent of evangelical democracy at home and abroad during the Eisenhower administration would be the reorganized and revitalized U.S. armed forces.

The Military's Promotion of Evangelical Democracy

The first indication that the military was preparing to undertake this new, vital mission was found in the Defense Department's Troop Information and Education programs, which were unified in policy direction but the individual services developed their own separate programs. Unlike the State Department, the military took NSC-68's call for government action to build a resolute national will seriously and attempted to mobilize the nation spiritually with a series of patriotic programs that incorporated the new psyops techniques being developed to fight international communism. Because of its historic concern with the maintenance of civic virtue (both political and moral) as essential to an effective fighting force during time of crisis and its key role in the developing civil-military religion, the armed forces became the most powerful formulator and promoter of national will and took seriously the need to shape what they considered an appropriate, patriotic American character. At home and abroad during the early Cold War, the military promoted an evangelical democracy as an antidote to atheistic communism. If the armed forces could revitalize the American people through an emphasis on their "Christian democratic heritage," military leaders believed that an adequate number of high-quality recruits would be forthcoming, thereby strengthening America's defenses and deterring an enemy attack. This policy, according to DOD, would have the added benefit of also increasing the nation's resistance to communist efforts to undermine American will through psychological infiltration. Infused with a crusading zeal to save the nation and the world, the armed forces set about applying their own psychological warfare techniques to service personnel in particular, and American society in general.

Despite the Chaplain Corps's Character Guidance Program, AFIE programs had failed as morale builders during Truman's first administration. Designated a command responsibility, but with considerable variance between commands and services and with no clearly defined ideology, these programs underwent a shift in focus: the anticommunist motif was grafted onto the original citizenship and morality emphasis. A 1949 report on the program from the chief of chaplains to the secretary of the army claimed that AFIE accomplished the twin goals of "develop[ing] the individual's sense of responsibility and to counteract alien philosophies."[41] Thwarting "alien philosophies" ultimately became AFIE's dominant emphasis during the Cold War.

Immediately after becoming secretary of defense, George C. Marshall ordered AFIE to develop a citizenship and world affairs course for all branches and instructed commanders to begin experimenting with new lecture techniques to make information hours more stimulating for the men and women under their command. To accomplish this task, DOD turned to civilian experts in citizenship education at Columbia University's Teachers College, then under the direction of Columbia's new president and national war hero, Dwight D. Eisenhower.[42]

Eisenhower, who at this stage in his career had no qualms about increasing the military's role in American life, claimed he accepted the Columbia presidency to pursue civic-minded programs that would simultaneously improve the American character and promote the interests of the armed forces. Columbia, however, had sought the retired general in hopes of capitalizing on his skills as a fund-raiser. Despite his success at raising money, his tenure at the university was unhappy. Eisenhower irritated the faculty with his superpatriotism and continuing dedication to military interests. The university's regents had not been deceived regarding the general's loyalties, for he had clearly indicated to all that he was less concerned with producing first-rate scholars at Columbia—which he called his new military headquarters and which he staffed with two former Pentagon aides—as he was with creating "exceptional Americans." The armed services constituted "the bulwark of democracy," he told students in his first address as president of Columbia. "I believe in one thing only—this United States is the greatest force and the greatest power for good in the world and we have to be strong enough to extend its influence where it needs to go to protect ourselves." Moreover, he added, "The time has come when every one of us from 17 to 60 is going to have to place his time at the disposal of the government. . . . Everyone . . . must place first his obligation to his country in regard to school or anything else."[43]

As president of Columbia, Eisenhower launched a series of programs to advance anticommunism citizenship education. Among the most important of these were the American Assembly—a forum in which prominent conservative businessmen met with Columbia scholars to find solutions to the nation's problems—and, more important to this study, the Citizenship Education Project (CEP). Funded by the Carnegie Corporation under the influence of George C. Marshall, the CEP was an attempt to improve citizenship education in the nation's public school system. The president of Columbia's Teachers College, William Russell, a militant anticommunist, administered the program and imposed a curriculum on its experimental schools that simultaneously stressed critical thinking and instructed students in doctrinaire anticommunism. After two years of operation in hundreds of high schools, Eisenhower contacted Marshall about adapting the CEP for use in the armed services' AFIE programs.

Teacher's College and DOD held several meetings that ultimately produced a series of fifteen teaching units called "Hours of Freedom" that taught recruits citizenship with situation ethics. Despite an enthusiastic beginning, the relationship between the CEP and DOD was short-lived. The Carnegie Corporation became uncomfortable with the idea of funding a military project and DOD grew dissatisfied with a program that taught GIs to think creatively. When critics charged that the CEP was infected with the leftist politics of Columbia's professors and after Eisenhower went on indefinite leave from the university to assume command of North Atlantic Treaty Organization (NATO) forces in Europe, DOD severed its ties to the civilian project. This episode, while of short duration, was not without significance. The CEP provided Eisenhower an important credential as a formidable foe of international communism when he announced his candidacy for the presidency in January, 1952, making it possible for the increasingly vocal and politically active evangelical community to rally to his candidacy as the nation's savior. In addition, after their involvement with the CEP, the armed forces increased the anticommunism segments of their AFIE programs while eliminating any suggestion of leftist philosophy implied in the critical thinking portions of the "Hours of Freedom" instruction as the military came under the scrutiny of Sen. Joseph McCarthy and his cohorts.[44]

President Truman, the State Department, DOD, and right-wing politicians were not alone in perceiving an ideological crisis within the nation. Neoevangelicals, already in much agreement with the "military mind," which stressed obedience and loyalty as the highest democratic virtues, promoted a religiously oriented form of militant Americanism as a means of solving the nation's spiritual crisis.[45] Members of the Christian community were disturbed by foreign policy setbacks they perceived as evidence that the United States was no longer God's chosen nation and blamed the Truman administration for America's fall from grace. This environment of fear, anxiety, and blame fostered a series of revivals starting in 1949 that combined the salvation message with militant anticommunism and promoted the extraordinary career of a Youth for Christ evangelist named Billy Graham—the premier spokesman of America's civil-military religion.

At the end of the decade, the revival spirit kept alive since the end of World War II by neoevangelicals of the Youth for Christ movement flourished in the atmosphere of national fear surrounding communist advancements. Graham attracted little public notice before 1949, when his Los Angeles "Canvas Cathedral" crusade brought him to the attention of William Randolph Hearst and Henry Luce, prominent publishers who enthusiastically endorsed and promoted Graham's religiously oriented anticommunism. Throughout his early crusades, Graham claimed that America was losing the Cold War because of its materialism and wickedness. He saw Soviet triumphs as signs of divine punishment and was convinced the nation's only hope was to sanctify itself with an old-fashioned revival. "Tonight may be the last time that Jesus will pass your way," Graham warned as he urged crusade audiences to come forward and accept Christ as their personal savior.[46]

The tall, masculine Graham was tremendously popular because— along with his hard-hitting critique of American mores—he seemed to epitomize the national character sought by the religious community and government officials alike. His confident manner imbued his followers with a sense of security during an age of increasing anxiety and reassured them that they could do something about the communist threat even if the Truman administration seemed unable to do so. According to Graham, if the people humbled themselves and prayed, God, who had rejected America because of its immorality, would hear his people, forgive their sins, and lead the nation to victory against the communist forces. In addition, Graham appealed to a large segment of the American population that did not necessarily attend his crusades but supported his call for strong military measures against the Red Army. "Because Christianity needs a show of strength and force," Graham claimed, "we must maintain the strongest military establishment on earth."[47]

As a proponent of American civil-military religion, Graham not only enthusiastically supported aggressive foreign policies, he also recommended military training to solve the nation's social ills—especially the growing juvenile delinquency problem. Graham later claimed that teenage offenders, who lacked proper discipline at home, could be redeemed if taught Americanism, obedience, and religion. Youth "need something to believe in, they need a cause," he preached. "[T]hey need a flag to follow, they want a master, they want someone to control them."[48]

Graham should not be viewed as a mere opportunist. One might charge him with insincerity because he called for aggressive military policies to save the nation from the evil forces of communism while arguing that the only way that the American people could truly be safe was by accepting Jesus' invitation to be "born again." According to this thesis, Graham capitalized on anticommunist scare tactics to fill his coffers with donations and surround his stage with converts. If the nation's only hope was to turn to God, were not atomic bombs unnecessary and even immoral? No insincerity was apparent, however. Graham, as did many people at the time, perceived little conflict between religious and military solutions. In 1950, Sen. Edward Martin (R-Pennsylvania) called for the nation to move forward with the atomic bomb in one hand and the cross in the other. Later, Eisenhower's secretary of state, John Foster Dulles, claimed that America needed "a righteous and dynamic faith" along with its nuclear arsenal.[49] Graham gained supporters not because he was shrewd, although there is no doubt that he was, but because he articulated in an emotional, clear, and perhaps even simplistic style the prevailing—albeit somewhat contradictory—public opinion regarding how best to deal with the communist threat.

Graham held considerable power in the civil-religious atmosphere of the early Cold War. Although he accorded the president of the United States the special honor of being the leader of the New Israel, Graham reserved for himself, as the nation's foremost evangelist, the right to judge each politician's spiritual fitness for the sacred office. In the early 1950s, when a group of conservative North Carolina Democrats urged Graham

President Eisenhower (right) *meets with evangelist Billy Graham.*
Courtesy Billy Graham Center Archives.

to enter the primary, he retorted, "Why should I demote myself to be a Senator?"[50] Presidents who listened to his counsel benefited from Graham's endorsement, whereas those who refused to do so, such as Truman, limited their effectiveness as leaders of the American people. Graham initially gave Truman his blessing because of the president's general interest in religious matters, his strong stand against communism, and, more importantly, because Truman had granted the evangelist a thirty-minute meeting in July, 1950. Truman subsequently became disenchanted with Graham after the evangelist knelt before reporters on the White House lawn to falsely demonstrate how he had led the president in prayer. Privately describing Graham as just another "street-corner, Bible banging, phony son-of-a-bitch," Truman refused any further consultations, ignored the minister's incessant invitations to appear at one of his crusades, and rejected Graham's emotional appeal for a national day of prayer—religious/political mistakes that Eisenhower would not make. To retaliate, Graham launched a public campaign pointing out the Democratic Party's failings and portraying Truman as the personification of those shortcomings. Thoroughly disgusted with the president's unwillingness to assume his religious responsibilities, Graham turned to Eisenhower, whom the evangelist claimed would be the people's Moses and save them from Truman, the "hard-hearted pharaoh."[51]

Eisenhower as the Nation's High Priest

Unlike Truman, Eisenhower understood the importance of the president's symbolic duties as the nation's spiritual leader. Within American civil-military religion, the president functioned as a high priest in much the same way that the Jewish priesthood did in Old Testament accounts. According to the Bible, the priest understood the correct method of worship and how to properly appease God's anger with sacrifice. The president, acting as high priest, called the nation to sacrifice during times of crisis and orchestrated the national rituals that many believed identified the United States as the New Israel. According to this thesis, the president, more than any other single individual, possessed the power to restore the moral and spiritual basis of American unity.[52]

Throughout the presidential campaign, Eisenhower benefited from Graham's counsel on how best to shape his religious image and to counteract his reputation as a hardened military commander. Graham's support dovetailed with the image of the general promoted by his growing number of supporters: a latter-day George Washington whose prayers at Valley Forge saved a troubled nation. Eisenhower did nothing to disavow this religious/patriotic imagery and actively encouraged its promotion during the 1952 campaign. Reared in a home where Bible reading but not church attendance was stressed, Eisenhower had shown little interest in religious matters until World War II. As a presidential candidate, he recalled "the most agonizing decision" of his life when he had spent hours in prayer before giving the final order for the invasion of France: "If there were nothing else in my life to prove the existence of an almighty and merciful God, the events of the next twenty-four hours did it. This is what I found out about religion. It gives you courage to make the decisions you must make in a crisis, and then the confidence to leave the result to higher power. Only by trust in one's self and trust in God can a man carrying responsibility find repose."[53] After the war, Eisenhower claimed that his six years of fighting had rekindled his early faith and made him the "most intensely religious man" that he knew.

Although he did not affiliate with any particular denomination during his army career, he did espouse the common denominator religion promoted by the military chaplaincy.

Eisenhower's 1952 campaign took on the character of a moral crusade and a religious revival. When Graham gave the candidate a Scofield Bible, thus assuring the public that a Republican president would not be reading liberal interpretations of scripture, fundamentalist Christians overwhelmingly embraced Eisenhower.[54] Throughout the election, Eisenhower promised a crusade to rid the government of corruption, to end the war in Korea, and to take aggressive measures to defeat ungodly communism. The general's supporters were more specific: they promised that "Ike" would begin the nation's "spiritual recovery." Adlai Stevenson, the Democratic candidate, also invoked religious metaphors during the campaign, but his political and religious liberalism, along with his divorced status, made him unelectable in the eyes of the nation's evangelicals. On election eve, Eisenhower charged that America was God's chosen nation, destined to fight the "organized evil challenging free men in their quest of peace." This was neither a "political nor a military enemy," according to Eisenhower, but a "moral" one that threatened America's "very definition of life itself."[55] By identifying with the American civil-military religion and by capitalizing on the public's fear of communism at home and abroad, Eisenhower secured a landslide victory. Analysts have attributed his victory, in part, to a record voter turnout (a 25 percent increase) that included a great number of conservative Christians who went to the polls to elect a candidate representing their views. The Eisenhower presidency was the golden age of American civil-military religion. Patriotism and piety combined to serve as an ideological weapon against atheistic communism throughout his two terms.[56]

Acting on Graham's advice, Eisenhower took concerted steps to secure his position as the nation's high priest and to organize national unity along civil-military religious lines. At the inaugural—the most important ritual in the civil-military religion—the new president went beyond the traditional acknowledgement of God's authority and need for divine guidance, to offer his own personal prayer to the "almighty God."[57] Eisenhower took the oath of office with his hand placed atop not one but two Bibles. The first had belonged to George Washington and was opened to Psalm 127, which begins, "Except the Lord build the house, they labour in vain that build it."[58] The new president beseeched the nation to rededicate itself to God during his inaugural address, for "[w]hatever America hopes to bring to pass in the world must first come to pass in the heart of America."[59] Eisenhower ordered every cabinet meeting opened with prayer (Ezra Taft Benson, one of the twelve apostles of the Church of Jesus Christ of Latter-Day Saints, preformed the ritual the first time), and periodically attended presidential prayer breakfasts.[60]

The close personal relationship between Eisenhower and Graham proved to be mutually rewarding. As the new president's spiritual adviser, the evangelist helped to make the general/president appear more "godly," while gaining considerable prestige himself in the process. Eisenhower not only rewarded Graham with office space in the White House, he also ordered the State Department to brief the preacher before and after each of Graham's international crusades. Eisenhower provided Graham a ready ear, one that listened to his advice on a wide range of subjects, such as Vietnam (hold it at all costs) and how to respond to *Sputnik* (with more sacrifice and a tougher American character). It was clear, however, that the president conferred with Graham not because he needed direction on foreign policy and domestic issues, but because the minister told him what he wanted to hear and gave religious legitimacy to his policies. The Eisenhower-Graham alliance never stymied presidential initiatives, however, for when the evangelist's views differed from the president's, Graham always recognized his subordinate position and pledged to do his part in "selling the American public" on Eisenhower's programs.[61]

Critics claimed that Eisenhower and Graham headed a Christian movement that was purely superficial. William Lee Miller charged the administration with manipulating religion for its own purposes. "Officialdom prefers religion which is useful for national purposes, but undemanding and uncomplicated in itself. It also wants religion which is negotiable to the widest possible public." Miller's charges appear accurate, for despite the general's call for national repentance, he appears to have personally reflected only a superficial Christian faith. Besides his clandestine relationship with his wartime driver, Kay Summersby, there was other evidence of the president's lack of piety. Elmer Davis recalled that while the president had supported Graham's call for a national day of prayer, on the date appointed for America's supplication and consecration, Eisenhower "caught four fish in the morning, played eighteen holes of golf in the afternoon and spent the evening at the bridge table."[62] The most revealing story regarding Eisenhower's apparent lack of piety involved his church affiliation. After the inaugural celebrations ended, Eisenhower had been baptized and then joined, again on Graham's recommendation, the National Presbyterian Church of Washington. When the press quoted his new evangelical minister, Rev. Edward L. R. Elson, boasting that he pastored the church of presidents, Eisenhower reportedly told an aide, "You go tell that goddamn minister that if he gives out one more story about my religious faith I won't join his goddamn church." Privately, the minister begged the president's forgiveness. Publicly, he praised Eisenhower's "masculine Christian testimony" and "disciplined habits of worship."[63]

Although the president's irreverence appears contradictory to his public statements, adherents of America's civil-military religion did not necessarily espouse personal piety but instead saw, often quite sincerely, that America's Christian heritage served as a useful organizing principle. In this light, his rhetoric seems more authentic. There is little doubt that Eisenhower recognized the power of the American civil-military religion as a means to establish ideological goals for the nation. He used its precepts to define what it meant to be an American (patriotic and capitalistic) and what codes of conduct (political and moral) were expected of the people. Evangelicals such as Lt. Gen. William K. Harrison Jr., Chaplain (Maj. Gen.) Charles I. Carpenter, AFIE director John C. Broger, Adm. Arthur W. Radford, and others prospered in the civil-religious environment encouraged during the Eisenhower presidency and believed, as Harrison did, that "Biblical prophecies concerning the end of the age and the second advent of Christ" were evident in world events.[64] Most significantly, Eisenhower's attempt to fully incorporate civil-military religion into his administration did not create any public controversy. The public did not charge the president with breaching the separation of church and state because few believed he had acted inappropriately.[65] Religion of the civil-military religious variety could not be separated from the politics of the day, for the national government was operating in an overtly religious society. "Recognition of the Supreme Being," according to the president, "is the first, the most basic, expression of Americanism. Without God, there could be no American form of government nor an American Way of Life." In 1952, Justice William O. Douglas of the Supreme Court ruled, "We are a religious people whose institutions presuppose a Supreme Being." An American atheist, claimed a leading clergyman in Washington, D.C., was a contradiction in terms.[66]

Strengthening the Eisenhower administration's connection to American civil-military religion was the president's choice for secretary of state, John Foster Dulles. A devout Presbyterian who believed that the Cold War was a spiritual contest as well as an economic, political, and military one, Dulles was the quintessential Cold Warrior. As international tensions intensified, his attitude, like that of Eisenhower and so many other national security planners, evolved in a manner that reflected an increasing interest in the utility of the American civil-military religion.[67] The son of a minister and grandson of an international lawyer-diplomat, Dulles studied government at Princeton University under Woodrow Wilson and incorporated the idealized Wilsonian worldview into his philosophy of foreign policy. Dulles's early writings before and during World War II were influenced by his involvement with the liberal Federal Council of Churches (he chaired its Commission on a Just and Durable Peace) and warned against religious nationalism. Instead of deifying the state and demonizing competitor states, which he claimed often resulted in war, Dulles suggested substituting a universal, ecumenical, but foremost Christian religion for the people's former spiritual nationalism. This universal religion would stress "the concept of a duty to fellow man" and would promote "the welfare of the human race" instead of the narrow interests of any individual government. "[T]he willingness to sacrifice which demands an outlet," Dulles claimed, would be absorbed and "spiritual forces [would then be released] into a sphere of greater universality."[68]

Despite his discourse, Dulles found it difficult during the Cold War to escape from America's belief that God had ordained it as a "city on the hill." Like so many other policy makers who used the American civil-military religious precepts to secure congressional appropriations and public approval for aggressive foreign policies, Dulles came to believe and act upon his own rhetoric. Faced with an international communist foe, Dulles (by then a delegate to the United Nations and serving on a series of foreign minister councils) contradicted his earlier dictums and identified America as the nation of righteousness in opposition to the evil forces of Soviet communism. Dulles, as a "Priest of Nationalism," claimed that Americans during the period of the early republic "were imbued with a great faith. We acted under a sense of moral compulsion, as a people who had a mission to perform in the world. . . . We availed of every opportunity to spread our gospel throughout the world."[69] Regrettably, in

Dulles's view, the American people had become materialistic and were now "less concerned with conducting a great experiment for the benefit of mankind and . . . [were] more concerned with piling up . . . material advantages." In short, American wealth—which was, according to Dulles, "the rust that corrodes men's souls"—had endangered national security.[70]

Dulles condemned the American character while celebrating its potential for greatness. "United States foreign policy is made at home," he told a Chicago audience in 1951. "It is the projection abroad of our national will. . . . Our will flows from the fundamentals of our faith." The following year, Dulles proclaimed that a foreign policy devoid of spirituality would betray American principles: "Whether we like it or not—and I like it—our people are predominantly a moral people, who believe that our nation has a great spiritual heritage to be preserved." As Eisenhower's secretary of state, Dulles advocated mounting a political and psychological offensive (along with a military stalemate enforced by the threat of massive retaliation) that used "ideas as weapons" against communism to weaken it from within.[71]

Eisenhower and Dulles both appreciated the value of using religious emblems to legitimize national and international goals of the secular state. The president in particular understood the significance of imagery in the current ideological struggle. One of the most popular public measures during his administration was the two-word addition to the Pledge of Allegiance that symbolically institutionalized the American civil-military religion into the nation's domestic and international policies. After Rev. George M. Docherty claimed that the flag salute was devoid of any statement that distinguished the American way of life from that of the Soviets, the president supported a congressional measure to insert the phrase "under God" into the pledge.[72] Representative Overton Brooks (D-Louisiana) claimed that the new pledge "declared openly that we denounce the pagan doctrine of communism and declare 'under God' in favor of free government and a free world."[73] After signing the legislation into law, Eisenhower wrote: "from this day forward, the millions of our school children will daily proclaim in every city and town, every village and rural schoolhouse, the dedication of our Nation and our people to the Almighty. To anyone who truly loves America, nothing could be more inspiring than to contemplate this rededication of our youth, on each school morning, to our country's true meaning. . . . In this way we are reaffirming the transcendence of religious faith in America's heritage and future; in this way we shall constantly strengthen those spiritual weapons which forever will be our country's most powerful resource in peace or in war."[74]

Furthermore, the phrase "In God We Trust," which had been imprinted on the nation's coins since the Civil War, became the national motto in 1954. Congress ordered the Postal Service to cancel all first- and second-class mail with "pray for peace" the following year, and Capitol Hill built its first prayer room the year after that.[75]

Conclusion

Eisenhower succeeded in gaining public support where Truman had failed because he understood how best to capitalize on the nation's social and cultural forces. By establishing himself as the high priest of the American civil-military religion rather than an international Christian coalition, Eisenhower not only gained considerable political support that helped ensure his reelection in 1956, he also secured public approval for radical foreign policy departures, including his "New Look" defense initiative, which emphasized massive retaliation and aggressive psychological warfare operations. In addition, it was during Eisenhower's two administrations that the military and religious forces calling for the active shaping of the public character by the federal government finally matured. More specifically, this character-shaping campaign would be planned and implemented by influential high-ranking evangelical officers within the U.S. armed forces, the branch of government most receptive to psyops after World War II. The armed forces, unified and strengthened by the National Security Act and imbued with a missionary impulse created by its central role in the civil-military religion during the Cold War, embarked on a moral crusade during the late 1950s intended to save the nation from its communist foe by strengthening the character of its people. All that the services needed to begin their unprecedented public outreach was a catalyst. The catalyst came in the summer of 1953 when the media reported the shocking news that twenty-one Americans held captive in North Korea had refused repatriation.

CHAPTER 4

Evangelical Democracy and the Reshaping of the American Character

The will to resist the enemy could not be taught overnight, for it

rests on character traits instilled in our homes, our schools, [and]

our churches.

—The U.S. Fighting Man's Code, 1955

The Boy Scouts of America (BSA) ended their "Crusade to Strengthen the Arm of Liberty" in 1950 with a national encampment on the very same grounds that the Continental Army had occupied during the winter of 1777–78. This second National Boy Scout Jamboree at Valley Forge was a resounding success in large part because the military provided the equipment and personnel needed for efficient and disciplined operations. The army had secured congressional appropriations for the 625-acre gathering (as it had for the first national jamboree at Fort Myer, Virginia, in 1937) in the belief that such patriotic gatherings played an important role in creating a unified national will. During that week, the enthusiastic scouts entertained and edified thousands of visitors with nightly historic pageants and religious services. One evening, the forty-seven thousand uniformed campers pledged allegiance to the flag in unison and, on another, each boy lit a candle to symbolize American freedom of worship as the light for the rest of the world to follow.[1]

The significance of such patriotic/religious imagery no doubt was greatly intensified by fast-breaking and disturbing world events. Less than a week before the Valley Forge jamboree began on June 30, North Korean forces crossed the 38th Parallel and began rampaging through South Korea behind an armored spearhead of Soviet-supplied tanks. The two principal speakers at the encampment, Pres. Harry S. Truman and Gen. Dwight D. Eisenhower, commented on the developing crisis. Truman did so only indirectly, with utopian calls for human brotherhood and international fellowship as an alternative to war.[2] A few days later, however, Eisenhower won the scouts' enthusiastic support with a hard-hitting speech calling for U.S. intervention to prevent communism from enslaving the world. "How can we doubt eventual success if we meet these issues firmly?" the general asked the wildly cheering crowd.[3]

Like the military, the Valley Forge Park Commission embraced the opportunity provided by the 1950 jamboree to educate the Cold War public regarding its political-religious heritage. At the end of the week, park officials presented each youth with a package of Valley Forge dogwood seeds and a special jamboree edition of the park's *Historical Record and Guidebook*. "Read it. Keep it. It is precious," the booklet entreated. "Its pages tell why we must continually do our best to 'Strengthen the Arm of Liberty.'" If each boy returned to his hometown spreading the gospel of Americanism learned at the jamboree, park officials claimed, the nation's "dedication and re-dedication to the principles and traditions of historic Valley Forge" could be awakened.[4]

The BSA returned to Valley Forge for its annual jamboree in 1957. During the intervening seven years, the Korean War had ended and Eisenhower had defeated Adlai Stevenson. At the beginning of his second term, the popular president faced increasingly difficult international and domestic challenges. Despite his use of civil-military religious precepts to foster a unified and revitalized national will as a deterrent to international communism, there had been little ideological progress in rolling back the iron curtain. In fact, reports of widespread disloyalty among American troops during the Korean War convinced many that the United States was in the midst of a serious crisis. The BSA believed that another Valley Forge experience for American youth was in order. "It is the earnest desire of all jamboree leaders that each boy should go home inspired and filled with a deep appreciation of what this historic setting means to every American," a map issued by the BSA to troop leaders instructed. "Make it live in the hearts of your boys."[5]

The 1964 jamboree was the biggest, the most spectacular, and the last national Boy Scout encampment at Valley Forge. The mood differed significantly from that of previous gatherings: the civil rights movement, Pres. John F. Kennedy's assassination the year before, Lyndon Johnson's "War on Poverty," and America's growing involvement in the Vietnam conflict had revealed deep divisions in American society. The civil-military religious message, however, was still clearly evident at Valley Forge that week. The Jamboree began with a historical pageant that featured six thousand of the fifty-two thousand campers reenacting the Revolutionary War followed by a $30,000 fireworks display and the arrival on stage by helicopter of BSA president Thomas J. Watson Jr. and Lady Baden-Powell, widow of Sir Robert Baden-Powell, founder of the Boy Scouts. Despite the BSA's best efforts, religious nationalism had become considerably muted. Opposing segments of society contested the parameters of civil religion and openly questioned what it meant to be an American in light of the social and political turmoil of the decade.[6]

Soon after the 1964 jamboree, the Valley Forge Park Commission, worried about damage to subterranean artifacts during large-scale gatherings, moved to end its involvement with the BSA. The Valley Forge Historical Society argued passionately against the move, however, claiming in its official journal that if the Boy Scouts taught "a lasting sense of American patriotism and liberty," they would advance the nation's security and the cause of "human liberty." would be advanced. According to the historical society, "the immortal dead who sleep at Valley Forge will forgive the 'desecration'" to park grounds, for when the "knowledge of the meaning of Valley Forge dies, the death-knell of human freedom is probably imminent."[7]

Before the futility of their efforts became clear, "Cold War Progressives," that is, those men and women within and without the military who believed that the U.S. military was the linchpin of American civil-military religion and the architect of the national will, argued for concerted steps to fashion a patriotic and increasingly evangelical national character. Moral and resolute, this revitalized American character would be willing, according to its proponents, to sacrifice for the common good as did the Continental soldier at Valley Forge. Cold War Progressives combined the old Progressive notion that military service instilled in the nation's youth the democratic, masculine, and moral values believed essential for national defense with the more pragmatic needs of the Cold War—the necessity of convincing the public to fund a large peacetime military as a deterrent to international communism.

In the turn-of-the-century muckraking tradition, these religious nationalists called the public's attention to a perceived degeneracy in the nation's youth serving in Korea in their attempt to purify the military's ranks and to reach out to the public with aggressive new character education programs. Additionally, Eisenhower's New Look defense policy, the energized National Security Council structure, and activist psychological warfare strategies coalesced at the same time Sen. Joseph McCarthy launched an attack on the army's masculinity. McCarthy's charges, while leading to his downfall, at the same time strengthened a "cult of toughness" that was already developing in American society. It was in this atmosphere that the Korean POW scandal became a catalyst for creating the national character and will long sought for by the U.S. armed forces.

Eisenhower's New Look Strategy

When Dwight David Eisenhower took the oath of office in 1953, the army looked to its former chief of staff and commander of NATO forces to protect its interests from encroachments by the air force and navy. Most of its officer corps had served under Eisenhower and in-service morale had greatly improved after he kept his campaign promise to personally go to Korea in an effort to end the war. However, the army's faith in the new president was based more on wishful thinking than reality. Following World War II, Eisenhower had supported UMT and a large reserve and National Guard force structure rather than increased manpower ceilings for the regular army as a cost-effective means of providing national security. In addition, when Defense Secretary James Forrestal selected Eisenhower in 1949 to serve as his adviser on defense appropriations, the retired general had championed the air force's—and to a lesser extent the navy's—strategic-bombing capabilities over the army's conventional ground forces. Perhaps the Korean War experience, coupled with Eisenhower's call during that conflict for the rapid expansion of ground troops, misled those in the army hierarchy to believe that he would be the protector and promoter of their service's interests. In any case, confidence plummeted after Eisenhower publicly announced his national security policy commonly referred to as the "New Look."

The final New Look policy paper (NSC-162/2), originating in the secret Operation Solarium study, based the nation's defenses on a modified pre–NSC-68 strategy; that is, an economically minded defense posture that relied on the nation's nuclear arsenal to contain communism and "roll back" the iron curtain. The authors of NSC-68 had called for the rapid buildup of conventional and nonconventional military forces in preparation for a year of "maximum danger" in 1954, when experts predicted that the Soviet's technological and production capabilities would peak. The New Look discounted any specific year for concern. It was based on the assumption that America should plan for the "long-haul" with steady, managed defenses. While reminiscent of Truman's containment doctrine in scope, the New Look differed significantly from the previous administration's national security policy in emphasis. It placed considerably less dependence on conventional weaponry and, in order to keep defense costs down, supported an airpower strategy of "massive retaliation" with nuclear weapons. Additionally, by not specifying where or when nuclear bombs would be deployed, but implying that the primary target would be Moscow (which was believed to be the source of all communist aggression), the New Look remained ambiguous enough to keep the Soviets off balance and uncertain about the U.S. response to any future offensives.[8] According to New Look advocates, the threat of massive retaliation would not only contain the Soviets in the short run, it would also deter the Kremlin from retaliating when Eisenhower initiated his rollback policy. Truman had attempted a military rollback in Korea with disastrous results. The Eisenhower administration hoped to liberate captive nations by threatening to use America's burgeoning nuclear arsenal and by fully incorporating political, economic, paramilitary, and psychological warfare operations into a comprehensive offensive strategy.[9]

The chief reason the army rejected the New Look was Eisenhower's decision to cut the army's funding, and to a lesser extent the navy's, in favor of the air force. As the air force's influence increased, the army and navy struggled to protect their budgets and manpower ceilings from the massive cuts needed to fund Eisenhower's New Look. General Maxwell D. Taylor, who served as army chief of staff from 1955–59, actively campaigned for a "flexible response" strategy that would keep the army from degenerating into little more than an occupation force. Taylor warned the president that massive retaliation actually threatened national security because nuclear parity would destroy the power of deterrence and only a preventive war could stop the Soviets from eventually matching America's atomic advances. If the United States obliterated half the civilized world, what possible objective would be achieved? Taylor attempted to carve out an important mission for the army by emphasizing the service's guided-missile program (centered at Redstone Arsenal, Alabama, under the direction of Werner von Braun) and its elite airborne units. Defense Secretary Charles E. Wilson countered by limiting the range and restricting the army's use of its missiles and planes.[10] Taylor also tried to improve the army's public image with an aggressive publicity campaign that highlighted the masculinity and courage of the American GI. Despite his best efforts, enlistment rates dropped and early retirements increased within the demoralized army.[11]

Cold War Progressives responded to public apathy to the army, and the armed forces in general, as military progressives traditionally did during peacetime: by emphasizing the character-education function of military service. Because they also operated during the fifties under the belief that communism presented a very real internal and external threat, such character education became considerably more political and religiously oriented. By this method—that is, an emphasis on evangelical anticommunist ideology—religious nationalists argued that the armed forces could develop the patriotic morality and democratic citizenship that would foster the determined national will needed to support a strong defense establishment. While earlier historians marveled at what they perceived as an "overreaction" to the internal communist threat by American policy makers during the era, recent declassifications have revealed that such fears were not totally ungrounded. In the 1990s, the National Security Agency (NSA) published the Venona translations of Soviet intelligence messages sent from 1940–48, proving that Moscow had indeed established a communist spy ring in the United States during World War II that was "aggressive, capable, and far-reaching," with "at least some wartime spies and agents of influence remain[ing] unidentified" during the Cold War.[12]

Admiral Arthur Radford, chairman of the Joint Chiefs of Staff from 1953–57, also moved to protect the navy's interests under the New Look. He did so by fully supporting the president's defense initiative and calling for even further cuts in the army's budget. By this method, the JCS chief helped preserve the navy's nuclear capabilities and, in particular, its *Polaris* submarine-launched intercontinental ballistic missile program. Radford, outspoken, partisan, and a leading spokesperson within the military hierarchy for evangelical democracy, neutralized opposition to his proposals by demanding that the JCS reach consensus before sending recommendations to the president. Army staff officers blocked the admiral's plans to reduce their service to a mere 575,000 (capable of operating only as a small task force) by leaking news of the move to the press and by publicly supporting Taylor's flexible response proposal. The president became so aggravated by this so-called Revolt of the Colonels (which he perceived as merely interservice rivalry) that he limited the military's future presence at NSC meetings to the JCS chairman. Radford and his successor, air force general Nathan F. Twining (1957–60), communicated to the president the interests of their own services, increasingly shutting the army out of key policy-making decisions. Despite this reduction in overall military representation at NSC meetings, the presence of Radford, an ardent proponent of evangelical democracy, ensured the continuing influence of civil-military religious precepts at the highest level of government.[13]

In October, 1957, the United States suffered yet another in a series of public relations disasters when the Soviet Union successfully launched its *Sputnik* satellite. Headlines reading "Are We Americans Going Soft?" stirred public sentiment as Congress moved to increase the military budget in order to compete with the Soviet space program. The president, deluged with intelligence reports that proved there was no "missile gap," refused to abandon his cost-effective New Look strategy and instead responded to *Sputnik* by extending federal aid to public education and by making only limited increases in the nation's missile program, primarily by creating the civilian-directed National Aeronautics and Space Administration (NASA). According to historian Robert Divine, Eisenhower failed during the crisis because he did not disavow the notion in the public mind that "Sputnik represented a fundamental shift in military power and scientific achievement from the United States to the Soviet Union." The president sought to "rekindle the trust and confidence" of the American people, shaken by *Sputnik*'s success, *Vanguard*'s failure, and rumors of a missile gap with his 1958 reorganization of the Defense Department and by stepping up his administration's efforts in the psychological warfare realm.[14]

Psychological Warfare under Eisenhower

"Don't be afraid of that term [psychological warfare] just because it's a five-dollar, five-syllable word," Eisenhower reassured the nation. "Psychological warfare is the struggle for the minds and wills of men."[15] The president highlighted the critical importance he placed on psychological warfare operations when he named Charles Douglas "C. D." Jackson as his special assistant for psychological warfare and by creating the President's Committee on International Information Activities (the Jackson Committee) to study the psychological warfare policies of previous administrations in order to formulate more effective ones. The Jackson Committee's final classified report claimed that the Kremlin's primary weapon during the Cold War would be psychological. Because communism held "significant appeal to many people," the committee urged the administration to step up its efforts to identify America's own competing ideology. In order to avoid Truman's mistakes of using psychological warfare only defensively and presenting a confused picture of American intentions to target audiences, the committee recommended that Eisenhower assume personal control and direction of psychological warfare through the means of a reorganized and greatly strengthened NSC.[16]

The NSC thus became an instrument of Eisenhower's policies during his presidency. Under the Truman administration, the NSC had served primarily as a supplementary advising agency. Eisenhower responded to the Jackson Committee's recommendations by refashioning and expanding the agency's structure and functions into a comprehensive national security system. This system served as Eisenhower's chief mechanism for implementing national security policies and, because of Radford's intimate involvement in NSC procedures, inadvertently increased the influence of proponents of evangelical democracy in domestic and foreign policy decision making. Among other innovations, the president created a planning board to set agendas and to prepare briefing papers, appointed a special assistant for national security affairs to serve as a nonvoting member and preside over the planning board and to assist the president in NSC business, established a special staff to form "an unbiased point of view" of planning board papers, and created the Operations Coordinating Board (OCB) to take over from the Psychological Strategy Board the coordination and implementing of NSC decisions. While Eisenhower, more often then not, made final decisions through informal meetings with trusted advisors, he utilized the NSC bureaucracy to study, implement, and evaluate the effectiveness of his policies.

The most significant policy paper produced by the NSC system each year was the Basic National Security Policy (BNSP), which outlined the administration's strategic objectives for the coming year. Each BSNP, in addition to the traditional military and political aspects of national policy, always included a section on the psychological aspects of American security at home and abroad.[17] Once the newly revitalized and activist NSC structure was in place, military-inspired programs directed at the American public could occur without public debate. In 1958, after the yearly BSNP seemingly condoned activity of this nature, the influential and generally evangelical "true believers" in DOD felt fully authorized to conduct the joint military-civilian anticommunism seminars referred to in this study as Cold War seminars (to be discussed in the next chapter).

Eisenhower's psychological warfare policies and NSC system were still under construction when Stalin unexpectedly died in March, 1953. The previous year, Truman had approved a PSB-sponsored plan code-named Operation Cancellation, which hoped to exploit political instability within the Soviet bloc created by a succession crisis. However, the State Department, fearing the consequences of liberation in Eastern Europe, refused to implement the plan. Instead, State merely announced Stalin's death through its information programs, offered America's condolences to the Russian people, and adopted a "wait-and-see" strategy while the Kremlin scrambled to build a unified political front.[18] Eisenhower was furious with his "so-called experts" in psychological operations and, as the Jackson Committee had earlier recommended, assumed control of such activity shortly thereafter. The president announced his new strategy with two speeches in the spring of 1953. Taken together, "A Chance for Peace," presented at the annual meeting of the American Society of Newspaper Editors, and "Atoms for Peace," which the president delivered to the UN General Assembly, contrasted America's peaceful and magnanimous development of atomic energy to the Soviets' allegedly sinister intentions for nuclear weapons. In addition to this overt strategy, the Eisenhower administration attempted to undermine Soviet influence in third world nations with a series of unprecedented operations in the psychological realm that supplemented covert military actions already under way.[19]

McCarthyism and American Masculinity

Eisenhower enjoyed overwhelming public support for his foreign and domestic policies in large measure because of his shrewd management of the American civil-military religion. His manipulation of religious nationalism as an organizing mechanism secured popular support for his policies while at the same time neutralizing his opponents and potential critics. Indeed, the Eisenhower administration retained a high approval rating throughout both terms even though numerous federal agencies were in disarray as a result of Joseph McCarthy's rise to power as the nation's leading anticommunist zealot.

McCarthy, as other scholars have so aptly demonstrated, gained strength and prestige from each of his well-publicized attacks on the State Department until, overworked and drinking heavily, he finally succeeded in convincing himself that he was on a holy mission from God. "You don't understand," he told syndicated columnist Jack Anderson when asked about his investigations, "this is the real thing, the *real thing.*"[20] Although McCarthy undoubtedly exploited opportunities created by the civil-military religious consensus, there was little doubt that McCarthyism represented a considerably darker side of that consensus. Eisenhower "tolerated" and in some ways even "benefited" from McCarthy's investigations—as long as the senator refrained from looking beyond the "sins" of the previous administration. However, when McCarthy overstepped his boundaries by challenging the patriotism and even the "manhood" of the U.S. armed forces, the president moved quickly and decisively to neutralize this challenge to the civil-military consensus. Specifically, the Eisenhower administration had taken advantage of McCarthyism in purging Democratic appointees and programs that did not support or which attempted to operate independently of White House control, but it could not permit the undermining of the military's reputation or the usurpation of the president's priestly role.[21]

Empowered by his mission and no longer realistic about his objectives, McCarthy had inexplicably turned his attention to the center of America's civil-military religion: the U.S. Army. Historians have pointed to the army-McCarthy hearings as a triumph for the armed forces. Most scholars allege that McCarthy met his match, suffering defeat because of the service's incontestable patriotic credentials. However, they have paid little attention to how McCarthyism affected the army and was then used by the service's leaders to strengthen internal security measures, purge the ranks of undesirables, and help in their attempt to represent American ideals. The senator's charge that the army contained effeminate "commie-coddlers" implied that the most-revered uniformed Cold Warriors were weak and soft on communism simply could not be overlooked. Already under pressure because of the New Look cost reductions, the army could ill afford anyone questioning its ideological foundation. If the nation was to be safeguarded from communist infiltration, if not outright attack by the Soviet Union, then it was essential, according to Cold War Progressives, that the U.S. military shape the critically important moral and patriotic components of American character. At all costs, the Kremlin must be kept from suspecting any vulnerability—material or psychological—in the nation's defenses.[22]

Traditionally projecting an image of masculinity, the services were particularly sensitive about charges of weakness. Old line officers had denounced George C. Marshall's attempts to "democratize" the army after World War II. They worried that Marshall's "civilizing" and "sanitizing" of the military experience had emasculated America's Cold Warriors and, through them, all of society. Popular culture blamed "momism," the belief that American mothers had coddled their sons and robbed them of their manly characteristics, for the reported decline in masculinity. Even the nation's comic strips seemed to reflect the image of a "cowed and eunuchoid" American male. Dagwood Bumstead, the bumbling husband in *Blondie,* was unable to command the respect of his wife and two children, his boss Mr. Dithers, or his neighbors, coworkers, door-to-door salesmen, and mailman. Even his dog "Daisy" paid little heed to the master of the house.[23]

A "cult of toughness" developed in opposition to the "feminization" of society. Historian Donald J. Mrozek claims the War Department promoted physical training and recreational sports during World War II as a means of developing the physical and moral "combative qualities" necessary to survive in battle. After the war, the public viewed this same toughness or "aggressive, action-oriented attitude" as one remedy for improving the decadent postwar society. Pain and suffering would solve the national crisis in character and will, according to "toughness" proponents. Football, which had been the source of much concern to Progressive reformers earlier in the century, was heralded as the moral equivalent to on-the-job training for modern life. Football, according to an article in *Look* magazine in 1962, "demonstrates the value of work, sacrifice, courage, and perseverance," that was so desperately needed "in our modern society with its delinquency problem, lack of discipline and physical softness."[24]

The rhetoric of the new effeminate American male played heavily in the charges of McCarthy and other "red hunters" who built their cases on "the assumption that patriotism and masculinity were synonymous." The equating of sexual perversion with communist subversion grew in intensity as a "lavender [homosexual] scare" developed in the same month—February, 1950—that McCarthy first "discovered" there were communists in the State Department. The Federal Bureau of Investigation (FBI) responded by intensifying sexual surveillances during security checks and the armed forces began purging their ranks of those who exhibited the slightest "tendency" toward homosexuality. The annual discharge rate for personnel with homosexual tendencies doubled during the 1950s as the military sought to rid itself of the image of softness and moral corruption. This was a significant departure in policy from World War II. When full mobilization needs dictated less scrutiny, homosexuals generally remained in uniform—often placed in "gender-specific" jobs. After the war, the Truman administration identified homosexuals as security risks, but the stress was on the possibility that such individuals would be susceptible to blackmail rather than the idea that their sexual preference was a corrupting influence on the government.[25]

The public, with little exception, applauded the results of the lavender scare. Billy Graham praised all those who, "in the face of public denouncement and ridicule, go loyally on in their work exposing the pinks, the lavenders and the reds who have sought refuge beneath the wings of the American Eagle."[26] Similar sentiments were expressed in the popular culture. Author Mickey Spillane's best-selling detective novels featured the adventures of a macho hero named Mike Hammer. Hammer, bragging in *One Lonely Night* (1951) about the villains he had killed, explained: "They were commies, Lee. They were red sons-of-bitches who should have died long ago. . . . They never thought that there were people like me in this country. They figured us all to be as soft as horse manure and just as stupid."[27]

Having exploited the lavender scare to rid itself of the image of "softness" and "moral corruption," the army, not surprisingly, reacted strongly to McCarthy's assault on its manliness. In the aftermath of its public relations victory in the army-McCarthy hearings, DOD became extremely sensitive to any criticism of its character and determined to increase its emphasis on patriotism and masculinity as a bulwark against communist aggression. Any perceived character weakness in American soldiers was the fault, according to the services, of American homes, schools, and churches and not on changes in military training. American youths corrupted by wealth and momism made poor material with which to work. The "Cult of Toughness" had its roots in the army's call for instructing "soft" Americans in values shorn of any ambiguity, but it was in the climate of McCarthyism that the crisis of American toughness entered its most extreme phase, prompting DOD to take extraordinary measures to ensure that masculine values were incorporated into the American spirit.[28]

Despite McCarthy's challenge to the patriotism and manliness of the nation's armed forces, DOD itself was ultimately responsible for what became the military's greatest public relations crisis of the decade. In 1955, the Defense Department developed a "Code of Conduct" for service personnel after learning that twenty-one Americans subjected to communist "brainwashing" in prisoner of war (POW) camps in North Korea, had defected to the enemy.[29] While internal division over how to interpret the Korean War POW experience existed in the military from the beginning of the scandal, in the end, the Pentagon capitalized on a developing POW myth in its attempt to reshape the American character. According to the myth, not only had the twenty-one defectors betrayed their country, a significant number of the Americans held captive in North Korea had been guilty of serious misconduct. In Korea, the myth concluded, American democracy had been found lacking. Because the nation's homes, schools, and churches had failed to teach the traditional American values of patriotism and moral leadership, soldiers had been unprepared for the ideological battle with their communist captors.

Proponents of the myth, such as journalist Eugene Kinkead, author of *In Every War but One* (1959), alleged that unlike POWs in previous conflicts, "soft" Americans had collaborated en masse, refused to escape, and died at an alarming rate from the disease of "give-up-itis." Newspapers and magazines published the views of an army psychiatrist, Lt. Col. William E. Mayer, who charged that up to a third of all American POWs were guilty of collaboration. Virginia Pasley's immensely popular book *21 Stayed* (1955) investigated the background of the infamous defectors and concluded that their treason derived from broken homes and an ill-defined concept of what it meant to be an American. Kinkead, Mayer, and Pasley all blamed the scandal on the nation's premilitary environment and inadequate troop information programs rather than on the particular rigors of enemy POW camps.[30]

Official DOD investigations, as did the findings of sociologist Albert Biderman in *March to Calumny* (1963), found that the charges against the American POWs held in North Korea had been greatly exaggerated; they had behaved no less patriotically than prisoners in any other war. Such findings, however, had little effect on the public perception that widespread treason had occurred. Biderman wondered why the POW myth, which attacked the very character of the military, would be spread so passionately by the armed forces through the Code of Conduct program. The military clearly was aware that in all previous wars Americans undergoing torture had collaborated, yet it actively and enthusiastically promulgated the idea that something new and disturbing had occurred in Korea. It did so in its attempts to provide the American public with an ideological blueprint for survival. According to Biderman, a small group of old line army officers capitalized on the collaboration myth in order to reverse George C. Marshall's democratic reforms, which they believed had undermined discipline. More importantly, however, DOD hoped that the new Code of Conduct would both instruct recruits on proper POW behavior and serve as a springboard for the military's larger goal: that of providing a unified national ideology. "I am an American fighting man," the code proclaimed, "responsible for my actions, and dedicated to the principles which made my country free. I will trust in my God and in the United States of America." It was ironic, according to Biderman, that in its effort to fortify the character of all Americans, the military had tarnished the reputations of those Americans who had endured the worst treatment during the war.[31]

An official military investigation revealed the basic facts of the Korean War POW experience. After surviving a number of death marches, torture, intolerable living conditions, and inadequate medical care at the hands of the North Koreans, the UN captives had been turned over to the Red Chinese in the spring of 1951. The Chinese alleviated some of the physical suffering, but increased efforts to undermine the traditional beliefs of the various nationalities held prisoner for propaganda purposes. They forced each man to submit to "self criticism" sessions and to attend daily two-hour political lectures on the virtues of communism. Although a number of Americans resisted cooperating with their captors in any fashion (reactionaries), most passively endured ideological "instruction" and learned to mimic the "right" responses to critiques of the United States. The POWs employed such actions in an effort to obtain the food, clothing, and essential medical treatment desperately needed for survival. Whether or not such cooperation was treason is highly suspect. "The University of Pyuktong," as the prisoners derisively referred to their indoctrination, produced few real communists. Nonetheless, U.S. officials were greatly alarmed when they learned of Chinese attempts at psychological indoctrination. Especially disturbing—and certainly more damning—was the revelation that a handful of POWs became discussion leaders (progressives) and aided the communists in instructing their fellow prisoners on the "evils" of America.[32]

American POWs had never before encountered such intense political indoctrination. However, the real difference in this war, and the catalyst for much of the POW scandal, was the fact that UN representatives had fought hard for voluntary repatriation during truce negotiations. They did so in order to facilitate the large group of communist prisoners who wanted to stay in noncommunist hands once the war ended. Military leaders were aware that a few Americans in every war had chosen to remain behind. However, the United States had never before adopted voluntary repatriation as official policy, thereby making any defections headline news. The ultimate result was that twenty-one American, one British, and 305 South Korean prisoners freely chose to remain with the communists, whereas more than twenty-five thousand Chinese and North Korean prisoners, who had received instruction in American democratic principles during their UN captivity, voluntarily remained in the South. With a bit of public relations work, such a lopsided scorecard could easily have been presented as an overwhelming victory for the free world. Yet somehow the number twenty-one stuck in the craw of Americans, who were encouraged by the military to view the scandal as a general failure and indicative of the dismal state of American character and will.

Up to a year before news of the infamous twenty-one hit the press, the Korean War POW myth began to take shape. The public first became concerned about the conduct of American prisoners in 1952, when the Chinese published statements by captured air force pilots who "confessed" that they had used biological weapons against the Korean people. The negative publicity surrounding these statements prompted Assistant Secretary of Defense for Manpower Anna Rosenberg to conduct a survey of current Armed Forces Information and Education programs. In 1953, her successor, Dr. James H. Hannah, released the survey report, which recommended a massive overhaul of troop information programs so soldiers would better know why they were fighting.[33]

Shortly after the Rosenberg survey became public, the army treated the first Americans released during Operation Little Switch (April 21–May 3, 1953) for communist brainwashing. Believing that the Chinese had handpicked a number of these sick and wounded POWs as part of a plot to infiltrate all of American society with communist philosophy, the army took great precautions to protect the public from ideological contamination. After flying the alleged traitors back to the United States "under a cloak of military secrecy," officials placed them on a sealed ward at the Valley Forge Army Hospital in Phoenixville, Pennsylvania, where they underwent "political psychiatric therapy" as an antidote to brainwashing. Unsure if brainwashed individuals could be held responsible for their actions, yet concerned that a large number of the remaining prisoners waiting to be released in Operation Big Switch in the fall of 1953 had betrayed their country, the military alternately sequestered then paraded the debilitated and emotionally traumatized men two-by-two before the press as evidence of the communist depradations.[34]

Valley Forge Army Hospital became a center of media attention, overwhelming the medical staff. Newspapers reported that the army doctors assigned to treat the POWs were less concerned with the service's search for traitors than they were with the normal psychological problems associated with reintroducing the former prisoners to American society. The staff noted that the men, who had spent up to twenty-eight months in communist hands and lived daily under the threat of torture and death, did manifest "a moderate to marked degree of blandness, retardation, and apathy." However, these qualities had also been observed in returning prisoners following World War II and were not evidence of any new method of brainwashing or mind-changing process. "I don't know where this idea [that the hospital was "debrainwashing"] started," one furious Valley Forge doctor claimed, "but there's one thing for sure—we're not running a damned Laundromat here." The only explanation for the lack of confidentiality regarding the former POWs, he added, was that the army was exploiting the situation "for political propaganda and publicity purposes."[35]

Protests regarding the army's treatment of the repatriated men emerged from several quarters. On May 7, Rep. Edith Nourse Rogers (R-Massachusetts) argued that the patients were being stigmatized unfairly. The former POWs, "bitter beyond expression," rejected charges that they had collaborated with the enemy. They argued instead that they had been instructed prior to their capture that "conversation beyond the 'name, rank, number, only' proviso could be excused" if they revealed no military information.[36] Moreover, while the enemy had "tried to show us that they had something," Pfc. Rogers Herndon, twenty, of Jacksonville, Florida, explained to reporters, "they had nothing compared to what we have in the United States."[37] *The Nation* published an especially poignant editorial regarding the army's mishandling of the Operation Little Switch POWs and concluded that their treatment was "a sorry episode . . . to be associated with the great name of Valley Forge."[38]

The army had little time to evaluate its treatment of the Valley Forge POWs before newspapers and the popular press broadcast the shocking news that the notorious twenty-one had refused repatriation during Operation Big Switch. While the NSC recommended that the armed forces ameliorate the damage to the American psyche caused by the twenty-one turncoats through greater efforts to educate troops on proper POW conduct, its subordinate psychological warfare agency, the Operations Coordinating Board, suggested that the military maintain public morale by minimizing the public attention focused on collaborators.[39] At first the army also vacillated. Were the POWs who had been brainwashed unable to resist manipulation or did they willingly collaborate with the enemy because of inadequate prewar training? Although there were always individuals in the military ready to speak out in defense of the general patriotism of the Americans held in North Korea, the second explanation clearly provided the most benefits.

In time, DOD, genuinely fearing that the American male no longer possessed the toughness needed for national defense, minimized the voice of doubters within and without of uniform and, in much the same fashion as Progressive Era muckrakers, enthusiastically publicized reported cases of disloyalty to gain approval for its national regeneration plans. The Defense Department had helped Eugene Kinkead with his research and writing,[40] while the army, though disclaiming any official endorsement, had given Lieutenant Colonel Mayer free reign to travel the country and publicly question the patriotism of the American POWs and U.S. service personnel in general. All of the services incorporated Mayer's audiotapes into their troop information programs.[41] The military's acceptance of the POW myth was separate but quite compatible with the evangelical impulses within DOD; that is, not all who called for POW reform based on the myth were evangelicals. Those who were, however, saw the reported POW misconduct as proof that the armed forces should take immediate and drastic action to implement their civil-religious version of Americanism.

The Code of Conduct

After first learning of the twenty-one defections, Eisenhower explained to reporters that the military had been unable to prepare soldiers psychologically for communist indoctrination because the young men and women entering the services no longer possessed "knowledge of what America is . . . and why they were fighting."[42] Taking the commander in chief's cue, Defense Secretary Charles Wilson appointed an eleven-member committee chaired by Carter L. Burgess, assistant secretary of defense for manpower and personnel, to investigate the POW scandal in Korea and to draft a new unified code of conduct to supplement existing regulations governing the proper treatment of prisoners. The Geneva Conventions of 1929 and 1949 set forth detailed protections for prisoners but did not specify what conduct was expected of them. Although each of the services had its own regulations regarding POW behavior, there had never been a clearly defined code of conduct applicable to all military personnel.

The Burgess Committee did two things. First, it investigated to see if widespread treason had actually occurred in Korea. Interestingly, the committee's final report, *POW: The Fight Continues After the Battle*, claimed that "the record [of the prisoners] was fine indeed," incidents of collaboration had been exaggerated, and that American POWs held in North Korea had not behaved markedly different from prisoners in earlier wars. Yet, it inexplicably issued the Code of Conduct, the committee's second task, presumably so that the Korean War story would never be repeated.[43] The committee's inconsistencies aptly demonstrated the military's dilemma: at heart the services wanted to defend their war record, but at the same time they desired to alert the nation to the need for greater character education through the medium of the POW myth.

Writing the code presented certain problems. Expert testimony had made clear that the Spartan code of giving only one's name, rank, and serial number when questioned by captors had always been impossible for servicemen to meet. Now, however, only the air force, as the committee's proceedings revealed, opted for a more "compassionate" stance. The other services were convinced that they needed an inflexible standard to "toughen up" recruits and revitalize the nation spiritually.[44] The Burgess Committee concluded that a "line of resistance must be drawn somewhere and initially as far forward as possible. The name, rank and service number provision of the Geneva Convention was accepted as this line of resistance."[45] One army general, parodying Thomas Jefferson, claimed that the future depended on "young men who have iron in their souls and guts in their beliefs. . . . The tree of liberty survives only when it is watered by the blood of the patriots."[46]

The Burgess Committee worded the final code ambiguously with regard to what actions POWs would be held accountable for, but at the same time, it clearly implied that a strict standard of conduct would henceforth be expected of all Americans. During the drafting, S. L. A. Marshall tried to make the code a simple list of general orders, but Assistant Defense Secretary Carter Burgess repeatedly interrupted the work to demand the inclusion of "certain phrases to please him." Marshall said Burgess claimed that by flowering up the wording, the military "would get good publicity and would put the thing over with the press."[47] It is worth noting that while the wording of the Code of Conduct remains virtually the same today as it was when first drafted, during the Vietnam War its interpretation by DOD to troops departing for the battlefront was considerably refined to reflect the well-known realities of torture.

Like the failed UMT plan, the early Cold War military used the new Code of Conduct and its strict interpretation and implementation by the various services as a vehicle for greater character education. If public outrage toward the Korean War POW scandal could be managed and turned inward, DOD believed it could rally the support it needed to indoctrinate the nation's youth in patriotism and moral leadership. Lieutenant Colonel Mayer said the code should not be considered a formula for learning how to be a POW, but rather "the first principle of American society."[48] After distributing copies to all members of the armed forces, DOD ordered the Defense Advisory Committee on Prisoners of War to submit bimonthly reports on the status of code instruction in each of the services, court-martial cases against collaborators, and efforts to extend the code to the American public.

According to the three progress reports submitted by the advisory committee, the military initially attempted to teach proper POW behavior to service personnel through survival training and by publicizing the trials of the collaborators. However, the services' early attempts to instruct men on how to resist brainwashing and learn resistance through "instructive" torture proved to be dismal failures. Especially troubling were reports coming from the Advanced Survival Training Course conducted at Stead Air Force Base in Reno, Nevada. Airmen subjected to mock torture at Stead were unable to withstand training sessions in "vertical Coffins" and other devices imported from North Korean POW camps. Grown men had even been reduced to tears when no simulated torture occurred and they were merely interrogated aggressively by army personnel portraying communists. Although survival training continued at Stead, with twenty-nine thousand men completing the course by 1955, it was clear that little could be done to teach servicemen to withstand physical and mental torture. Mock torture sessions at Stead did not solve the collaboration dilemma, but they still proved useful to the military because men who had "volunteered" for the experience viewed the course as a "rite of passage" and a validation of their manhood.[49]

Instead of revising the Code of Conduct to reflect the realities of torture, the army hardened its stance and issued a report in May, 1956, that claimed POWs held in North Korea had been neither brainwashed nor tortured (despite the air force's use of Korean torture devices in survival training), but instead had betrayed their country after merely being exposed to group indoctrination. Perhaps the army was more comfortable dealing with an American character crisis than it was with something it believed it could do little about.

The Supreme Court foiled the military's attempt to use the courts-martial of collaborators as a deterrent when it ruled in *United States ex rel Toth v Quarles* (1955) that once separated from the armed forces, one could not be tried for offenses that had occurred while in the service. Because the army had dishonorably discharged all twenty-one defectors at an earlier date, the Supreme Court overturned decisions against three of the "turncoats" who had returned to the United States in July of that year. Three more of the twenty-one subsequently left China, and the army found itself in the difficult position of having court-martialed and imprisoned eleven POWs who had collaborated but not defected, while those who had refused repatriation remained free. To remedy this inconsistency, the army reversed many of its previous courts-martial decisions and reduced some of the men's prison sentences. This new leniency resulted in the failure of the military's plan to use court proceedings as a deterrent, as the services could no longer use the courts as a public forum to keep the scandal alive.[50]

Failing in these two avenues of code training, the military fully embraced its motivational qualities, giving leading evangelicals in the armed forces an opportunity to exert themselves. By March, 1956, the services had incorporated a series of films (including a cartoon) based on the Korean War POW scandal into AFIE programs. The Defense Department distributed six posters exemplifying the spirit of the code to bases throughout the country, and chaplains preached the code from the pulpit and through character guidance programs. Because all service personnel had by that year reportedly received instruction in the code, the Defense Advisory Committee on POWs directed future efforts toward retired service personnel and the general public. The committee recommended "that the services find an effective means for coordinating with civilian educational institutions, churches and other patriotic organizations to provide better understanding of American ideals"[51]

One reason that enemy indoctrination had been so successful, according to the Burgess Committee, was because the communists possessed a single party line. American POWs had been unable to forcibly counter their discussion leaders' criticisms of democracy because the prisoners were the product of a pluralistic society that valued differences of opinion. Since the Code of Conduct implied that the nation had a single standard to live by, but had not articulated exactly what that standard was, the military now attempted to identify a unified American ideology to propagate through code training.[52]

An ideological program already being discussed by evangelicals at the Pentagon seemed perfectly suited to the needs of the Code of Conduct program.[53] In 1954, Admiral Radford, in his second year as chairman of the JCS, championed an international propaganda program authored by John C. Broger, a World War II veteran and president of the evangelical Far East Broadcasting Company. "Militant Liberty," as Broger's concept was most often known, taught the seventy freedoms and seventy responsibilities of the "free world" to third world nations threatened by communism. Broger emphasized "personal evangelism in the political rather than the religious field" by comparing democracy's "sensitive individual conscience" to communism's "annihilated individual conscience."[54] Defense Secretary Charles Wilson enlisted Kenneth Wells of the Freedoms Foundation at Valley Forge to share his marketing expertise with Broger in promoting the concept throughout the military and various other federal agencies.

In addition, Radford hired the Jam Handy Agency, a public relations firm whose clients included General Motors and Coca-Cola, to further adapt Militant Liberty for the domestic market.[55] Assistant Defense Secretary Carter Burgess and Assistant Secretary of the Army Hugh Milton joined the team in promoting the ensuing "Battle for Liberty" program— written at an eighth grade level and touted as a supplement to the Code of Conduct—to military personnel and civic organizations across the nation.[56] Secretary Wilson not only endorsed both the Militant Liberty– Battle for Liberty concept and the Code of Conduct as "unified and purposeful guiding precepts for all members of the Armed Forces," he also recommended disseminating Broger's principles to the American public.[57]

The military attempted to reach the American people with the evangelical democracy contained in the Code of Conduct and Militant Liberty through a number of creative means. Historian Francis Stonor Saunders claimed that the JCS met in December, 1955, to discuss means to introduce Militant Liberty themes into the motion picture industry. The top-secret report following the session claimed that films could

Adm. Arthur W. Radford, chairman of the Joint Chiefs of Staff.
Courtesy National Museum of Naval Aviation, Pensacola, Florida.

"awaken free peoples to an understanding of the magnitude of the danger confronting the Free World; and to generate a motivation to combat this threat." The following year, JCS officials traveled to the Metro-Goldwyn-Mayer offices in California to meet with a number of notable members of the anticommunist Hollywood elite, including John Wayne and John Ford. Wayne agreed to insert Militant Liberty themes "carefully" into his film projects. Ford, a former chief of the Field Photographic Branch of the Office of Strategic Services (OSS), asked for numerous copies of the Militant Liberty booklet to send to "his script writers so that they can learn the nomenclature of the concept."[58]

A month later, DOD called together the heads of all relevant governmental agencies for a briefing on the Code of Conduct and Militant Liberty programs for the purpose of offering the military's assistance in organizing an effective preservice motivational training program for the nation.[59] Groups such as AmVets, the Veterans of Foreign Wars, and the American Legion had intensified their citizenship training programs in the wake of the Korean War POW scandal, but DOD was also interested in introducing code training into Sunday schools, public education, and the general work force.[60] The Department of Health, Education, and Welfare accepted the challenge and designated a forthcoming White House Conference on Education as a national forum "to elucidate and amplify the Code of Conduct." The Commerce Department promised to report to DOD on business efforts to educate workers in Americanism and anticommunism. The Religious Education Association of America recommended that its members include "lessons on responsibility to God and Country into Church curriculum."[61] Even a "Code of an American Mother" was developed. It proclaimed: "I am an American mother, responsible for my actions, and dedicated to impart to my child the principles which made my country free. Together we will trust in our God."[62]

Attempts were also made to integrate the spirit of the code and Militant Liberty into the nation's foreign policy. Copies of the code were sent to more than twenty-two UN member countries in the hope that they would each adopt a similar policy for fighting the spread of communism. In addition, the military introduced a classified form of the Militant Liberty concept, "Project Action," in such far-flung places as French Indochina and Latin America. Broger claimed that third world nations were particularly receptive to ideological propaganda. "Most religions of these areas have lost their appeal [and] . . . traditional cultures have become unable to furnish an acceptable comprehension of existence in the world today," Broger told the JCS. If America did not provide "a new faith, militantly propagated by articulate natives" communism would. Evangelical democracy had to be covert in Vietnam because the United States feared overt operations would anger the French. In Ecuador, trainees listened to lectures and watched films before discussing democratic principles. A comic book was used to propagate the concept in Guatemala because that nation's soldiers were largely illiterate.[63]

The armed forces presented Militant Liberty, the Battle for Liberty, and Project Action as an American ideology to combat communism at home and abroad. Although the promotion of Radford's and Broger's beliefs demonstrated the growing influence of evangelicals in the JCS and DOD, the episode also defined the limits of ideological programs within the American government. Considerable reaction against Militant Liberty emerged immediately within the State Department, the CIA, and the U.S. Information Agency (USIA), which all opposed the concept's "motivational" qualities. To Admiral Radford's dismay, the individual services also offered considerable opposition. The military academies refused to incorporate Militant Liberty into their curricula and the Marine Corps argued that the concept was inappropriate for its use because it was based on a fear approach. One Pentagon colonel complained that the program was "just another front office boondoggle. The Admiral says we need an ideology, so they hire a guy and appoint a committee that unanimously agrees we're all for clean living and American Motherhood and the rest of it." The colonel claimed that such principles, better said by the Boy Scouts, were wrapped "up into a capsule, and now they think they've got something like ideological little liver pills."[64]

Additionally, Militant Liberty became closely tied with political and religious extremists. Along with the more acceptable Kenneth Wells of the Freedoms Foundations at Valley Forge, Fred C. Schwarz of the Christian Anti-Communism Crusade, a leading member of the 1960s radical right, admired the evangelical aspect of the concept.[65] In the end, the concept's motivational or evangelical underpinnings doomed not only Militant Liberty but also, because of its close association, the entire Code of Conduct program. By the early 1960s, advocates of greater character education bemoaned the fact that code training had degenerated into a short film for new recruits and a wallet-sized card that most of the services required their personnel to memorize and carry on their person at all times.

Despite the failure to turn the Korean War POW scandal and the Code of Conduct into a vehicle for public character education, evangelicals continued to solidify their positions in DOD. In her excellent study of evangelicals in the military, historian Anne Loveland noted that Eisenhower's appointee for the office of chief of chaplains, Brig. Gen. Frank A. Tobey, a Baptist, worked diligently to minimize Catholic influence in the military. Parachurch organizations such as the Overseas Christian Servicemen's Centers, the Christian Military Fellowship, the Navigators, and Campus Crusade for Christ also intensified their efforts with service personnel and effectively targeted high-ranking military officials. Despite DOD's rejection of his program, John C. Broger became deputy director of Armed Forces Information and Education in 1956 and director in 1961. While Broger did not officially promote evangelism in the AFIE program, behind the scenes he kept the spirit of Militant Liberty alive in the halls of the Pentagon and advocated its principles overseas while serving with People to People, a type of international Code of Conduct program that waged peace by making American "principles understood throughout the world." People to People originated in the offices of the USIA and was independent of military control, but Broger headed the Armed Forces Committee, which became the most active of all committees in the program, from 1956–61.[66] Broger also joined forces with Abraham Vereide's International Christian Leadership (ICL), an organization that showed considerable finesse in increasing evangelical influence in Washington, D.C., through weekly prayer groups in all branches of the government, including the armed forces.[67]

Conclusion

Cold Warriors attempted to reshape the American character along civil-military religious lines with the Code of Conduct and Militant Liberty programs. Although this attempt to increase public civic virtue proved ineffective, it did provide the services with valuable experience in conducting a preservice motivational program. When the Code of Conduct failed to create the national will believed essential for American security, evangelicals in the armed forces sought direct authorization from the NSC to reach out to the American people with a series of Cold War seminars. By 1958, the JCS, convinced that the nation was losing its ideological battle with communism, promoted highly aggressive, military-sponsored, public anticommunism programs that often embraced the sensational rhetoric of political extremists. Until DOD ended the campaign in 1962–63, active and reserve officers appeared on panels with leading members of the radical right who pointed to the example of the American POWs held in North Korea as proof that only immediate and drastic action to revitalize the national character and will could save the nation. Sociologist Albert Biderman continued to speak in defense of the character of the American soldier in Korea, but his voice was drowned out by the wave of anticommunist hysteria created by these joint civilian-military seminars.

CHAPTER 5

The U.S. Military
and the Radical Right

The least I can do is absolve [active-duty military officers present]

from any responsibility for anything I hope to say this morning.

They can get into an awful lot of trouble if they are involved in any

such statements.

—Rear Adm. Chester Ward, 1961

Students and faculty at the University of Arkansas–Fayetteville attended the April 14, 1961, "Strategy for Survival" conference free of charge. The Fayetteville Chamber of Commerce advertised this Cold War seminar, which alerted the public to the dangers of communism, as being "authorized by the Secretary of Defense and the Joint Chiefs of Staff" and not connected "with any of the less responsible 'anti-communist' elements." The conference featured Dr. Clifton Lloyd Ganus Jr., the vice president of Harding College in Searcy, Arkansas. Ganus, who was in demand at anticommunist meetings across the country, represented Harding's National Education Program (NEP), a hard-hitting, ultraconservative information service endorsed by Kenneth Wells and the Freedoms Foundation at Valley Forge for promoting the civic values epitomized by George Washington during the American Revolution. After delivering his early-morning address on "The Moral Foundation of

Freedom," Ganus flew over the Boston Mountains at the navy's expense to repeat his speech at the afternoon session of the Fort Smith "Strategy for Survival" gathering.

Anticipation ran high throughout the crowd of more than one thousand that waited in the local high school's auditorium to hear Ganus. Fort Smith's mayor, Robert R. Brooksher, had proclaimed the occasion "Freedom Day" so that area residents could inform themselves of the part they must play in America's survival. The event's morning program, full of rousing, anticommunist rhetoric, had prepared the audience for Ganus's speech. Like the people of Fayetteville, Fort Smithians were outraged to learn that America had "lost China because of a lack of comprehension on the part of our prevailing policy molders" and that it had "lost Cuba more recently in the same way and are beginning to lose Africa." Ganus then asked, "How many righteous people will it take to save America?"

Other seminar speakers representing military and governmental agencies—such as Robert Morris, former chief counsel of the U.S. Senate Internal Security Subcommittee and naval reserve intelligence officer in World War II, and Brig. Gen. Clyde J. Watts, World War II veteran and former commanding general of the U.S. Army Reserve's XIX Corps Artillery (Oklahoma, Louisiana, and Arkansas)—lent credibility and prestige to the occasion, but Ganus clearly was the big draw of the day. He warned his audience to be alert to the insidious nature of communism. If America continued "on the same road that we are now traveling, increasing liberalism in religion and . . . in government . . . it won't be long," the former Texan and Tulane graduate declared, "before we won't have any of our liberties left." The United States, he cautioned, would crumble from within, just like the Roman Empire.

"What can we do as individual citizens to help solve this Communist problem?" a young girl asked during the question-and-answer period. Ganus advised checking local officials' voting records more closely. Despite the area's conservative reputation, he pointed out, a representative of the Fort Smith district had "voted eighty-nine percent of the time to aid and abet the Communist party." The people were shocked at what they believed was tangible evidence that communism had invaded their own small community.[1]

Too long unmindful of their patriotic duties, Fort Smith's citizens were now ready to act, to "draw the line and not negotiate away anymore of our friends or our national interests." A "Strategy for Survival Council," organized out of the office of the local Merchants National Bank, distributed literature claiming that the United Nations was the brainchild of the Soviet Union, that peaceful coexistence was impossible, and that the opinions of the Supreme Court, led by Chief Justice Earl Warren, served the enemy. Rumors that a junior high school civics teacher was but one of "twenty card-carrying communists" in town fed the growing panic. Fort Smith, like many other communities throughout the United States hosting Cold War seminars, became a hotbed of anticommunist sentiment.[2]

Arkansas's more moderate citizens, fearful of the oppressive, McCarthy-like atmosphere, questioned the propriety of active and retired members of the armed forces participating in programs at which the NEP and other, less-savory organizations promoted extremism. Did not military participation validate the radical right's claims? After a brief investigation, Sen. James W. Fulbright (D-Arkansas), chairman of the Senate Foreign Relations Committee, discovered that the situation in Fort Smith was not isolated. From Pensacola to San Diego and from Pittsburgh to San Antonio, a national network of anticommunism seminars thrived that linked the military's character-shaping goals with those of ultraconservatives. "We the people are prepared to pray and fight. But is our government?" Retired army brigadier general Wallace P. Campbell asked his Searcy, Arkansas, audience at a 1962 Cold War seminar. "The future of America and of Christianity is up to dedicated patriots like you. Will you accept the challenge? If so, with God's help, we will win!"[3]

Frustrated at the end of the Korean War by their inability to revitalize the American character and will through less activist means, a handful of politically oriented officers joined forces with civilian ultraconservatives.

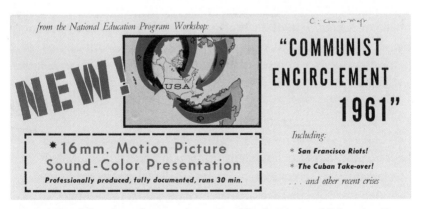

Promotional flyer for a short movie produced by the National Education Program in Searcy, Arkansas, entitled Communist Encirclement: 1961.

Between 1958 and 1963, a series of military-sponsored Cold War seminars combined public moral and anticommunism education in such a way that the gatherings often became public forums for members of the radical right. For the most part, officers participated in Cold War seminars with a clear conscience and under the assumption that they did so with presidential approval and even direction. Although Eisenhower denied ever authorizing the notorious anticommunism conferences, no plot existed within DOD to form a partnership with extremists. Instead, the military was attempting to fulfill an ideological goal expressed by both the Truman and the Eisenhower administration: American policy makers sought an effective means to strengthen the national character and will of the American public as an ideological bulwark against communist advancement.

The unfortunate alliance with the radical right occurred without strategic planning. Cold War seminars completely under military control generally operated with little controversy. However, when the services invited civilian anticommunism experts to participate and employed no effective quality control measures over the numerous and widespread proceedings, the seminars often became havens for political extremists. Additionally, high-ranking active and reserve officers appearing on programs with members of the radical right had the effect of legitimizing the extremists' views in the eyes of those attending and led to anticommunism hysteria in towns visited by such conferences. In the end, this embarrassing episode, though of short duration, played a pivotal role in undermining the character-shaping goals of evangelicals within DOD. Public exposure of the conferences made the military sensitive to charges of evangelical political indoctrination, leading to "tamer" religiously oriented character education programs during the Vietnam War. Although no major realignment of the fundamental role of the military in American society ever occurred, when news of the Cold War seminars first broke in the early 1960s, a number of journalists took it as a sign that just such a realignment was taking place.

Senator Fulbright's "Secret Memo"

In July, 1961, Senator Fulbright informed Defense Secretary Robert McNamara in a "secret memo" (as the media later referred to it) that a classified 1958 National Security Council directive sanctioning the use of "military personnel and facilities to arouse the public 'to the menace of the cold war'" had spawned numerous joint military-civilian anticommunism programs.[4] Fulbright claimed that, in the aftermath of the directive, "Strategy for Survivals," "Freedom Forums," "Project Alerts," and numerous other anticommunist seminars were spreading extremist views across the nation. Especially troublesome, wrote Fulbright, was a series of navy seminars under the direction of Vice Adm. Robert L. Goldthwaite, chief of naval air training at Pensacola, Florida. Speakers at such gatherings had condemned U.S. foreign policy makers past and present and admonished civilians to "DEMAND a more patriotic attitude" from "public officials and policies displaying 'softness' toward Communism."[5] After conducting his own investigation to substantiate Fulbright's charges, McNamara quietly issued a DOD directive ordering the armed forces to cease all involvement with extremists at Cold War seminars.[6]

The general public became aware of the controversy surrounding the seminars when Cabell Phillips of the *New York Times* disclosed the contents of the Fulbright memo and DOD's new restrictions on military personnel participating in civilian anticommunism education. Senator Strom Thurmond (D–South Carolina), an army reserve general, demanded a congressional investigation into Fulbright's and McNamara's attempt to "muzzle the military." Radical-right organizations drummed up support for Thurmond's efforts with an aggressive letter-writing campaign. Patriotic emotions quickly flared, as exemplified by a Tennessee housewife who advised Fulbright to "go somewhere and blow out . . . your rotten, perverted communist brain."[7]

Fulbright reassured his constituents that, contrary to Thurmond's implications, he was not conspiring with the communists by questioning the military's role in Cold War seminars. His sole objective in writing the memorandum had been to reveal the dangers inherent in the 1958 NSC directive. The Arkansan argued that the government should reconsider its policy given that the military's traditional role in American society was to obey orders, not mold public opinion. Although many throughout the nation wrote the senator expressing their support, Fulbright turned the politically dangerous issue over to the Senate's internal investigation subcommittee, chaired by John Stennis (D-Mississippi), and concentrated instead on his forthcoming reelection.[8]

After thirty-six days of hearings at which sixty-four witnesses appeared, the Senate investigators substantiated many of Fulbright's charges but refused to condemn the basic principle underlying Cold War seminars. Political extremism had indeed been evident in the conferences, but the majority report claimed that "qualified military men, because of their experience and specialized knowledge," were especially suited for the anticommunism indoctrination of the American public. The Stennis Subcommittee did, however, advise closer DOD supervision of future conferences. If the military eliminated partisan politics and maintained "quality control," the subcommittee opined, Cold War seminars could serve the valuable function of informing the American people about the dangers of communism.[9]

Despite the Senate's support, the phenomenon of military-sponsored anticommunism seminars was already waning. Faced with the constant scrutiny of investigative reporters, the Pentagon removed even the suspicion of extremism by limiting further civilian seminars to tightly controlled meetings directed by the Industrial College of the Armed Forces (ICAF). A few days after the Stennis Subcommittee issued its final report in October, 1962, Pres. John F. Kennedy revealed that the Soviets were arming missiles in Cuba. Frightened by the serious international crisis, the public soon forgot the controversy surrounding Cold War seminars.[10]

Critics like Cabell Phillips charged that a cabal of officers at the highest levels of the Pentagon had organized Cold War seminars for their own covert purposes. This charge gained credence after Eisenhower revealed in the aftermath of Senate hearings that his administration had never formally authorized the military to educate the public about communism. "Unless material has been taken out of context, or general language interpreted very loosely," Eisenhower theorized to the Stennis Subcommittee, "I think there is no basis for these assertions involving the National Security Council." According to the president, the armed forces had conducted public anticommunism seminars without explicit instructions to do so.[11]

Individuals within DOD, and the JCS in particular, frustrated by the quality of national defense policies against the Soviets and inspired by evangelical influences within the current administration, had interpreted an ambiguous NSC directive that spoke of the need for programs to improve the national character and will as authorization for such activity by the military. They did so because there was ample evidence that they were operating within the parameters of current national security policy. A number of events had occurred that warranted, in the opinion of key officers, the appropriation of the services and grassroots political structure of ultraconservatives. Unaware of the potential dangers of relying on these civilian anticommunism "experts," Cold War seminars gave the military, a traditionally silent partner in shaping policy, a public means to promote its own domestic strategic objectives.

Although it is impossible to trace the idea for conducting the Cold War seminars to a single source, it is clear that as the ideological conflict between the free world and the communist bloc intensified, a consensus emerged among policy makers that the time had come for drastic and immediate action that would result in the creation of a national will strong enough to withstand communism. Since the beginning of the Korean War POW scandal, policy makers circulated a number of plans to inform the American public about the dangers of domestic and international communism. Especially notable was a memorandum on Cold War planning from the JCS chairman, Adm. Arthur Radford, to Defense Secretary Charles Wilson. Radford, a firm believer in evangelical democracy who had championed the failed Militant Liberty and Battle for Liberty programs, not only welded considerable power through the NSC, he also led an increasingly influential JCS during Eisenhower's presidency. Truman had preserved the JCS's wartime structure to advise him on policy. Eisenhower, on the other hand, increased the agency's activism by requiring the service chiefs, as he did members of the NSC, to be instruments of his policy initiatives.[12] Radford ignored outgoing chairman Gen. Omar Bradley's warnings against political involvement and enthusiastically supported Eisenhower's New Look defense initiatives by assisting the president in making and implementing decisions regarding "ideological armor" of the American public.[13]

Radford's memorandum to Wilson, written in August, 1957, expressed concern that the United States had not faced the fact that it was not winning the Cold War. Along with traditional military concerns, the admiral claimed, the armed forces needed planning in "collateral military responsibilities."[14] Initially, Radford's "collateral military responsibilities," or "cold war activities" as the services' political, psychological, social, and economic activities during the Cold War were often called, were directed at foreign nationals (such as "Good Will" cruises that demonstrated American naval superiority and free medical care and literacy training that highlighted democratic benevolence). However, these responsibilities quickly began to focus on American service personnel, who, through rigorous training and indoctrination in the tenets of evangelical democracy would, according to Radford, exemplify to other peoples of the world both the nation's military might and its highest ideals. Deputy Defense Secretary Donald A. Quarles promoted Radford's memorandum, concurrent with the JCS's own study on the military's role in the Cold War, as it was being processed through the DOD bureaucracy. Meanwhile, as DOD considered Radford's memorandum, the JCS, the military agency most active in promoting domestic political indoctrination and moral uplift, issued its own memorandum in June, 1958, instructing each branch of service to increase its Cold War activities.[15]

The month before the JCS issued its memorandum, Adm. Arleigh Burke, the chief of naval operations, formed an advisory panel consisting of senior naval and Marine Corps officers in order to stimulate ideas on how best to advance the sea services' new collateral responsibilities. Burke, in a move that facilitated the involvement of political extremists in naval Cold War planning, refused to limit the panel to self-generated ideas and invited civilian guest panelists to offer suggestions. Shortly thereafter, the army followed the navy's example by creating its own advisory board to solicit collateral ideas from army officers. A year later, the Pentagon completed the triad of advisory panels when it established the Department of Defense Coordinating Board "to further U.S. objectives in the cause of freedom and to create better understanding and cooperation with our friends and allies throughout the world."[16]

Among other proposed foreign and domestic Cold War activities, the navy's Cold War Advisory Panel recommended that its officers pattern their public statements on the speeches of Dr. Frank Barnett, director of research for the ultraconservative Richardson Foundation. According to Barnett's "Fourth Dimensional Warfare" concept, Americans were fighting an ideological battle with communism. "The front is everywhere," the Rhodes scholar and foreign policy enthusiast claimed. "If here at home we lose the will to sacrifice or cynically disregard our spiritual traditions our physical wealth will not safeguard American civilization." Barnett further stated: "national defense begins at the level of domestic political morality, the quality of citizenship training for our youth, and the reputation of American business growth both here and abroad. These 'intangibles' are the clear responsibility of private citizens."[17]

In addition to fighting the Cold War on the psychological warfare front (with ideas generated by advisory panels and boards), the military attempted to defeat communism spiritually with religious nationalism. In May, 1958, Navy Secretary Thomas Gates moved to improve the moral character of his service with General Order No. 21. Designating moral education as a command responsibility instead of merely the job of unit chaplains, Gates endeavored to restore historic American civil-religious values. Far from being "just another leadership program," General Order No. 21 sought to create "a movement amongst top-level leadership to bring back values of virtue, honor, [and] patriotism, . . . that had fallen by [the] wayside in American life." More intensive than similar programs in the army and the air force, General Order No. 21 integrated moral education throughout all echelons of the navy and Marine Corps and gave individual officers greater latitude in formulating programs of instruction for the men and women under their command.[18]

To implement General Order No. 21, the navy established the Naval Leadership Working Group (NLWG) and made available to all commanding officers seven training teams from Task Force 21 that taught the "nuts and bolts" of leadership. "It was obvious," according to the NLWG, "that thorough training of personnel from the bottom up in the finer qualities of naval leadership [indoctrination in American heritage, the military's role in world affairs, and the reasons for the recent Korean POW scandal] would produce salutatory effects, not only within the navy itself, but ultimately in the whole nation." After just a year's operation, General Order No. 21, according to the NLWG, had replaced "dry, humdrum lectures by uninspired speakers" with innovative group discussions. All of the services participated in formulating and broadcasting anticommunist themes through Cold War seminars, but the navy, because of its involvement in the Cold War Advisory Panel, General Order No. 21, and the inspirational leadership provided by Admiral Radford, by far played the most conspicuous role.[19]

In early 1958, while the various military advisory panels and General Order No. 21 were still in their planning stages, Deputy Defense Secretary Quarles submitted a plan for public anticommunism education to the NSC's Armed Forces Policy Council (AFPC). The Stennis Subcommittee later revealed that Quarles's objective was to "raise the level of Cold War ideological education and sophistication at the grassroots level, with the initial target to be [the] American serviceman and his dependents . . . and through them, Americans generally." Quarles inadvertently left the door open for the radical right's involvement in his plan when he suggested that the government could save time and money by relying on "some of the world's outstanding persons experienced in these fields and in these techniques," instead of training its own experts.[20]

The AFPC forwarded the seminar plan to the NSC, where it was debated and then circulated through a series of committees. In the final classified document, NSC-5810/1, the Basic National Security Policy for 1958, all that remained of the original recommendation was a brief reference to the need for civilian anticommunist education. Although considerably more forceful than previous BSNPs regarding the national character and will, it contained no explicit instructions calling for the military to take action. General Nathan Twining, who succeeded Admiral Radford as JCS chairman in 1958, sat with the NSC by Eisenhower's invitation. Twining, too, would have understood that no explicit consent was ever given. Nevertheless, the JCS welcomed NSC-5810/1 as an endorsement of military anticommunism indoctrination of the American public and instructed installation commanders to expand troop information programs to include local civilian groups. Section 46 of the BSNP, "Support by U.S. Citizens," claimed that a resolute American character was "essential to the success of a national strategy to meet the threat to our national security. ... Our nation, our institutions, the principles we hold dear, and our very lives are now in great danger," a danger, according to the 1958 BSNP, that would persist for many years. "While this threat is taking on new dimensions, the determination of U.S. citizens to face the risks and sacrifices, and their willingness to support the demands on their spiritual and material resources, necessary to carry out this national strategy will be crucial." In order to achieve the high level of national will necessary for defense, the NSC recommended continuing efforts to "develop a comprehension among the American people of these needs and of the fact that our national strategy provides the best hope that war can be averted and our national security objectives achieved." This was a forceful statement of the need to provide anticommunism education for the American public, but it did not specifically assign responsibility for such activity to DOD.[21]

The Pentagon clearly could not interpret the BSNP policy paper's vague wording as explicit authorization for the intensive military indoctrination of Americans. Interestingly, Quarles sat on the Operations Coordinating Board, the committee charged with translating classified NSC decisions and overseeing their implementation by federal department heads. Perhaps Quarles chose to interpret the BSNP's reference regarding civilian anticommunism education as authorization for the military to proceed with his original plan, for upon receiving an explanation of the classified directive from the OCB, DOD commissioned the Cold War seminars by issuing a series of guidance papers for all commanders in the various services. These directives coincided with the military's stress on evangelical democracy as the answer to the American character crisis, as evidenced by the various military collateral activities boards and panels,

General Order No. 21, and by the number of civil-military religionists in positions of power in the military hierarchy.[22]

The Stennis Subcommittee's final report concluded that initial seminars posed little threat to American democratic traditions. The earliest defense seminars, sponsored by the ICAF, focused less on anticommunism than on coordinating public and private strategies in the event of a national emergency. In fact, officers at the ICAF first began conducting "National Defense Seminars" in 1948. These two-week traveling training sessions for active and reserve officers and selected private citizens, with titles such as "A Businessman's Briefing on National Security," had by 1963 instructed seventy thousand in the strategies necessary for military and civilian cooperation during national emergencies. The National Defense Seminars differed from later Cold War seminars in that they stressed orthodox defense policies (military strategy, economic resources, science research, technical skills, sound management, and good organization) rather than emphasizing the military's Cold War collateral activities.[23]

The first Cold War seminar—that is, the first public seminar organized by the military in an effort to create the national will and character believed necessary to promote evangelical democracy as a rival to Soviet communism around the world through an ever-expanding network of anticommunism conferences—originated in a suggestion Frank Barnett of the Richardson Foundation made to Adm. Arleigh Burke. In September, 1958, Barnett approached Burke, then chief of naval operations, with a solution to the public apathy to the threat of communism. According to Barnett, reserve officers, free of constraints against political statements, "could be utilized to spread the word to their civilian connections," while taking directions behind the scenes from the regular military.[24] The JCS "enthusiastically" accepted Barnett's suggestion, along with the financial backing of the Richardson Foundation and the management skills of the University of Pennsylvania's Foreign Policy Research Institute (FPRI) for its first "Defense Strategy Seminar." The university established the FPRI in 1955 to study long-range foreign policy issues. The Defense Strategy Seminars, later renamed "National Strategy Seminars," were initially based on the book *Protracted Conflict,* written by FPRI director Dr. Robert Strauz-Hupe. The FPRI's deputy director was

Adm. Arleigh A. Burke, chief of naval operations.
Courtesy United States Naval Academy.

a retired lieutenant colonel, William R. Kintner, an expert in POW inter-
rogation and brainwashing. Admiral Radford sat on the organization's
advisory committee. In partnership with the Institute of American Strategy, cochaired by Barnett, the FPRI distributed its manifesto, *American
Strategy for the Nuclear Age,* to the American public.[25] Burke claimed that
the basic purpose of the two-week summer conference, first held at the
National War College (NWC) in 1959, would be "to train cadres of citi-
zen-soldiers who are active in civic and public affairs and who can, through
their positions in civilian life, help create a resolute national climate of
opinion. According to Burke, "This will . . . strengthen national defense
programs and bolster the national will to resist communist 'peace' and
propaganda stratagems."[26]

Defense Strategy Seminar faculty members came from a variety of
governmental, military, and civilian agencies but its speakers were more

heavily represented on the Right rather than the Left of the political spectrum. Instructors taught, among other subjects, communist theory and strategy, propaganda analysis, psychology, economic and political warfare, the positive aspects of American ideology, and factors bearing on national will and national character. Most important, the first Defense Strategy Seminar, as did all subsequent Cold War seminars, urged its "graduates" to return to their homes and host additional meetings. A network of anticommunism conferences would strengthen the national will, according to the organizers, by rallying Americans at the grassroots to improve the contents of public school curricula, upgrade citizenship and youth physical fitness training, and increase community understanding of the communist threat and the blessings of American heritage.[27] The Richardson Foundation and the FPRI promised to update seminar alumni with the latest anticommunism literature, but the DOD hierarchy never created a follow-up policy to oversee this ever-expanding Cold War seminar network. In November, 1959, Cold War seminars received further encouragement when DOD issued a directive that described the services' collateral activities as command responsibilities that should be "approached with vigor, imagination, and enthusiasm."[28]

Cold War seminars proliferated in the wake of the first conference held at the NWC and as a series of "Weekend Strategy Seminars" spread across the nation. Fourteen reserve officers who had attended the first conference at the NWC organized a "*Reader's Digest*" version of their anticommunism instruction for other officers in the New York City area. Weekend Strategy Seminars for reserve officers, usually conducted on military installations but open to the public, quickly multiplied across the nation and had little if any direction or control from DOD. According to the Stennis Subcommittee's highly conservative estimates, only two seminars were held in 1959, followed by more than a hundred the next year and almost twice that number by 1961. In reality, however, hundreds of additional meetings occurred as the network of seminars extended beyond DOD's ability to track them. Generally given little more guidance than a list of suggested resources and orders to report back on their progress, army and navy officers scrambled to develop their own, often highly personalized, anticommunist programs.[29]

According to Defense Secretary McNamara's 1961 investigation, three categories of Cold War seminars existed. The National Defense Seminars held at the ICAF stressed orthodox defense policies and caused DOD little concern. The Defense (or National) Strategy Seminars conducted yearly at the NWC, as well as the weekend conferences they spawned, were more troubling. While these seminars had varying degrees of radical-right involvement, they remained under the direction of military officers—many of whom promoted extremist political stances. With proper guidance, these seminars could operate in a responsible fashion. Finally, the McNamara report identified a large group of seminars organized and conducted by the radical right but with notable military participation. Although the armed forces had only initiated these conferences, because the services provided speakers, films, literature, and meeting facilities, the public considered such events to be DOD sanctioned. Among the well-known members of the radical right who organized Cold War seminars falling into this "cock-a-doodle" category—as it was called by the McNamara investigators—were Fred C. Schwarz, Billy James Hargis, and George S. Benson. According to the McNamara report, such radical-right meetings were "rabid, bigoted, one-sided presentations . . . [that preached the] adoption of methods similar to those of communists."[30]

The Radical Right and the U.S. Military Connection

Members of the early 1960s radical right (also known as ultraconservatives or ultras, the far right, the lunatic fringe, or simply superpatriots) have been identified as "individual[s] who sought refuge from . . . reality in the conspiracy theory of history and the either-or cosmology of the paranoid." More specifically, the radical right included political extremists of both parties who longed for the "good old days," a time when, they believed, Americans were ruled by less government and possessed considerably more freedom. They differed from other conservatives by degree. Whereas conservatives discerned complexities in economic, social, and political issues, members of the radical right were monists, meaning that they reduced the nation's perceived degeneracy to a single source—communism, in the case of the 1960s extremists. The radical right frequently accepted any source, no matter how spurious, that supported its belief that a communist plot was underfoot to destroy American freedoms. Extremists saw a communist conspiracy behind every government action, whether it was something as momentous as the creation of the United Nations or as obscure as the fluoridation of the country's water supply. It would be naïve to think that all conservatives who participated in Cold War seminars fit this definition, but enough of them did that the more moderate conservatives became tainted by association.[31]

Evidence of common ground between the radical right and the military can be found in the air force training manual scandal of 1960. The scandal erupted over statements in Air Reserve Center training manual NR 45-0050 claiming that the National Council of Churches was a communist front organization. The air force withdrew the publication after journalists traced the source of the charges back to Billy James Hargis and the "Circuit Riders," a radical anticommmunist movement at one time associated with the Methodist Church. Although most service personnel rejected the notion that America's mainline denominations were infiltrated with communists—a charge that was, in fact, atypical—other statements within the training manual were illustrative of the military's religious-political mind-set during the early Cold War. In lesson fifteen, the reader was told to be aware that "loyal American citizens have sometimes inadvertently collaborated to make valuable information available to our potential enemies." Subversion, according to the manual, was "any activity by which any person or group willfully attempts to interfere with or impair the loyalties, morale, or discipline of any member of the Armed Forces, or American citizens in general." According to this definition, anyone critical of the military was suspect. "First of all, don't aid or encourage subversion by being a chronic complainer yourself," the manual urged. "The enemy wants you to become dissatisfied. . . . He hopes that such complaining will destroy the Air Force *esprit de corps,* bring about disunity in our ranks, and thus severely impair the effectiveness of the Air Force as a fighting unit."[32]

Despite the fact that a significant number of military officers joined forces, in varying degrees, with members of the radical right at Cold War seminars and shared some philosophical affinity with them, military officers for the most part were not political extremists. True believers of the American civil-military religion shared common concerns regarding the national will with the radical right, but they did not embrace the conspiracy theory that the U.S. government was riddled with communist sympathizers. Nor, for that matter, did they oppose civil rights to the same degree as did members of the radical right. There were, of course, a few notable exceptions. The presence of high-ranking radical-right officers in the armed forces during the early 1960s, no matter how small the number, greatly alarmed critics after the release of Fulbright's secret memo.

The most notorious extremist officer of the day was Maj. Gen. Edwin A. Walker, commander of the 24th Infantry Division in Augsburg, Germany. Walker indoctrinated soldiers and their families with hard-line anticommunism, citizenship, religion, and traffic safety instruction through his 1960 "Pro Blue" program. Before assuming command of the division in November, 1959, Walker prepared to implement NSC-5810/1 by traveling across America gathering information from various civilian anticommunist organizations, including the John Birch Society and Harding College's National Education Program in Searcy, Arkansas. More adventurous than most army officers, Walker took steps to eliminate "alien influences" from religious services held in military chapels. He also distributed radical-right literature, denigrated many leading political and public figures of the day, and recommended that the men and women under his command vote for ultraconservative candidates. Initially called "Citizenship in Service," the religiously oriented Pro Blue program enlisted the aid of the Chaplains Corps in preaching that each individual form a "right relationship with God." Walker also reached out to military spouses by organizing women's study groups at each of his subordinate units' installations. Finally, he contacted local parent-teacher associations to enlist their help in getting schools to incorporate the tenets of Pro Blue in their classroom instruction.[33]

When the military reprimanded Walker for blatantly violating federal laws and military orders that forbade political activities within the service, the thirty-year veteran resigned from the army and launched an aggressive anticommunist lecture tour and unsuccessful campaign for political office. Walker traveled throughout the nation, complaining that his superiors had gagged him. Communist sympathizers within the government, the former general explained, were trying to nullify the 1958 NSC directive. By silencing America's vigilant defenders on the front lines of the Cold War, Walker charged, liberals had effectively removed those best qualified to warn the nation of the dangers of communism.[34]

Captain Kenneth J. Sanger, commander of the Sands Point Naval Air Station in Seattle, Washington, agreed with Walker that the military played a crucial role in disseminating anticommunist information to the public. Americans, according to Sanger, were exposed to communist propaganda each day. He attempted to stop "militantly atheistic, communistic, Soviet imperialism, and our own materialism" by emphasizing American ideals and values. Sanger testified to the Stennis Subcommittee that reservists attending his Cold War seminars responded "way beyond our expectations."[35] In their capacities as members of local Lion's Clubs or Chambers of Commerce, Sands Point reservists propagated anticommunist programs throughout the Pacific Northwest. Acting as coordinator for his weekend citizen-sailors, Sanger helped community groups book radical-right celebrities, maintained a pool of navy speakers that delivered four hundred canned speeches in less than a year, and indoctrinated leading citizens with radical-right literature and two controversial films, *Operation Abolition* and *Communism on the Map*. When publicly criticized for overstepping his boundaries, Sanger indicated that he operated with the full knowledge and approval of his superior, Vice Adm. Robert Goldthwaite, chief of naval air training at Pensacola, Florida.[36]

Admiral Goldthwaite's leadership course at Pensacola Naval Air Station was already five years old in 1958 when both the navy's General Order No. 21 and the mysterious NSC-5810/1 directive seemingly authorized Cold War seminars. The admiral issued a pamphlet entitled *What Can I Do?* in December, 1960. It admonished officer and enlisted students undergoing flight training to demand that the nation "immediately estab-

Vice Adm. Robert Goldthwaite, chief of naval air training at Pensacola, Florida. Courtesy National Museum of Naval Aviation, Pensacola, Florida.

lish a foreign policy based on Godly, moral principles and supporting freedom for all mankind to replace the policy of coexistence with evil."[37] According to the navy, not only did enlistments increase and courts-martial decline after the new focus on leadership and anticommunism began, the venereal disease rate also dropped. Moral leadership became "more important to our combat-readiness than any weapons system ever developed," one officer claimed. "This time we are dealing with the very heart of our whole combat capability—the man."[38]

As commanding officer of the 150,000 naval airmen assigned to Pensacola and a dozen other bases throughout the United States, Goldthwaite exercised tremendous influence over the content of naval leadership programs. The admiral's ultraconservative political views led him to associate his Cold War education efforts with "Project Alert," a radical-right program sponsored by reserve officers in the Navy League of the United States, and its companion organization, the Advisory Council on Naval Affairs (ACONA).[39] By the end of 1962, Pensacola was the center of a right-wing revival. There were thirteen Project Alert committees in Florida and a hundred nationwide that employed the films *Operation Abolition* and *Communism on the Map*, as well as a series of NEP cartoons, at Cold War seminars throughout the United States.[40]

Anticommunism Materials used at Cold War Seminars

Although DOD issued its own series of propaganda films, many commanders preferred to use commercially produced movies. Cold War seminars often illustrated the domestic communist threat by showing *Operation Abolition,* a House Un-American Activities Committee (HUAC) film that documented the San Francisco student riots in May, 1960. The committee alleged that hard-core communists had conspired with radical students in California to block HUAC's probe of the state's education system. Hoping to legitimize its efforts and squelch a growing movement intent on abolishing HUAC, the committee subpoenaed all existing news coverage and pieced together a forty-five minute exposé of the purportedly communist-inspired riots.[41]

Operation Abolition drew enormous criticism, for despite HUAC's claims to the contrary, the student demonstrations had been spontaneous. Known communists did appear at the committee's request to testify about their influence in California's schools, but the riots did not begin until *after* students were denied seating at the hearings. Although it was clear that *Operation Abolition* had been deliberately doctored, the Stennis Subcommittee refused to criticize the HUAC production and instead recommended that it be shown at anticommunist seminars.[42]

In conjunction with *Operation Abolition,* many Cold War seminars alerted their audiences to international danger by showing *Communism on the Map*. This best-selling filmstrip—in demand at military bases, public schools, and fundamentalist churches across America—equated communism with socialism and grossly distorted the extent of Soviet advances across Europe. *Communism on the Map,* the *Arkansas Democrat* advertised, traced "the growth of communism from the time of the Bolsheviks . . . to the present day encirclement of our own nation."[43]

The controversial filmstrip was clearly inaccurate, but even more troubling was the revelation that *Communism on the Map* was privately produced by Harding College of Searcy, Arkansas. Harding, a Church of Christ–affiliated institution located in the heart of the state, had recently blossomed into the top anticommunist training headquarters of the nation. Investigative reporters revealed that military and civilian groups, often at taxpayer's expense, flew into Searcy to train with NEP instructors and materials before launching a Cold War seminar or adopting "Americanism" programs designed by the NEP staff. From fees charged for these services, as well as contributions from businesses pleased with the college's efforts, Dr. George S. Benson, the school's president, raised an average of $1 million a year.[44]

Benson was able to keep contributions flowing into Harding's nonprofit bank account by promoting the free-enterprise system, moral leadership, and anticommunism with an avalanche of informational literature, more than fifty films, and the *Adventure Series,* which consisted of ten animated cartoons.

Paid for by the General Motors Corporation's Sloan Foundation, the cartoons taught basic economic concepts and equated New Deal liberalism with the evils of communism. They were shown primarily to young people in the classroom and at special youth-oriented Cold War seminars. In the cartoon "Fresh Laid Plans," Dr. Owlsly Hoot tricked the town of Eggville to accept price and wage controls. The power of the state then increased until all of the chickens in the corn-based economic system found their liberties destroyed. Children learned in "The Devil and John Q." that Satan invented inflation to destroy America's values and spirit. "Dear Uncle" warned against expensive government services. "All of us must do without some of the things we want," a disheartened Uncle Sam explained as a red hammer and sickle formed on the screen. "Only in that way can we preserve our strength and remain free." The award-winning cartoons reached an audience far wider than the Cold War seminars when MGM Studios distributed the series to more than ten thousand theaters across the nation.[45]

Aided by Kenneth Wells of the Freedoms Foundation at Valley Forge, Benson originally designed the NEP in 1941 and his nationwide Freedom Forums in 1949 with a general conservative audience in mind. However, Benson's emphasis switched from damning the New Deal to vilifying communism when it became apparent that the latter, more sensational segments of the Freedom Forums elicited the most enthusiasm. Not only did corporate heads from Kraft, Montgomery Ward, and Morton Salt continue to support Harding College, Benson's new agenda also attracted the attention of companies with large defense contracts. Boeing and General Electric, with $1 billion and $900 million respectively, hoped to alert "the country and the people to the dangers around us" by distributing NEP materials to their employees.[46]

As time went on, the NEP's reputation became tainted as Benson defended radical-right groups that bought his goods and appeared on the same Cold War seminar circuit as his NEP speakers. Benson denied periodic charges that the radical right influenced the NEP by explaining that his anticommunism predated that of other groups. George Benson and Harding College were, by implication, the philosophical foundation of the 1960s radical right.

Religiously Oriented Anticommunist Crusades

Dr. Fred C. Schwarz, an Australian physician who headed the Christian Anti-Communism Crusade and authored the bestseller *You Can Trust the Communist (To Be a Communist)*, often appeared at NEP Freedom Forums. In his own weeklong traveling anticommunist schools that netted millions of dollars in the 1960s, Dr. Schwarz instructed predominately college-educated Americans about the "satanic" Soviet threat. Schwarz himself refused to accuse government leaders of communist sympathies, but the "faculty members" featured at his schools were quick to identify a "pacifist" conspiracy that was allegedly responsible for the State Department's recent foreign policy disasters. The Christian Anti-Communism Crusade developed an effective grassroots political structure that organized dozens of small study groups in each community visited by one of his traveling schools. Once indoctrinated in communist-style intimidation tactics, anticommunist converts neutralized critics, influenced voters, and ran for office—all the while proclaiming Schwarz's apocalyptic message.[47]

Billy James Hargis of Tulsa, Oklahoma, the best-known radical-right spokesman, looked to Benson and the NEP for inspiration and legitimacy. Unlike Schwarz's upper-middle-class supporters, Dr. Hargis's following consisted of members of the white Protestant working class attracted by his flagrant anti-intellectualism. The portly founder of the Christian Crusade surrounded himself with retired military men and used radio and television broadcasts to spread the word that America was strong only because its leaders believed in God. Hargis also charged that the nation's future was in jeopardy because "godless leaders have infiltrated and subverted practically all phases of the American way of life."[48] He appealed to nativist sentiment by charging that the civil rights movement was creating a "crisis bred in the pits of Communist debauchery and conspiracy . . . for segregation is a law of God."[49] His most notorious charge, that the National Council of Churches was a communist front, brought him support from fundamentalist congregations frightened by new liberal trends in religion.[50] In 1962, Hargis organized a gathering in Washington to coordinate right-wing efforts. The result was the creation of the Anti-Communist Liaison, headed by Edward Hunter, a Korean War POW brainwashing "expert."

Hunter, the best-selling author of *Brainwashing in Red China,* was also a frequent speaker at Cold War seminars. Part of his fame derived from his appearance before the Senate Internal Security Subcommittee in July, 1961, regarding a particularly troubling foreign document. *The Statement of the Eighty-one Communist and Workers' Parties, Which Met in November and December of 1960 in Moscow,* or the *New Communist Manifesto,* as the Moscow pamphlet was quickly dubbed, marked the beginning of a highly coordinated "anti-anti-Red drive" designed by the Soviets, according to Hunter, to destroy America's dynamic grassroots anticommunism movement of the 1960s. Because of the manifesto, communists were "swarming over America," Hunter claimed, "infiltrating the White House, and even dictating what postage stamps are being circulated." Hunter agreed with other ultraconservatives that the Soviet architects of the *New Communist Manifesto* formulated the document to counter the recent success of the American military in educating the public on the dangers of communism.[51]

Poster promoting an "Operation: Alert" rally in Little Rock, Arkansas, at which Maj. Gen. Edwin A. Walker and Dr. Billy James Hargis were the featured speakers.

In the May, 1962, issue of *Reader's Digest,* the FPRI's William Kintner wrote of the emergence of an "insidious campaign to silence anti-Communists." Because the Moscow conference convened shortly after DOD initiated its Cold War seminars and the popular meetings were aborted soon after Premier Nikita Khrushchev issued the manifesto, many of

Kintner's readers became convinced that communist operatives within the United States had implemented instructions contained in the document. Unless the American public became aware of the true nature of this statement, Kintner warned, the Kremlin would soon succeed in destroying the nation's unity.[52]

Central to the ideology of Benson, Schwarz, Hargis, Hunter, and many other radical-right leaders was a Christian fundamentalist background. Fundamentalism and political extremism, though closely related in the early 1960s, were not synonymous terms. Not all fundamentalists were politically active, nor were all members of the radical right religious. However, when the two elements combined, as they often did in the early Cold War, they produced a powerful right-wing force. Soviet imperialism proved that the end of the world was near, Billy Graham–style evangelists proclaimed, as thousands flocked to revivals that won souls for Christ by capitalizing on Cold War fears. During the phenomenon of the Cold War seminars, the sacred and secular worlds merged in the rhetoric of anticommunism.[53]

The 1960s Red Scare

Resentment that could not easily be contained often surfaced when religious patriots unleashed their moral indignation on communities. In Brookfield, Connecticut, near hysteria broke out in the summer of 1961 after a showing of *Operation Abolition* at a Cold War seminar cosponsored by the PTA and local civil defense unit. Those brave enough to question the extremist statements of the speaker, Dr. Carlton Campbell, formerly associated with both the NEP and Schwarz's Anti-Communism Crusade, were shouted down from the podium and followed out to their cars by uniformed members of the civil defense unit, who recorded their license plate numbers. In the aftermath of the meeting, Brookfield, like many other communities visited by Cold War seminars, formed its own anticommunist committee that aggressively smeared anyone who dared to oppose it.[54]

Dr. Fred Schwarz conducted a five-day anticommunist school at Glenview Naval Air Station in Illinois to fight against "moral decay, political apathy and spiritual bankruptcy."[55] In addition to military officers, the faculty of "Education for American Security," included Herbert Philbrick, a former FBI agent and author of *I Led Three Lives;* Richard Arens, director of HUAC; and Merrill Root, of *Collectivism on the Campus* fame. The Illinois Division of the American Civil Liberties Union (ACLU) requested an official investigation after it learned that Capt. Isaiah Hampton, the

Glenview commander, screened both *Communism on the Map* and *Operation Abolition* on government property during the conference. The ACLU feared that a program claiming the nation's universities were breeding grounds for communists would turn "Americans against Americans."[56] Dr. Schwarz and Captain Hampton showed they cared little about the ACLU's qualms when they declared that they were willing to "suppress any civil liberties necessary" if it would prevent the Soviets from conquering America within the next five to ten years. [57]

After Dr. Tyler Thompson, a professor of religion at Northwestern University and Democratic candidate for Congress, complained to the navy secretary about the situation at Glenview, anticommunist forces began a smear campaign that played a part in his later defeat at the polls. The Glenview Village Board asked Mrs. Norma Morrison to resign her seat after she cast the only vote against a resolution commending the anticommunist school. The civic-minded housewife "received a number of nasty telephone calls . . . most of them anonymous and at night. They accused me of being a 'Red,' or 'pink.'" Recalling the bitterness that followed the controversy, Morrison later said, "Our town is divided in a way I've never seen it before."[58]

The intolerance shown in Brookfield and Glenview appears typical of communities visited by Cold War seminars. In Houston, schools purged liberal references from their textbooks during the summer of 1961 in the wake of anticommunist propaganda and intimidation.[59] When it was announced that same year that San Antonio's "Americanism Seminar" would feature Sen. Strom Thurmond, the local chapter of the National Association for the Advancement of Colored People denounced the endeavor for headlining "the worst race-baiter that anyone knows," while conservatives in the community declared that it was now "time for the American people to decide who is going to run this country—patriots or pinks."[60] Stan Twardy, a reporter for the *Progressive,* left Oklahoma City's Christian Crusade, which featured Billy James Hargis, Robert Welch, and General Walker, "convinced that the 'Crusade' had unleashed a flood of hatred and suspicion whose corroding effect on society can be regarded only as a major triumph for Communism."[61]

Project Alert

The most extreme manifestation of Cold War hysteria occurred in Pensacola, Florida, where the Navy League and ACONA's Project Alert joined forces with Admiral Goldthwaite's moral leadership course. Goldthwaite claimed that "'Project Alert' [was] . . . an educational plan for victory in the Cold War through community action in alerting all citizens to the dangers of the international communist conspiracy."[62] This morality and anticommunism program reportedly held 520 meetings with a total estimated attendance of fifty thousand in its first year alone. With the aid of NEP materials and speakers, Goldthwaite trained military personnel, their dependents, and civilians to become active red hunters.[63]

The first Project Alert meeting was held in Lubbock, Texas, in 1959 under the auspices of Rear Adm. Walter G. Schindler, commandant of the Eighth Naval District. From its inception, Project Alert—unlike earlier morality programs that focused primarily on building the character of military personnel—embraced extremism. By virtue of the enthusiastic response at Lubbock, the national chair of ACONA, retired admiral John W. Reeves Jr. proposed to center the program in Pensacola for the purpose of extending the benefits of "Americanism" to every U.S. citizen. Admiral Goldthwaite illustrated how this feat could be accomplished by quoting Dr. Fred Schwarz: "If . . . I were to speak to one person a week and could convince, inform and instruct that person, and if we each convinced, informed and instructed another person the following week, and the four of us each enlisted another the following week, by this process, everyone in the world could be reached in less than twelve months."[64]

Members of the Pensacola Project Alert planning committee, dominated by Goldthwaite and his senior officers, regularly flew to Searcy, Arkansas, at the navy's expense to train with Harding College's Clifton Lloyd Ganus Jr. and Glenn A. Greene. Greene, a card-carrying member of the John Birch Society, designed Pensacola's initial two-day introductory seminar and follow-up series of three-hour meetings to stress "Communism in the world today and the need to build internal defense by strengthening American knowledge and moral leadership."[65]

Goldthwaite left most of the daily work in Pensacola to local civilians while he and other naval personnel concentrated on spreading the program across the nation. Not only was Project Alert associated with Schwarz's anticommunism school at Glenview and Sanger's operation at Seattle, it also appeared at naval air stations in Corpus Christi; Minneapolis; South Weymouth, Massachusetts; Memphis; Grosse Ile, South Carolina; Los Angeles; and Dallas. Goldthwaite extended the program even farther by offering Project Alert speakers and materials for use in army-sponsored Cold War seminars.[66]

Although Project Alert went nationwide, its most concentrated effort remained in Florida. The Pensacola Project Alert committee blanketed the state with its conservative message and pressured politicians to accept their proposals. "To combat world aggression and to support the freedom of man," Project Alert called for a patriotic rebirth in Pensacola. Superpatriots pressured community clubs to indoctrinate their members with a whole series of anticommunism meetings. Project Alerters contacted schools to plan classroom programs that reached all the way down to the fifth grade. Parent-Teacher Associations won over by the program asked parents: "How long has it been since you discussed your country over the breakfast table with your children?"[67] Religious leaders preached anticommunism, commended the navy's role in the program, and showed *Communism on the Map* to their congregations. Pensacola's major industries, including Gulf Power, Sherrill Oil, and the Chemstrand Corporation, donated heavily to the program and held employee anticommunism meetings at their plants.[68]

Decals, such as this, produced by the Freedoms Foundation at Valley Forge were used to promote Project Alert.

Project Alert placed tremendous psychological pressure on the people of Pensacola in an effort to get them to conform to its ultraconservative viewpoint. Candidates for the Project Alert speaker's bureau who voiced misgivings about the program's content were immediately dropped. Goldthwaite had the July 20, 1961, issue of the *Reporter*, which featured an article critical of his propaganda activities, removed from the shelves of the local library on the grounds that it was a "Communist magazine."[69] A leaflet widely distributed by Project Alerters stated: "our experience has shown that there will be certain forms of opposition to a PROJECT ALERT effort. In most instances it will come from well-intentioned sources, people who fail to fully understand the critical world situation and the need for education NOW. It will also probably stem from sources with motives NOT consistent with the nation's best interest. IT IS HARD TO BELIEVE . . . BUT . . . IN ALL PROBABILITY THERE IS A COMMUNIST CELL OPERATING IN YOUR COMMUNITY."[70] Many who opposed Project Alert privately felt forced to support it publicly. One teacher at the junior college claimed that he wrote speeches for the program because Alerters had "threatened to call me a communist if I didn't."[71]

Professional women's organizations such as the United Church Women, the League of Women Voters, and the American Association of University Women (AAUW) were especially hostile to the program's excesses. Project Alerters sprang into action when Louise Jacobson, president of the Pensacola AAUW, refused to substitute a Project Alert meeting for a talk on the United Nations by Dr. William G. Carleton, a professor of political science at the University of Florida, in October, 1960. Notices were sent to AAUW members condemning Carleton's political views. "As the speaker presents his interpretation of the UN and its accomplishments," Project Alert warned, "remember the words of Karl Marx: 'Before the proletariat fights out its battles on the barricades, it announces the coming of its rule with a long series of intellectual victories.'"

After Dr. Carleton gave his scheduled talk, Jacobson and the AAUW became the chief target for the fury of Pensacola's radical right. Those AAUW members who did not immediately resign were socially ostracized and frequently called communist sympathizers. In the early spring of 1961, Jacobson openly challenged Project Alert's stranglehold over the community by arranging for syndicated columnist Drew Pearson to speak at the Pensacola Municipal Auditorium. A liberal spokesman of Pearson's caliber apparently was more than some Pensacola's extremists could stomach, for on the night of the speech, unidentified vigilantes burned a cross in the front yard of the house where Pearson had earlier dined with leading liberals of the community.[72]

The JCS became aware that problems had occurred with a number of the Cold War seminars after the ICAF reported in July, 1961, that "some of the regional conferences . . . [had taken] extreme positions on certain controversial issues."[73] In order to prevent further embarrassment, the service college called for centralized control over future seminars. Goldthwaite, too, recognized problems with Project Alert and apologized to Admiral Burke that some of his officers had "[run] away with the program and brought upon the Navy some unfavorable criticism."[74] However, neither the navy nor DOD took any disciplinary action until Senator Fulbright's secret memo made the seminars a public issue.

In the beginning, Project Alert speakers were careful not to make radical statements likely to be published by the press. Later, after the release of the Fulbright memo and publication of a series of investigative reports on Cold War seminars had clearly documented Goldthwaite's close ties to both the military and the radical right, Project Alerters dropped their guard and openly criticized governmental policies and leaders. In the fall of 1961, Project Alert attempted to boost its declining reputation by inviting World War I hero and Eastern Airlines chairman Eddie Rickenbacker to speak at a rally. Rickenbacker shocked even his overwhelmingly conservative audience by calling for a preventive nuclear war against the Soviet Union and blasted the income tax, foreign aid, and the United Nations. The fighter ace predicted that the nation would one day erect a monument to the memory of Joe McCarthy "for his heroic efforts to awaken the American people to the danger this country, its people, and generations to come would have to face."[75] Local newspaper editors, emboldened now that Project Alert was in decline, jumped into the fray and openly criticized Rickenbacker's statements.[76]

The intensity behind Project Alert, like most other anticommunist organizations of the early 1960s, dissipated shortly after the Stennis Subcommittee concluded its hearings. Without active military participation, the radical right could no longer use the seminar structure to claim legitimacy. However, the underlying principle behind the Cold War seminars, the belief that the maintenance of civic virtue and the creation of a national will was a military responsibility, remained. Although Project Alert never regained its former status, the program continued to promote conservative politics throughout the early 1960s with some success. Not only did

the Ugly Truth

About Drew Pearson

BY DR. BILLY JAMES HARGIS
A CHRISTIAN CRUSADE PUBLICATION
TULSA 2, OKLAHOMA

Cover of an early 1960s pamphlet.

the state of Florida pass a law requiring that an anticommunism course be taught in its high schools, it also created the Florida Center for Cold War Education, a state anticommunist propaganda office. Other states followed suit as the federal government backed away from pursuing further civilian indoctrination in the wake of the Cold War seminar scandal.

Although the military had joined forces with the radical right to produce the Cold War seminars, the services were never able to control, or truly support, those political extremists. The Defense Department had made a commitment to the civil rights movement because of its chronic manpower shortages and need for order within the ranks during the Truman administration, no matter how individual officers might have felt about the issue. The radical right, however, generally held that the civil rights movement had been orchestrated by Moscow to destroy the nation's existing social structure. Because of this basic clash in philosophy, any partnership between the U.S. armed forces and the radical right was sure to be short lived. In addition, the radical right was unable to sustain itself because of internal religious divisions in the anticommunism movement. Fundamentalist groups, which were largely nativist, could not take advantage of the potent anticommunism forces within the Catholic Church because of their inherent anti-Catholicism. Religiously isolated and lacking the official sanction of the U.S. military after the Cold War seminars ended, the radical right was destined to remain on the fringes of American society.

Conclusion

Anticommunism seminars passed from the American scene after 1964 and were soon forgotten by liberals, conservatives, and even most historians. The phenomenon of the Cold War seminars, however, was not an insignificant episode. For a short period, civilian supremacy over the military was indeed strained. There is no data indicating that any organized conspiracy endangered democracy; no military cabal planned a coup of the Eisenhower or Kennedy administrations. Nevertheless, the military leaders discussed here—at the center of the American civil-military religion and believing themselves to be the nation's moral conscience—participated in programs outside of the services' traditional parameters. Cold War seminars were illustrative of the dangers inherent in efforts to incorporate a religious mission, without proper restraints, into the nation's military policies.

The armed forces had overstepped their traditional boundaries because leaders feared for their own and the nation's survival. Declining public morals seemed to prove that the real threat of communism was not from without but from within the American people themselves. Cold War Progressives believed that they could win the ideological struggle by combining moral outreach with anticommunism education. This observation is not meant to romanticize the military's actions. The active and reserve officers who accepted speaking invitations were fully aware that their presence validated members of the radical right, who railed against what they believed were the treasonous actions of all presidents and policy leaders from Woodrow Wilson forward. Military participation in Cold War seminars thus gave the impression that the U.S. military sanctioned the information being presented.

The U.S. armed forces, claiming to be the "guardian" of national values during the early Cold War, attempted to fortify the nation for a battle of "isms" by shaping the character and citizenship of the men and women under their control. When this attempt proved ineffective, the military extended its psychological warfare efforts directly to the American public through the medium of Cold War seminars. Ironically, by adopting many of the same propaganda techniques that they found so reprehensible when used by the communists, the services opened themselves up to charges that they had participated in the subversion of vital American principles. Whatever their original motivations, critics claimed that military leaders' attempts to shape the public's character and promote an American ideology at home and abroad had unleashed forces that threatened the very precepts that servicemen and women had pledged their lives to defend.

Epilogue

THE CITIZEN SOLDIER IN RETROSPECT

Like the winter soldiers of 1776 who stayed after they had served

their time, we veterans of Vietnam know that America is in grave

danger.

—William Crandell of the VVAW, January, 1971

In 1969, the Valley Forge Park Commission met in special session to consider a controversial petition by the Vietnam Veterans Against the War (VVAW). The VVAW was seeking permission to hold an antiwar protest rally at the park to climax "Operation RAW" (Rapid American Withdrawal), an eighty-six mile march retracing the Continental Army's historic route from Morristown, New Jersey, to Valley Forge, Pennsylvania. The park commission initially was reluctant to grant permission because Valley Forge had, in recent years, attracted a number of "hippies" in search of marijuana plants that were falsely rumored to be growing wild in the park. Hippies, in the opinion of one commissioner, had turned the Continental Army's winter encampment into a "no man's land." "[S]cattered whiskey and beer swillers" and "heated love scenes being enacted on blankets here and there in view of moving traffic," according to a 1965 report by the aptly named Subcommittee on Sex, Hippies, and Whiskey Swillers, were on the increase and detracted from Valley Forge's historic purpose.[1] The park commission approved the VVAW request nonetheless. No precedent could be found to bar it; various special interest groups had been allowed to use the park to promote their particular causes over the years. If the VVAW obtained proper insurance and provided its own parking attendants and sufficient toilets for the expected crowds, the RAW rally could proceed as planned.[2] Ultraconservative Carl McIntire, an area pastor and founder of the American Council of Christian Churches, the Twentieth-Century Reformation Hour, and numerous other fundamentalist organizations, encouraged the veterans to come to Valley Forge. "The more they talk," the prowar, political activist clergyman claimed, "the more people will turn from the defeat and surrender they champion and demand that the nation win the peace by victory and honor."[3]

The VVAW chose the Valley Forge site in order to identify itself with the traditional American values of patriotism and civic virtue. Organized late in the antiwar movement, the veterans used Revolutionary War imagery to highlight their citizen-soldier credentials. Borrowing a reference from Tom Paine's *Crisis*, VVAW leaders referred to themselves as the "new winter soldiers," who had answered their nation's call to duty, not once, but twice: first as soldiers in the field and now as antiwar warriors battling to overcome middle-class apathy toward the Vietnam War.[4] Having personally experienced the grim realities of combat (often, they claimed, as participants in the very war crimes they now condemned), the veterans pleaded with the nation to end the war before American freedoms and virtue were destroyed. "[E]ven though I'm a first lieutenant . . . on active duty," one West Point graduate and VVAW marcher explained, "I'm many things before I'm an Army officer. . . . As a human being, as a citizen, as a military officer, I reject the Vietnam War in its entirety."[5]

During the Labor Day weekend march, Operation RAW attracted considerable media attention with its "Guerilla Theater." Performed at shopping malls, town squares, and other high-traffic locations along the old Continental Army route, Guerilla Theater emphasized the reported brutality of the American soldier by simulating the search-and-destroy missions conducted in Southeast Asia. To the shock of onlookers, longhaired, bearded veterans dressed in jungle fatigues and armed with rubber knives and plastic M16s "roughed up" and "detained" civilians played by professional actors who had infiltrated the unsuspecting crowds. Other VVAW members followed closely behind, distributing leaflets that read: "A U.S. infantry company has just come through here. If you had been Vietnamese, we might have burned your house, shot you and your dog, raped your wife and daughter, burned the town and tortured its citizens." The war must be stopped, the VVAW warned parents, before their sons became murderers or returned home in a body bag.[6]

Valley Forge park police, armed with shotguns and backed by state troopers and the FBI, prepared for trouble as the veterans approached the historic encampment on the final day of the RAW march. In a dramatic ceremony, the protestors, some on crutches or in wheelchairs, formed a battle line on the ridge leading into the historical park. Chanting "Peace! Now!" they descended from the hill, greeting fifteen hundred supporters with hugs and tears before solemnly forming ranks, presenting arms, and then, on command, smashing their toy rifles to the cheers of the crowd. After listening to speeches by Jane Fonda, Donald Sutherland, and other VVAW celebrities, the veterans left their inspirational surroundings determined to spread Guerilla Theater and the winter soldier message across the nation.[7] After the RAW demonstration, the VVAW made headlines with its "Winter Soldier Investigation," held in Detroit from January 31–February 2, 1971, which featured alleged firsthand accounts of war crimes. The organization also sponsored "Dewey Canyon III," a weeklong demonstration that spring in Washington, D.C. In December, 1971, a group of antiwar veterans returned to Valley Forge. Although the turnout at the park was considerably lower than at the earlier RAW demonstration, the weeklong encampment brought the antiwar crusade considerable publicity, especially when Reverend McIntire led 150 of his followers in a counterprotest at the historic site.

The use of Valley Forge imagery during the VVAW's RAW protest was indicative of contesting definitions of patriotism during the Vietnam War. Escalating body counts, news of atrocities committed by American troops, and the inability of policy makers to end the war honorably, led a number of Americans to challenge the prevailing civil-military religious consensus at its core. By questioning the role of the armed forces as an instrument of God's will, a new interpretation of the citizen soldier as a soldier who questioned rather than obeyed his government was fighting for recognition in the American consciousness and mission. According to the recollections of one eyewitness to the 1970 RAW march at Valley Forge, the VVAW protested against the war not to undermine the American Way of Life, as critics like McIntire claimed, but "to protect the principles those men [the Vietnam veterans] had fought to establish by insisting that the Vietnam War . . . be stopped."[8]

A number of factors that coalesced during the early Cold War resulted in the short-term phenomenon of military-sponsored Cold War seminars. The military's historic role as a character-shaping institution, the general belief that America's character and will were woefully lacking in the masculine and patriotic values necessary for an ideological battle with communism, the rise of evangelicals within American society, and a greatly strengthened military establishment prompted a number of high-ranking DOD leaders to take concerted and organized steps to articulate an American ideology and to shape the national character along lines that supported a conservative military mind-set. These trends came to maturity during the Eisenhower presidency when the Pentagon formulated "Strategy for Survival," "Project Alert," and other joint military-civilian anticommunist seminars that often became public platforms for members of the radical right to attempt to legitimatize their extremist political views. When it became clear that a lack of quality control had allowed this public outreach to spin out of control, DOD ended its active participation.

In the aftermath of the Cold War seminars, military indoctrination efforts came under the close scrutiny of investigative reporters and DOD severely curtailed its efforts to shape a national character. While the maintenance of civic virtue and the creation of a national will are current concerns of the military, DOD largely suspended such attempts during the Vietnam War. Evangelicals who were still well positioned in the DOD hierarchy channeled their religious efforts into more acceptable directions.

Although the Cold War seminars are illustrative of the dangers inherent in efforts to incorporate a religious mission into the nation's military policies without proper restraints, it would be wrong to conclude that the armed forces have no proper role in the American civil religion. Civil religion in a democracy sustains the nation. The military, by necessity, needs to be included in its parameters. Military character education, conducted within the ranks and under proper direction, appears to be an essential component of an effective defense establishment in a democracy. In fact, the reduction of civil-military religious education as a means of strengthening the national will and character may have contributed in some degree to the declining morale and widespread drug use among American troops during the Vietnam era. If military historian and analyst Harry Summers's observation that President Johnson's "failure to invoke the national will was one of the major strategic failures of the Vietnam War" is correct, perhaps a revival of national character studies is in order, especially those studies that differentiate between its various components and extrapolate the critical role each plays in a democratic republic. Such studies are critical to the successful management of the national will in a pluralistic, evolving democracy.[9]

Notes

Introduction

1. George Washington to John Hancock, Sept. 25, 1776, in *The Papers of George Washington,* ed. Dorothy T. Wohig, 6:394–400.
2. John B. B. Trussell Jr., *Birthplace of an Army: A Study of the Valley Forge Encampment,* 39–47; John Shy, *A People Numerous and Armed: Reflections on the Military Struggle for American Independence;* James Kirby Martin and Mark Edward Lender, *A Respectable Army: The Military Origins of the Republic, 1763–1789.*
3. Charles Royster, *A Revolutionary People at War: The Continental Army and the American Character, 1775–1783,* vii–x, 3–18.
4. Thomas Paine, "The American Crisis," in *Thomas Paine: Collected Writings,* ed. Eric Foner, 91.
5. Fredric M. Litto, "Addison's *Cato* in the Colonies," *William and Mary Quarterly* 20, no. 3 (July, 1966): 447.
6. Barry Schwartz, *George Washington: The Making of an American Symbol,* 170; Matthew Spalding and Patrick J. Garrity, *A Sacred Union of Citizens: George Washington's Farewell Address and the American Character,* 77.
7. George Washington, quoted in David E. Wheatley, "The Chaplains of the American Revolution," unpublished paper, 1987, U.S. Army Military History Institute, Carlisle Barracks, Pa. (hereafter MHI); Royster, *Revolutionary People at War,* 234.
8. Schwartz, *George Washington,* 188.
9. James D. Scudieri, "The Continentals: A Comparative Analysis of a Late Eighteenth-Century Standing Army, 1775–1783" (Ph.D. diss., City University of New York, 1993), 164.
10. General Order, Mar. 1, 1778, in John C. Fitzpatrick, ed., *The Writings of George Washington from the Original Manuscript Sources: 1745–1799,* vol. 11, 11:8–12.
11. Royster, *Revolutionary People at War,* 194–96.
12. Rita Kirk Whillock, "Dream Believers: The Unifying Visions and Competing Values of Adherents to American Civil Religion," *Presidential Studies Quarterly* 24, no. 2 (spring, 1994): 375–76.
13. Catherine Albanese, *Sons of the Fathers: The Civil Religion of the American Revolution,* vii, 95–99.

14. Robert Neely Bellah, "Civil Religion in America," in Robert Neely Bellah, *Beyond Belief: Essays on Religion in a Post-Traditional World,* 9–15.

15. B. Edward McClellan, *Schools and the Shaping of Character: Moral Education in America, 1607–Present,* 27.

16. Albanese, *Sons of the Fathers,* 99.

17. Schwartz, *George Washington,* 114.

18. Benjamin Franklin, "Proposals Relating to the Education of Youth in Pennsylvania," in *The Papers of Benjamin Franklin,* ed. Leonard W. Labaree, 36–37.

19. Tamar Frankiel, "Ritual Sites in the Narrative of American Religion" in *Retelling U.S. Religious History,* ed. Thomas A. Tweed, 69.

20. Conrad Cherry, *God's New Israel: Religious Interpretations of American Destiny;* Robert Neely Bellah, *The Broken Covenant: American Civil Religion on Trial;* Richard G. Hutcheson, *The Churches and the Chaplaincy,* 131–32; Richard R. Gilbert, *The Nation with the Soul of a Church: A Critical Reflection,* 20; Robert D. Linder, "Civil Religion and Baptist Responsibility," *Southwestern Journal of Theology* 18, no. 2 (spring, 1976): 25–39; Adam Gamoran, "Civil Religion in American Schools," *Sociological Analysis* 51, no. 3 (1990): 235–56; F. Michael Perko, *Schooling and the American Civil Religion,* 1–26.

21. Allan R. Millett and Peter Maslowski, *For the Common Defense: A Military History of the United States of America,* 94–95; Morris Janowitz, *The Professional Soldier: A Social and Political Portrait,* 48; Charles Moskos, *A Call to Civic Service: National Service for Country and Community,* 16.

22. Moskos, *Call to Civic Service,* 13; Mary Ann Glendon and David Blankenhorn, *Seedbeds of Virtue: Sources of Competence, Character, and Citizenship in American Society,* 1–2; Eric B. Gorham, *National Service, Citizenship, and Political Education,* intro, 168; John Hardin Best, "A History of the Development of the Concept of Citizenship Education in America, 1900–1950" (Ph.D. diss., University of North Carolina, 1967).

23. Francis C. Steckel, "Morale and Men: A Study of the American Soldier in World War I and II (Ph.D. diss., Temple University, 1990), v.

24. Hutcheson, *Churches and the Chaplaincy,* 131–32; James Brooks, "Military Religion and Moral Ethos: An Ethical Analysis" (Ph.D. diss., Iliff School of Theology, Denver, 1994); Harvey Gallagher Cox, *Military Chaplains: From Religious Military to a Military Religion,* 89; John Helgeland, "Civil Religion, Military Religion," *Foundations and Facets Forum* 5, no. 1 (Mar., 1989): 41.

25. Steven Watts, *The Republic Reborn: War and the Making of Liberal America, 1790–1820,* 76; Albanese, *Sons of the Fathers,* 109.

26. "Benny Havens Ho," words by Lucius O'Brien, John T. Metcalfe, Ripley A. Arnold et al., U.S. Military Academy, 1838, in *Song Book of the United States Naval Academy,* ed. Alfred R. Taylor, Kenneth D. McCracken, and C. E. Beatty, 77.

27. Luther S. Luedtke, ed., *Making America: The Society and Culture of the United States,* 8–11; David Lownethal "Identity, Heritage, and History," in *Commemorations: The Politics of National Identity,* ed. John R. Gillis, 46–47.

28. Thomas Henry Bell, "The National Will" (Ph.D. diss., Claremont University, Claremont, Calif., 1996), 213–35.

29. Luedtke, *Making America,* 8.

Chapter 1

1. Lorett Treese, *Valley Forge: Making and Remaking a National Symbol,* 86.
2. Michael Pearlman, *To Make Democracy Safe for America: Patricians and Preparedness in the Progressive Era,* 11–14.
3. Theodore Roosevelt, *The Valley Forge Speech,* 19–21.
4. W. Herbert Burk, "The American Westminster," *Daughters of the American Revolution Magazine,* Dec., 1923, 701–707; Treese, *Valley Forge,* 101.
5. Treese, *Valley Forge,* 123; "Address of President Hoover at Valley Forge Park," May 30, 1931, in *Public Papers of the Presidents: Herbert Hoover,* vol. 3, *1931,* 272–77.
6. John Robbins Hart, *Valley Forge During World War II,* 2–3; Leonard Falkner, "We Relived the Miracle of Valley Forge," *American Magazine,* Dec., 1954, 98–103.
7. For more on this subject, see Clifford Wallace Putney, *Muscular Christianity: Manhood and Sports in Protestant America, 1880–1920;* and Gerald Franklin Roberts, "The Strenuous Life: The Cult of Manliness in the Era of Theodore Roosevelt" (Ph.D. diss., Michigan State University, 1970).
8. The definition of professionalism is still being debated. I have based my definition on one originally proposed by Samuel P. Huntington in *The Soldier and the State: The Theory and Politics of Civil-Military Relations,* 7–10.
9. Walter Millis, *Arms and Men: A Study in American Military History,* 198.
10. Pearlman, *To Make Democracy Safe,* 41; Francis A. Kellor, *Straight America: A Call to National Service,* 2–3, 182.
11. John Garry Clifford, *The Citizen Soldiers: The Plattsburg Training Camp Movement, 1913–1920,* 11.
12. Peter Karsten, *Soldiers and Society: The Effects of Military Service and War on American Life,* 227; Pearlman, *To Make Democracy Safe,* 38–41; Clifford, *Citizen Soldiers,* 16, 58.
13. Clifford, *Citizen Soldiers,* 16; Pearlman, *To Make Democracy Safe,* 82.
14. Clifford, *Citizen Soldiers,* 48–52.
15. John Patrick Finnegan, "Military Preparedness in the Progressive Era, 1911–1917" (Ph.D. diss., University of Wisconsin–Madison, 1969), 111–12.
16. Clifford, *Citizen Soldiers,* 185; Pearlman, *To Make Democracy Safe,* 111.
17. Penn Borden, *Civilian Indoctrination of the Military: World War I and Future Implications for the Military-Industrial Complex,* 18–19; Clifford, *Citizen Soldiers,* 84, 88.
18. Moskos, *Call to Civic Service,* 21; Clifford, *Citizen Soldiers,* 153.
19. Department of the Army Pamphlet no. 165-12, *A Brief History of the United States Army Chaplain Corps,* 7; Moskos, *Call to Civic Service,* 30; Millis, *Arms and Men,* 228–30, 233; Douglas Lincoln Clubine, "'Better Than They Were Before': Athletics and American Military Preparedness during the Great War" (M.A. thesis, Michigan State University, 1994), 27.
20. Millis, *Arms and Men,* 225.
21. Borden, *Civilian Indoctrination,* 98–99; Nancy K. Bristow, *Making Men Moral: Social Engineering During the Great War,* 40; Ronald Schaffer, *America in the Great War: The Rise of the War Welfare State,* 3–7.

22. Pearlman, *To Make Democracy Safe,* 156; Steven Wayne Pope, *Patriotic Games: Sporting Traditions in the American Imagination, 1876–1926,* 145; Thomas J. Hawley, "Committee on Training Camp Activities" (M.A. thesis: Arizona State University, 1992), 31, 44.

23. Bristow, *Making Men Moral,* 117.

24. Leonard Wood quoted in John Whiteclay Chambers, "Conscripting for Colossus: The Adoption of the Draft in the United States in World War I" (Ph.D. diss., Columbia University, 1973), 317–18.

25. Theodore Roosevelt quoted in ibid., 302, 320.

26. Chambers, "Conscripting for Colossus," 319–20; Nancy Gentile Ford, *Americans All! Foreign-Born Soldiers in World War I,* 74–76.

27. Borden, *Civilian Indoctrination,* 108–10; Stephen D. Wesbrook, *Political Training in the United States Army: A Reconsideration,* 11–12; Robert J. Higgs, *God in the Stadium: Sports and Religion in America,* 204; Bristow, *Making Men Moral,* 33.

28. Edward Lyman Munson, *The Management of Men: A Handbook on the Systematic Development of Morale and the Control of Human Behavior,* 8–9.

29. M. K. Henderson et al., "A Study of the Information and Education as it has been applied in the Past, with suggestions for Future Use of the Program," copy in MHI Library, 5; Jack Edward Pulwers, "The Information and Education Programs of the Armed Forces: An Administrative and Social History, 1940–1945" (Ph.D. diss., Catholic University of America, 1983), 5; Morris Janowitz, *The Reconstruction of Patriotism: Education for Civic Consciousness,* 54–55; Munson, *Management of Men,* 11.

30. Pulwers, "Information and Education Programs," 5.

31. Pearlman, *To Make Democracy Safe,* 155–56; Robert Jackall and Janice M. Hirota, "America's First Propaganda Ministry: The Committee on Public Information During the Great War," in *Propaganda,* ed. Robert Jackall, 9.

32. Pulwers, "Information and Education Programs," 11.

33. Clubine, "'Better Than They Were Before,'" 70–72; Pope, *Patriotic Games,* 151–54; Pearlman, *To Make Democracy Safe,* 172.

34. Gamoran, "Civil Religion in American Schools," 235–56; Robert Wood Lynn, "Civil Catechetics in Mid-Victorian America: Some Notes About American Civil Religion, Past and Present," *Religious Education* 68, no. 1 (Jan.–Feb., 1973): 5–27.

35. McClellan, *Schools and the Shaping of Character,* 57.

36. David C. McClelland, *Education for Values,* 4.

37. Jeffrey P. Hantover, "The Boy Scouts and the Validation of Masculinity," in *The American Man,* ed. Elizabeth H. and Joseph H. Pleck, 293.

38. Borden, *Civilian Indoctrination,* 132, 139; Joe P. Dunn, "UMT: A Historical Perspective," *Military Review* 68, no. 1 (Jan., 1981): 11–18.

39. Raymond C. McGath, "Service and Society: The Question of Universal Military Training in Congress, 1919–1920" (M.A. thesis, Arizona State University, 1992), 17.

40. Maj. M. J. Guner, memorandum for the commandant, U.S. Army War College, "Subject: Training of the C.M.T.C.," Mar. 18, 1930, file 367-26, archives, MHI; "Proposed Manual on Training Camps," 354.1 (7-2-25 to 6-26-25) folder, box 842, Central Decimal Files 1917–1925, Record Group (hereafter RG) 407, Adjutant General's

Office, 1917–, National Archives and Records Administration (hereafter NARA), College Park, Md.

41. Lt. Col. Louis Farrell, memorandum, "The Comparative Values of CMTC and ROTC Systems," course at the Army War College, 1929–30, file 367-19, Army War College curricula, archives, MHI; John William Killigrew, "The Impact of the Great Depression on the Army, 1929–1936" (Ph.D. diss., Indiana University, 1960), ix–12. For more on the CMTC, see Donald M. Kington, *Forgotten Summers: The Story of the Citizen Military Training Camps, 1921–1940.*

42. Aubrey Patterson Jr., telephone interview by author, July 28, 2003.

43. Borden, *Civilian Indoctrination,* 132; Wesbrook, *Political Training,* 15.

44. *Citizenship Training Manual* 2000-25; Arthur Alphonese Ekrich, *The Civilian and the Military: A History of the American Antimilitarist Tradition,* 224; Wesbrook, *Political Training,* 7–8.

45. Killigrew, "Impact of the Great Depression," iv.

46. Michael W. Sherraden, "Military Participation in a Youth Employment Program: The Civilian Conservation Corps," *Armed Forces and Society* 7, no. 2 (winter, 1981): 227–45; John A. Salmond, *The Civilian Conservation Corps, 1933–1942: A New Deal Case Study.* See also Charles William Johnson, "The Civilian Conservation Corps: The Role of the Army" (Ph.D. diss., University of Michigan, 1968).

47. Pearlman, *To Make Democracy Safe,* 231–32; George P. Rawick, "The New Deal and Youth: The Civilian Conservation Corps, the National Youth Administration, and the American Youth Congress" (Ph.D. diss., University of Wisconsin, 1957), 113.

48. Gorham, *National Service,* 129, 231.

49. Janowitz, *Reconstruction of Patriotism,* 98.

50. Rawick, "New Deal and Youth," 115–16; Johnson, "Civilian Conservation Corps," 233.

51. Pearlman, *To Make Democracy Safe,* 23; Robert K. Griffith Jr., *Men Wanted for the U.S. Army: America's Experience with an All-Volunteer Army Between the World Wars,* 213–15.

52. *Moral Leadership Program in the Air Force,* 5.

53. Eli Ginzberg, James K. Anderson, Sol W. Ginsburg, John L. Herma, *The Ineffective Soldier: Lessons for Management and the Nation,* vol. 1, *The Lost Divisions,* 27, 30.

54. Donald S. Napoli, "The Mobilization of American Psychologists, 1938–1941," *Military Affairs* 42, no. 1 (Feb., 1978): 33–34.

55. Francis C. Steckel, "Morale Problems in Combat: American Soldiers in Europe in World War II," *Army History,* summer, 1994, 317; Lee Kennett, *G.I.: The American Soldier in World War II,* 91–97; Ginzberg et al., *Lost Divisions,* 27, 30; William C. Menninger, M.D., *Psychiatry in a Troubled World: Yesterday's War and Today's Challenge,* 277.

56. George C. Marshall as quoted in Forrest C. Pogue, *George C. Marshall: Ordeal and Hope, 1939–1943,* 110, 118; Steckel, "Morale Problems in Combat," 317.

57. "Life Reporter Finds Many Gripes Have Lowered Army Morale," *Life,* Aug. 18, 1941, 17–18; Robert W. Coakley, Paul J. Scheips, and Emma J. Portuondo, *Antiwar and Antimilitary Activities in the United States, 1846–1954,* Office of the Chief of Military History, Mar. 11, 1970, 99; Thomas William Bohn, "An Historical and

Descriptive Analysis of the *Why We Fight* Series" (Ph.D. diss., University of Wisconsin, 1968), 93.

58. Russell O. Fudge, "Why? The Story of Information in the American Army" *Armored Cavalry Journal* 59, no. 2 (Mar.–Apr., 1950): 18; Pulwers, "Information and Education Programs," 35; Wesbrook, *Political Training*, 17–18.

59. Hilton H. Railey, "Morale of the United States Army: An Appraisal for the *New York Times*, 1941," archives, MHI, 7, 165, 172 (hereafter Railey Report).

60. Wesbrook, *Political Training*, 19; Railey Report, 180.

61. Railey Report, 182; Roger Barry Fosdick, "A Call to Arms: The American Enlisted Soldier in World War II" (Ph.D. diss., Claremont Graduate School, 1985), 40–42.

62. Arthur George Haggis Jr., "An Appraisal of the Administration, Scope, and Function of the United States Army Troop Information Program" (Ed.D. diss., Wayne State University, 1961), 18; Wesbrook, *Political Training*, 19.

63. Gen. Brehon Somervell as quoted in Thomas A. Palmer, "'Why We Fight': A Study of Indoctrination Activities in the Armed Forces" (Ph.D. diss., University of South Carolina, 1971), 20.

64. Forrest C. Pogue, *George C. Marshall: Organizer of Victory, 1943–1945*, 93.

65. Wesbrook, *Political Training*, 21; Fosdick, "Call to Arms," 53, 79.

66. Pogue, *Marshall: Ordeal and Hope*, 110. See also Edward Stuart Wells, "A History of the United States Army's Internal Information Program" (M.P.A. thesis, New York University, 1958).

67. Bohn, "Historical and Descriptive Analysis," 95–96; U.S. War Department, Information and Education Division, "Study of Information and Education Activities, World War II," Study no. 76, Bad Nauheim, Germany, Apr. 6, 1946, copy in MHI Library, 79.

68. Robert L. Gushwa, *The Best and Worst of Times: The United States Army Chaplaincy, 1920–1945*, 93.

69. David Culbert, "*Why We Fight*: Social Engineering for a Democratic Society at War," in *Film and Radio Propaganda in World War II*, ed. K. R. M. Short, 173.

70. Pulwers, "Information and Education Programs," 28.

71. Ibid., 244.

72. Fosdick, "Call to Arms," 288; Culbert, "*Why We Fight*," 174.

73. Pulwers, "Information and Education Programs," 336. See also Stefan Kuhl, *The Nazi Connection: Eugenics, American Racism, and German National Socialism*; Kenneth M. Ludmerer, *Genetics and American Society: A Historical Appraisal*; and Mark H. Haller, *Eugenics: Hereditary Attitudes in American Thought*.

74. James Edward Tobin, "*Why We Fight*: Versions of the American Purpose in World War II" (Ph.D. diss., University of Michigan, 1986), 89–93.

75. Clayton D. Laurie, *The Propaganda Warriors: America's Crusade Against Nazi Germany*, 235; Clayton R. Koppes and Gregory D. Black, *Hollywood Goes to War: How Politics, Profits, and Propaganda Shaped World War II Movies*, 59–60, 64.

76. Barry E. Cardwell, "Film and Motivation: The *Why We Fight* Series" (student paper, U.S. Army War College, 1991), 55.

77. Joseph McBride, *Frank Capra: The Catastrophe of Success*, 466; Bernard F. Dick, *The Star-Spangled Screen: The American World War II Film*, 4, 6; Bohn, "Historical and Descriptive Analysis," 75; Tobin, "*Why We Fight*," 113, 133, 118.

78. As quoted in Pulwers, "Information and Education Programs," 70.

79. Ibid., 216–17; Palmer, "Why We Fight," 21.

Chapter 2

1. Mason Weems, *A History of the Life and Death, Virtues & Exploits of General George Washington,* ed. Mark VanDoren, 182; Karal Ann Marling, *George Washington Slept Here: Colonial Revivals and American Culture, 1876–1986,* 3–4; Treese, *Valley Forge,* 100; Howell Walker, "Washington Lives Again at Valley Forge," *National Geographic,* Feb., 1954, 187–202.

2. Paul F. Boller Jr., *George Washington and Religion,* 10; Treese, *Valley Forge,* 12–13. See also Barbara MacDonald Powell, "The Most Celebrated Encampment: Valley Forge in American Culture, 1777–1983" (Ph.D. diss., Cornell University, 1983).

3. Alton Lee, "Army Mutiny of 1946," *Journal of American History* 53, no. 3 (Dec., 1966): 559; Jack Stokes Ballard, *The Shock of Peace: Military and Economic Demobilization after World War II,* 88, 93.

4. Kay Geiger, "The Demobilization of American Forces Following World War II" (M.S. thesis, Kansas State College of Pittsburgh, 1965), 13.

5. Ballard, *Shock of Peace,* 97; John C. Sparrow, *History of Personnel Demobilization in the U.S. Army,* 252.

6. Hanson W. Baldwin, "Military Chiefs Blamed: Low Morale in Services Held Partly Due to Soft Discipline of 'Democratic Army,'" *New York Times,* Sept. 3, 1953; *The Doolittle Report: The Report of the Secretary of War's Board on Officer-Enlisted Man Relationships,* 20–24; Mark R. Grandstaff, "Making the Military American: Advertising, Reform, and the Demise of an Antistanding Military Tradition, 1945–1955," *Journal of Military History* 60, no. 2 (Apr., 1996): 299–323.

7. "The Army Chaplain in the European Theater of Operations," App. 17, "Report of the General Board, United States Forces, European Theater," copy in MHI Library; Marshall as quoted in Gushwa, *Best and Worst,* 186; Merlin Gustafson, "The Church, the State, and the Military in the Truman Administration," *Rocky Mountain Social Science Journal* 2 (Oct., 1965): 6.

8. John Costello, *Virtue Under Fire: How World War II Changed Our Social and Sexual Attitudes,* 76–77; Joel T. Boone, "The Sexual Aspects of Military Personnel," *American Journal of Social Hygiene* 27, no. 3 (Mar., 1941): 116.

9. "Chaplains Condemn Army Entertainment," *United Evangelical Action,* March 15, 1946, 16; Thomas H. Bodie, "Character Guidance Program" (Ph.D. diss., St. John's University, Brooklyn, N.Y., 1953), xiv–xv.

10. Stanley High, "The War Boom in Religion," in *The Army Reader,* ed. Karl Detzer, 295–97; Gushwa, *Best and Worst,* 187; Hutcheson, *Churches and the Chaplaincy,* 147.

11. Stimson as quoted in Guy Oakes, *The Imaginary War: Civil Defense and American Cold War Culture,* 22.

12. Henry as quoted in Erling Jorstad, *Evangelicals in the White House: The Cultural Maturation of Born Again Christianity, 1960–1981,* 12–13.

13. Lawrence Leland Lacour, "A Study of the Revival Method in America (1920–1955) with Special Reference to Billy Sunday, Aimee Semple McPherson, and Billy Graham" (Ph.D. diss., Northwestern University, 1956), 274–76.

14. Joel A. Carpenter, "Fundamentalist Institutions and the Rise of Evangelical Protestantism, 1929–1942," *Church History* (Mar., 1980): 62–75; Richard John Neuhaus and Michael Cromartie, eds., *Piety and Politics: Evangelicals and Fundamentalists Confront the World;* Douglas A. Sweeny, "The Neo-Evangelical Movement, 1941–1960: Toward a More Thorough Historiographical Approach" (M.A. thesis, Trinity Evangelical Divinity School, 1984).

15. Joel A. Carpenter, "Youth for Christ and the New Evangelicals," in *Reckoning with the Past: Historical Essays on American Evangelicalism from the Institute for the Study of American Evangelicals,* ed. D. G. Hart, 354–75.

16. Steven Warren Guerrier, "NSC-68 and the Truman Rearmament: 1950–1953" (Ph.D. diss., University of Michigan, 1988), 3.

17. James A. Owre, "Unification of the Armed Forces: Derivation and Analysis of War Department and Navy Department Positions on Postwar Military Structure, 1945" (M.A. thesis, Queens College, 1970), 90.

18. William L. O'Neill, *American High: The Years of Confidence, 1945–1960,* 106; Charles B. Roberts, "Unification of the Armed Forces a Problem in Administration" (M.A. thesis, Duke University, 1953); Wells Brendell Lange, "The Army Position in the Unification Controversy Preceding the Passage of the National Security Act of 1947" (M.A. thesis, University of Rhode Island, 1961); Robert E. Fisher, "The U.S. Navy's Search for a Strategy, 1945–1947," *Naval War College Review* 58, no. 3 (summer, 1995): 73–86; Jeffery M. Dorwart, *Eberstadt and Forrestal: A National Security Partnership, 1909–1949;* idem., "Forrestal and the Navy Plan of 1945: Mahanian Doctrine of Corporatist Blueprint" in *New Interpretations in Naval History,* ed., William B. Cogar, 209–23.

19. Gaetano Vincitorio, ed., *Studies in Modern History,* 353; Herman S. Wolk, "The Battle of the B-36," *Air Force,* July, 1996, 60–65; "The Navy: Storm Over the Pentagon," *Newsweek,* Oct. 17, 1949, 23. See also Joseph J. Corn, *The Winged Gospel: America's Romance with Aviation, 1900–1950;* and Jeffery G. Barlow, *Revolt of the Admirals: The Fight for Naval Aviation, 1945–1950.*

20. Charles Pearre Cabell, "Power for Peace: Unification of the Armed Forces Speech to be delivered in Dallas, Texas, 15 May 1953"; Owre, "Unification of the Armed Forces," 90–93. See also Christopher C. Shoemaker, *The NSC Staff: Counseling the Council;* and "Statement by Fleet Admiral Chester W. Nimitz, USN Chief of Naval Operations before the Senate Naval Affairs Committee at Hearings on S. 2044," "Unification (1)" file, box 28, Lauris Norstad Papers, Dwight D. Eisenhower Presidential Library, Abilene, Kans. (hereafter Eisenhower Library).

21. Fred J. Cook, "Juggernaut: The Warfare State," *Nation,* Oct. 28, 1961, 286–87; John M. Swomley Jr., *The Growing Power of the Military,* 2–6. See also Richard Kevin Betts, "Soldiers, Statesmen, and the Resort to Force: American Military Influence in Crisis Decisions, 1945–1975" (Ph.D. diss., Harvard University, 1975).

22. The best treatment of evangelicals in the military is Anne C. Loveland, *American Evangelicals and the U.S. Military, 1942–1993.* See also Donald F. Crosby, S. J., *Battlefield Chaplains: Catholic Priests in World War II,* xvi–xvii; Israel Drazin and Cecil B. Currey, *For God and Country: The History of a Constitutional Challenge to the Army Chaplaincy,* 32, 34; Robert E. Klitgaard, "Onward Christian Soldiers: Dehumanization and the Military Chaplain," *Christian Century,* Nov. 18, 1970, 1377.

23. Neal C. Dirkse, "The Evangelical Emphasis in the United States Army Chaplaincy" (M.A. thesis, Pasadena College, 1956), 3–12; Klitgaard, "Onward Christian Soldiers," 1379; "Orphaned Chaplains," *Christian Century,* Nov. 22, 1944, 1342–43.

24. Gustafson, "Church, the State," 5; Dirske, "Evangelical Emphasis," 13; Cox, *Military Chaplains,* 94.

25. Robert C. Vickers, "The Military Chaplaincy: A Study in Role Conflict" (Ph.D. diss., George Peabody College for Teachers, Vanderbilt University, 1984); Cox, *Military Chaplains,* 107. See also Waldo W. Burchard, "Role Conflicts of Military Chaplains," in *Religion, Society, and the Individual: an Introduction to Sociology of Religion,* by J. Milton Yinger, 596–99.

26. Brooks, "Military Religion," 5–7, 18–19, 220–21; Cox, *Military Chaplains,* 94, 108.

27. George Dugan, "Military Church Decried as Trend," *New York Times,* Jan. 31, 1957; Drew Pearson, "One Church for Protestant GIs?" *Washington Post,* July 14, 1957; Anne Loveland, unpublished MS, copy in author's possession.

28. Brooks, "Military Religion," 5–7, 18–19, 220–21; Hutcheson, *Churches and the Chaplaincy,* 130; Cox, *Military Chaplains,* 89.

29. Carpenter, "Fundamentalist Institutions," 62–75.

30. Loveland, *American Evangelicals,* 2, 6–8; Hutcheson, *Churches and the Chaplaincy,* 123–24; "What Happens when Protestants are Caught Napping," *Christian Century,* July 5, 1944, 797; "Orphaned Chaplains," 1342–43; "Needed Chaplaincy Reforms," *Christian Century,* Feb. 28, 1951, 261–62; Marcia S. Littell, "Interfaith Rituals, Symbols and Experience: Working Reports on Their Promise and Problems," *Dialogue and Alliance: Journal of the International Religious Foundation* 3, no. 1 (spring, 1989): 76.

31. Loveland, *American Evangelicals,* 1, 4, 7; Gustafson, "Church, the State," 56.

32. Erving Goffman, *Asylums: Essays on the Social Situation of Mental Patients and Other Inmates,* 3–121; Hutcheson, *Churches and the Chaplaincy,* 45; Klitgaard, "Onward Christian Soldiers," 1377.

33. *A Ministry of Presence,* VHS (Fort Jackson, S.C.: U.S. Army Chaplain Center and School, 1990); "The Word at Work," Apr., 1945, "at an Induction Center," "Film Armed Forces" folder, unnumbered box, archives, Moody Bible Institute, Chicago (hereafter MBI); Cox, *Military Chaplains,* 106; Earl Parvin, *Missions USA,* 228–30.

34. "Air Force 'Pick-a-Faith' Drive Called Dictatorial," *Church and State,* Sept., 1955, 5.

35. Parvin, *Missions USA,* 226; Cox, *Military Chaplains,* 106; Hutcheson, *Churches and the Chaplaincy,* 1.

36. Grandstaff, "Making the Military American," 302; Robert H. Ferrell, ed., *Dear Bess: The Letters from Harry to Bess Truman, 1910–1959,* 356–67; Richard F. Haynes, *The Awesome Power: Harry S. Truman as Commander in Chief,* 14–16.

37. Pearlman, *To Make Democracy Safe,* 236; Richard Lawrence Miller, *Truman: The Rise to Power,* 364–68.

38. H. Kenaston Twitchell to Harry S. Truman, June 21, 1947, folder 109, box 611, Harry S. Truman Papers, Harry S. Truman Presidential Library, Independence, Mo. (hereafter Truman Papers); Merlin Gustafson, "The Religion of a President," *Journal of Church and State* 10, no. 3 (1968): 379–87.

39. "Address before a Joint Session of the Congress on Universal Military Training, Oct. 23, 1945, *Public Papers of the Presidents of the United States: Harry S. Truman,* vol. 1, *1945,* 408.

40. Harry S. Truman, *Memoirs of Harry S. Truman*, 1:511.

41. Lawrence R. Mallery Jr., comp., *Sourcebook: Peacetime Compulsory Military Training*, American Friends Service Committee, n.d., 16.

42. "Analysis of Ft. Knox Experiment U.M.T. Unit," *Conscription News*, May 15, 1947.

43. Ibid.; *The Fort Knox Experiment, 1947*, 4.

44. American Legion, *The Fort Knox Experiment*, 3.

45. Matthew H. Imrie, "The Fort Knox Experiment," *Army and Navy Chaplain*, Apr.–May, 1947, 2–6, 32; Mallery, *Sourcebook*, 18; "Analysis of Ft. Knox Experiment U.M.T. Unit—Part II," *Conscription News*, May 22, 1947, 3.

46. They were Morris E. Eson (Jewish), Charles J. Murphy (Roman Catholic), and Maury Hundley Jr. (Disciples of Christ). See Roger R. Venzke, *Confidence in Battle, Inspiration in Peace: The United States Army Chaplaincy, 1945–75*, 42.

47. War Department, Office of the Chief of Chaplains, Mar. 24, 1947, "Report on the Fort Knox Experiment with the Universal Military Training Proposal," folder 357x17, 17c, 17f 1947, box 357x3, Fort Knox Experiment, Lewis B. Hershey Papers, archives, MHI.

48. Venzke, *Confidence in Battle*, 42.

49. Lewis Minyon Durden, "The Army Character Guidance Program" (M.Th. thesis, Yale University, 1952), 17; Venzke, *Confidence in Battle*, 40.

50. The VD rate was 10.2 compared with 41.2 for all other white troops at this station during the same period. See John M. Devine, "Interim Report: UMT Experimental Unit, Fort Knox, Kentucky," Aug. 1, 1947, "(3) UMT Fort Knox Experiment" folder, box 41, President's Committee on Religion and Welfare in the Armed Forces, Harry S. Truman Presidential Library, Independence, Mo. (hereafter Truman Library), 11.

51. Ibid.; "Analysis of Ft. Knox Experiment—Part II," 3.

52. "Spiritually Busy," *UMT Pioneer*, May 1, 1948, copy in MHI Library, 8.

53. Devine, "Interim Report," 27.

54. "Analysis of Ft. Knox Experiment—Part II," 12.

55. "Remarks to the President's Advisory Commission on Universal Training, Dec. 20, 1946, *Public Papers of the Presidents of the United States: Harry S. Truman*, vol. 2, *1946*, 509; Haynes, *Awesome Power*, 84.

56. Report of the President's Advisory Commission on Universal Training, *A Program for National Security*, 72, 74.

57. Gena Elaine Mitchell, "Universal Military Training and the Truman Administration" (M.A. thesis, Georgia Southern College, 1971), 60, 68.

58. John Whiteclay Chambers II, *Draftees or Volunteers: A Documentary History of the Debate over Military Conscription in the United States, 1787–1973*, 361–62, 369–70; Jonathan Jacob Balkind, "Morale Deterioration in the United States Military during the Vietnam Era" (Ph.D. diss., University of California, Los Angeles, 1978), 68–69; Grandstaff, "Making the Military American," 302.

59. "Harry S. Truman's remarks at the Armed Forces Dinner, May 19, 1950," *Public Papers of the Presidents of the United States: Harry S. Truman*, vol. 6, *1950*, 423–25.

60. Balkind, "Morale Deterioration," 69.

61. Gustafson, "Church, the State," 3.

62. "Report to the President on Moral Safeguards for Trainees to be Inducted under

the Selective Service Act," Sept. 13, 1948, "Reports by Others" folder, box 37, President's Committee on Religion and Welfare in the Armed Forces, Truman Papers.

63. "Statement by the President Making Public a Report on Moral Safeguards for Selective Service Trainees," Sept. 16, 1948, in *Public Papers of the Presidents of the United States: Harry S. Truman*, vol. 4, *1948*, 488; Committee Meetings, Dec. 3, 1948, President's Committee on Religion and Welfare in the Armed Forces file, folder (2b), box 3, President's Committee on Religion and Welfare in the Armed Forces, Truman Papers.

64. "Urges Religious Support," *Army Navy Air Force Journal*, Oct. 14, 1950, newspaper clipping, "Press Clippings Re: Committee and its Members" folder, box 2, President's Committee on Religion and Welfare in the Armed Forces, Truman Papers.

65. *Information and Education in the Armed Services: A Report to the President by the President's Commission on Religion and Welfare in the Armed Forces*, 16.

66. Durden, "Army Character Guidance Program," 20, 38; Venzke, *Confidence in Battle*, 41.

67. Loveland, *American Evangelicals*, 10–11; Durden, "Army Character Guidance Program," 31.

68. "Great Lakes Recruit Command: The Chaplain's Program," *The Chaplain: A Journal for Protestant Chaplains* 9, no. 2 (Mar.–Apr., 1952): 34–35.

69. Bob Ohl, "Navymen: Characters with Character," *All Hands*, Sept., 1954, 14–17; Hutcheson, *Churches and the Chaplaincy*, 149–55.

70. Special Preparedness Subcommittee, Senate Armed Services Committee, *Military Cold War Education and Speech Review Policies*, 1808–10; John G. Hubbell, "Moral Build-Up Gives New Strength to the Navy," in *The Navy Blue Book*, ed. Tom Compere, 131.

71. James Burkhart Gilbert, *Redeeming Culture: American Religion in an Age of Science*, 138.

72. "Denies Air Force Plan Violates Conscience," *Church and State*, Oct., 1955, 2; Bodie, "Character Guidance Program," xvii, 116.

73. John W. Haas Jr., Irwin A. Moon, F. Alton Everest, and Will H. Houghton, "Early Links between the Moody Bible Institute and the American Scientific Affiliation," *Perspectives on Science and Christian Faith* 43, no. 4 (Dec., 1991): 249; Willard B. Gatewood Jr., "From Scopes to Creation Science: The Decline and Revival of the Evolution Controversy," *The South Atlantic Quarterly* 83, no. 4 (autumn, 1984): 364–65.

74. Wilbur M. Smith, *Will H. Houghton: A Watchman on the Wall*, 142–48; F. Alton Everest, "The Moody Institute of Science," *Journal of the American Scientific Affiliation* 5, no. 3 (Sept., 1953): 10–11.

75. Gene Arnold Getz, "A History of Moody Bible Institute and its Contributions to Evangelical Education" (Ph.D. diss., New York University, 1968), 486, 493.

76. "God of Creation," *Sermons from Science* ser., VHS, directed by Irwin Moon (Chicago: Moody Institute of Science, 1992).

77. Weldon D. Woodson, "Those Inspiring Sermons from Science," *Business Screen*, Apr., 1961, 39–40.

78. "Character Guidance Films," untitled folder, box 41, MBI, 24.

79. Getz, "History of Moody Bible Institute," 503; "God of Creation," *Sermons from Science* ser., VHS (Chicago: Moody Bible Institute, 1992); Hutcheson, *Churches and the Chaplaincy,* 147.

80. Gilbert, *Redeeming Culture,* 143.

81. John R. Wilkins, "Three days in the Pentagon," *Christian Century,* Mar. 12, 1952, 308–309. Among the speakers were Vice President Barkley, Defense Secretary Robert Abercrombie Lovett, and Assistant Defense Secretary Anna M. Rosenberg.

82. "A Day with the Navy," *Christian Century,* July 2, 1952, 777–78.

83. Bodie, "Character Guidance Program," 14.

Chapter 3

1. Kenneth Wells, "How Long Will the American Way Endure?" undated paper, copy in author's possession.

2. Kenneth Wells, "Two Hours Alone With Ike," undated paper, copy in author's possession; Kenneth Wells, interview by author, Mar. 31, 1995.

3. Eisenhower as quoted in Richard V. Pierard and Robert D. Linder, *Civil Religion and the Presidency,* 197.

4. George Todt, "George Todt's Opinion," *Los Angeles Herald Expositor,* Nov. 28, 29, and 30, 1960; William G. Wert, "Freedom Group Honors Our Way," *New York Times,* Nov. 22, 1949; George Thayer, *The Farther Shore of Politics: the American Political Fringe Today,* 276; Wells interview.

5. The remainder of Eisenhower's quote reads: "With us of course it is the Jud[e]o-Christian concept but it must be a religion that all men are created equal." See Patrick Henry, "'And I Don't Care What It Is': The Tradition History of a Civil Religion Proof-text," *Journal of the American Academy of Religion* 49, no.1 (Mar., 1981): 35–47.

6. Stephen J. Whitfield, *The Culture of the Cold War,* 100; Oakes, *Imaginary War,* 25.

7. George Kennan as quoted in *Foreign Relations of the United States, 1946,* vol. 6, *Eastern Europe and the Soviet Union,* 696–709; W. Scott Lucas, "Beyond Diplomacy: Propaganda and the History of the Cold War," in *Cold War Propaganda in the 1950s,* ed., Gary D. Rawnsley, 15.

8. Jill Edwards, "The President, the Archbishop and the Envoy: Religion and Diplomacy in the Cold War," *Diplomacy and Statecraft* 6, no. 2 (July, 1995): 490–511; Eugene F. Schmidtlein, "Relations between the Vatican and the Truman Administration," Working Paper Series, ser. 21, no. 3, 1989, Charles and Margaret Hall Cushwa Center for the Study of American Catholicism, University of Notre Dame, Notre Dame, Ind., 32.

9. As quoted in Martin E. Marty, *Modern American Religion,* vol. 3, *Under God, Indivisible, 1941–1960,* 200.

10. Jeannette Lea Williams, "Citizen Response to the Image of Savagery in Harry S. Truman's Korean War Rhetoric" (M.A. thesis, Texas A&M University, 1992).

11. Erik Monrad, "Ideological Continuity in American Foreign Policy and the Origins of the Cold War" (Senior Project, Antioch College, 1992), 42; Richard A. Melanson, "Paul H. Nitze to Norman Podhoretz: The Tradition of Anti-Commu-

nist Containment," in *Traditions and Values: American Diplomacy, 1945–Present,* ed. Kenneth W. Thompson, 147–79.

12. NSC-68 as quoted in Ernest R. May, ed. *American Cold War Strategy: Interpreting NSC 68,* 35.

13. Ibid., 54.

14. This definition is based on the work of Hans Morgenthau in *Politics Among Nations,* 134. See also Lawrence E. Key, *Cultivating National Will: An Introduction to National Will,* 2–8.

15. Oakes, *Imaginary War,* 21–22.

16. Along with May's *American Cold War Strategy,* see S. Nelson Drew, *NSC 68: Forging the Strategy of Containment;* and Keith C. Clark and Laurence J. Legere, eds., *The President and the Management of National Security: A Report by the Institute for Defense Analysis.*

17. Stuart J. Little, "The Freedom Train: Citizenship and Postwar Political Culture, 1946–1949," *American Studies* 34, no. 1 (spring, 1993): 40.

18. J. Wandress to author, May 3, 1996; David A. Pleiffer, "Riding the Rails up Paper Mountain: Researching Railroad Records at NARA," *The Record: News from the National Archives and Records Administration* 29, no. 1 (spring, 1997): 28.

19. Quoted in Little, "Freedom Train," 42.

20. American Heritage Foundation, *A Story of Citizenship in Action,* undated pamphlet, copy in "Eighth National Conference on Citizenship" folder, box 5, Freedoms Foundation Archives, Freedoms Foundation of Valley Forge, Valley Forge, Pa. (hereafter FFA); Jean Preer, "The American Heritage Project: Librarians and the Democratic Tradition in the Early Cold War" *Libraries and Culture* 28, no. 2 (spring, 1993): 165–88.

21. Oakes, *Imaginary War,* 38.

22. General Report, "Project East River," box 19, National Resources Board, RG 304, NARA, College Park, Md.

23. White House Office of Special Assistant for National Security Affairs, "Status of Projects," NSC-142 (4) file, box 3, NSC Series, Eisenhower Library.

24. "Valley Forge Foundation Report on 'Alert America Convoys,'" Feb. 22, 1953, FFA; White House Office of Special Assistant for National Security, "Status of Projects"; Valley Forge Foundation, *The Alert America Convoys,* 1952 pamphlet, copy in FFA; Wells interview; "Alert America Convoys Visited by over 200,000," *Civil Defense Alert* 1, no. 10 (Apr., 1952): 1.

25. Oakes, *Imaginary War,* 50–51.

26. Edward Lilly, "Report by Dr. E. Lilly, December 21, 1951," box 6, White House Office, NSC-OCB Secretariat ser., Eisenhower Library, 73; Lawrence Martin Thomas, "Truth at USIA: The Need for a Mandate" (M.A. thesis, Georgetown University, 1991), 34.

27. Shawn J. Parry-Giles, *The Rhetorical Presidency: Propaganda and the Cold War, 1945–1955,* 54–57.

28. As quoted in W. Scott Lucas, "Campaigns of Truth: The Psychological Strategy Board and American Ideology," *International History Review* 18, no. 2 (May, 1996): 301–302.

29. Terence H. Qualter, *Propaganda and Psychological Warfare,* 127.

30. Fritz G. A. Kraemer, "U.S. Capabilities in the Battle for Men's Minds," paper dated Feb. 3, 1960, box 15, President's Committee on Information Activities Abroad, Eisenhower Library. Emphasis added.

31. Department of State, *The Campaign of Truth: The International Information and Education Exchange Program, 1951,* 1; Wilson Compton, *Waging the Campaign of Truth,* 8.

32. Acheson as quoted in Lucas, "Campaigns of Truth," 287.

33. Parry-Giles, *Rhetorical Presidency,* 63.

34. Lucas, "Campaigns of Truth," 286; Gary Rawnsley, *Cold War Propaganda of the 1950s,* 36–37.

35. Barrett as quoted in Parry-Giles, *Rhetorical Presidency,* 60.

36. Qualter, *Propaganda and Psychological Warfare,* 130; Edward W. Barrett, *Truth Is Our Weapon,* 96; Angelo M. Codevilla, "Political Warfare," in *Political Warfare and Psychological Operations: Rethinking the US Approach,* ed. Frank R. Barnett and Carnes Lord, 80.

37. E. P. Lilly to C. Tracy Barnes, memorandum, Subject "Background Information, White House Office," "Dr. E. P. Lilly" reading file, box 6, NSC Staff, OCB Secretariat ser., Eisenhower Library.

38. Gray as quoted in W. Scott Lucas, *Freedom's War: The American Crusade against the Soviet Union,* 132.

39. George Morgan as quoted in ibid., 145.

40. Barrett, *Truth Is Our Weapon,* 260, 264.

41. Venzke, *Confidence in Battle,* 44.

42. "Comments on President's Committee Report on Information and Education in the Armed Forces," "(4) Reports, I and E Report" folder, box 2, President's Committee on Religion and Welfare in the Armed Forces, Truman Library.

43. Dwight D. Eisenhower, *At Ease: Stories I Tell to Friends,* 345–51; Steve Neal, *The Eisenhowers,* 240, 250–51; Travis B. Jacobs, "Dwight D. Eisenhower's Presidency of Columbia University," *Presidential Studies Quarterly* 25, no. 3 (summer, 1995): 555–60.

44. Richard William Streb, "A History of the Citizenship Education Project: A Model Curricular Study" (Ed.D. diss., Teachers College, Columbia University, 1979); Travis B. Jacobs, "Eisenhower, the American Assembly, and Columbia University," *Presidential Studies Quarterly* 22, no. 3 (summer, 1992): 455–68.

45. Richard R. Moser, *The New Winter Soldiers: GI and Veteran Dissent during the Vietnam Era,* 23–25.

46. Whitfield, *Culture of the Cold War,* 77; Jorstad, *Evangelicals in the White House,* 14.

47. Billy Graham as quoted in Marty, *Under God, Indivisible,* 330.

48. Graham as quoted in William G. McLoughlin Jr., *Billy Graham: Revivalist in a Secular Age,* 87–89.

49. Edward Martin and John Foster Dulles as quoted in Whitfield, *Culture of the Cold War,* 87.

50. Billy Graham as quoted in Keith J. Hardman, *Seasons of Refreshing: Evangelicalism and Revivals in America,* 252–53.

51. In later years, Graham took full responsibility for the misunderstanding over their

White House consultation. See Danny R. Day, "The Political Billy Graham: Graham and Politics from the Presidency of Harry S. Truman through the Presidency of Lyndon Baines Johnson" (M.A. thesis, Wheaton College, 1996), 47.

52. James H. Smylie, "The President as Prophet and King: Clerical Reflections on the Death of Washington," *Journal of Church and State* 18, no. 2 (spring, 1976): 95; James David Fairbanks, "The Priestly Functions of the Presidency: A Discussion of the Literature on Civil Religion and its Implications for the Study of Presidential Leadership," *Presidential Studies Quarterly* 11, no. 2 (spring, 1981): 214–32; idem., "Religious Dimensions of Presidential Leadership: The Case of Dwight Eisenhower," *Presidential Studies Quarterly* 12, no. 2 (spring, 1982): 260–67.

53. Eisenhower as quoted in Pierard and Linder, *Civil Religion*, 192–93; Robert D. Linder and Richard V. Pierard, *Twilight of the Saints: Biblical Christianity and Civil Religion in America*, 95.

54. Day, "Political Billy Graham," 7, 50.

55. Pierard and Linder, *Civil Religion*, 198.

56. Day, "Political Billy Graham," 53; Sydney E. Ahlstrom, *A Religious History of the American People*, 954.

57. Fairbanks, "Priestly Functions," 225; Linder and Pierard, *Twilight of the Saints*, 99.

58. Pierard and Linder, *Civil Religion*, 202.

59. Richard V. Pierard, "Billy Graham and the U.S. Presidency," *Journal of Church and State* 22, no. 1 (winter, 1980): 146.

60. Linder and Pierard, *Twilight of the Saints*, 97; Whitfield, *Culture of the Cold War*, 88.

61. Day, "Political Billy Graham," 53–54, 57, 60; Pierard, "Billy Graham," 146.

62. Marty, *Under God, Indivisible*, 302–303.

63. Pierard and Linder, *Civil Religion*, 203; Elson as quoted in Loveland, *American Evangelicals*, 35.

64. Lt. Gen. William K. Harrison Jr. as quoted in Loveland, *American Evangelicals*, 53.

65. Ahlstrom, *Religious History*, 954; Merlin Gustafson, "The Religious Role of the President," *Midwest Journal of Political Science* 14, no. 4 (Nov., 1970): 709–11; Fairbanks, "Priestly Functions," 214.

66. Quoted in Marty, *Under God, Indivisible*, 296.

67. Gustafson, "Religious Role," 709–11; Pierard and Linder, *Civil Religion*, 200–201.

68. Quoted in Stephen Wainwright Twing, "American Culture and the Cold War: An Exploration of the Cultural Shaping of Three Cold Warriors" (Ph.D. diss., University of South Carolina, 1995), 152.

69. Ibid.

70. Quoted in Oakes, *Imaginary War*, 23.

71. Twing, "American Culture," 153, 157, 163; Michael J. Devine, "The Diplomacy of Righteousness: The Legacy of John W. Foster," in *Traditions and Values: American Diplomacy, 1945–Present*, ed. Kenneth W. Thompson, 21–42. See also Brian Edward Klunk, "The Idea of America's Mission and its Role in the Beliefs and Diplomacy of John Foster Dulles and Jimmy Carter" (Ph.D. diss., University of Virginia, 1985).

72. Paul Allen Carter, *Another Part of the Fifties*, 114–15.

73. Marty, *Under God, Indivisible*, 301.

74. Linder and Pierard, *Twilight of the Saints*, 95; Carter, *Another Part of the Fifties*, 116.

75. Richard G. Hutcheson, *God in the White House: How Religion Has Changed the Modern Presidency*, 35.

Chapter 4

1. Walker, "Washington Lives Again," 187–202; *National Council Against Conscription, The Militarization of America: Report Issued by Albert Eisenhower, Dorothy Canfield Fisher, Reuben Gustavson, William J. Millor, S.J., Arthur Morgan, Ray Lyman Wilbur and Fifteen Others*, 26. The BSA had been conducting annual pilgrimages to Valley Forge on George Washington's birthday since 1913.

2. *Public Papers: Truman*, 5:513–16.

3. Treese, *Valley Forge*, 160–61; Valley Forge Park Commission, *Report of the Valley Forge Park Commission, Commonwealth of Pennsylvania, January, 1947, to January, 1951*, 14–19.

4. Quoted in Treese, *Valley Forge*, 159.

5. Quoted in ibid., 161.

6. "Jamboree Logistics are Biggest Camping Job," *Jamboree Journal*, July 21, 1964; John R. Murphy, "Scouts Thrill to VIPs Resume Hectic Pace," *Philadelphia Inquirer*, July 21, 1964; Senate Armed Services Committee, *Authorizing Military Support to the Sixth National Jamboree of the Boy Scouts of America, Valley Forge State Park, Pa.;* "Spectacular Show, Fireworks give Jamboree Brilliant Start," *Norristown Times Herald*, July 18, 1964; Treese, *Valley Forge*, 162.

7. "Question Box," *The Picket Post: A Record of Patriotism*, January, 1965, 29.

8. Grandstaff, "Making the Military American," 322; Douglas Kinnard, *President Eisenhower and Strategy Management: A Study in Defense Politics*, 8–9.

9. Thomas Bodenheimer and Robert Gould, *Rollback! Right-Wing Power in U.S. Foreign Policy*, 15–30.

10. Daun Van EE, "From the New Look to Flexible Response, 1953–1964," in *Against All Enemies: Interpretations of American Military History from Colonial Times to the Present*, ed. Kenneth J. Hagan and William R. Roberts, 329–31.

11. Andrew J. Bacevich, *The Pentomic Era: The U.S. Army Between Korea and Vietnam*, 19–24; Grandstaff, "Making the Military American," 313–14.

12. Robert Louis Benson and Michael Warner, eds., *Venona: Soviet Espionage and the American Response, 1939–1957*, xxxii.

13. Stephen Jurika Jr., ed., *From Pearl Harbor to Vietnam: The Memoirs of Admiral Arthur W. Radford*, 317–20; Kenneth W. Condit, *The Joint Chiefs of Staff and National Policy: 1955–1956*, 61–64; Willard J. Webb and Ronald H. Cole, *The Chairmen of the Joint Chiefs of Staff*, 45–49; Bacevich, *Pentomic Era*, 45.

14. Robert A. Divine, *The Sputnik Challenge*, 205.

15. Eisenhower as quoted in Blanche Wiesen Cook, "First Comes the Lie: C. D. Jackson and Political Warfare," *Radical History Review*, Dec., 1984, 42.

16. Shawn J. Parry-Giles, "Rhetorical Experimentation and the Cold War, 1947–1953: The Development of an Internationalist Approach to Propaganda," *Quarterly Journal of Speech* 80, no. 4 (Nov., 1994): 458–59; Clark and Legere, eds., *President and the Management*, 62–63; Lucas, "Campaigns of Truth," 294–96; Hans N. Tuch

and G. Lewis Schmidt, eds., *Ike and USIA: A Commemorative Symposium*, 10. The eight-member Jackson Committee was named for its chair, William Jackson, although C. D. Jackson was also a member.

17. "An Organizational History of the National Security Council," "NSC-General (Apr.–Dec., 1960) (7)" folder, box 5, Administration subser., White House Office of Special Assistant for National Security Affairs, NSC ser., Eisenhower Library; Kinnard, *President Eisenhower*, 16; Laura R. Gerber, "The People-to-People Program: A Case of Legitimate Goals vs. Government Bureaucracy" (History Senior Seminar paper, Goshen College, Goshen, Ind., 1993), 5.

18. John Joseph Yerechko, "From Containment to Counteroffensive: Soviet Vulnerabilities and American Policy Planning, 1946–1953" (Ph.D. diss., University of California–Berkeley, 1980), 212–81.

19. Bodenheimer and Gould, *Rollback!* 19–29.

20. McCarthy as quoted in David M. Oshinsky, *A Conspiracy So Immense: The World of Joe McCarthy*, 285.

21. Tuch and Schmidt, *Ike and USIA*, 17–18; Oshinsky, *Conspiracy So Immense*, 278; Richard Gid Powers, *Not Without Honor: The History of American Anticommunism*, 267–68; Robert Goldston, *The American Nightmare: Senator Joseph R. McCarthy and the Politics of Hate*, 152.

22. Goldston, *American Nightmare*, 151; Ellen Schrecker, *The Age of McCarthyism: A Brief History with Documents*, 64; Kyle A. Cuordileone, "Politics in an Age of Anxiety: Masculinity, the Vital Center, and American Political Culture in the Cold War, 1949–1963" (Ph.D. diss., University of California–Irvine, 1995), 148; Norman Dorsen and John G. Simon "McCarthy and the Army: A Fight on the Wrong Front," in *Decisions and Revisions: Interpretations of Twentieth-Century American History*, ed. Jean Christie, 280–85.

23. Joe L. Dubbert, *A Man's Place: Masculinity in Transition*, 254, 257; J. Robert Moskin, "Why do Women Dominate Him" in George Leonard et al., *The Decline of the American Male*, 3.

24. Donald J. Mrozek, "The Cult and Ritual of Toughness in Cold War America" in *Rituals and Ceremonies in Popular Culture*, ed. Ray B. Browne, 178–90.

25. Allan Berube, *Coming Out Under Fire: The History of Gay Men and Women in World War II*, 256.

26. Cuordileone, "Politics," 104; Geoffrey S. Smith, "National Security and Personal Isolation: Sex, Gender, and Disease in the Cold War United States," *International History Review* 14, no. 2 (May, 1992): 318–21.

27. Smith, "National Security," 327; Mary Ann Humphrey, *My Country, My Right to Serve: Experiences of Gay Men and Women in the Military, World War II to the Present*, 1; Cuordileone, "Politics," 105, 127.

28. Mrozek, "Cult and Ritual," 179.

29. Department of Defense, "Code of Conduct Program: First Progress Report," "Code of Conduct Program: Defense (1)" file, box 2, Subject subser., Special Assistant ser., Eisenhower Library, 2. (The three separate progress reports on the Code of Conduct program will hereafter be cited as either the First, Second, or Third Progress Report. The second report is in ibid., "Code of Conduct Program: Defense (2)" file, and the third report is in ibid., "Code of Conduct Program: Defense (3)" file).

30. Albert D. Biderman, *March to Calumny: The Story of American POWs in the Korean War*, 1–12; Eugene Kinkead, *In Every War but One*, 18, 148–49; Chip Young, "Name, Rank, and Serial Fiction: Korea and the First American POWs of Limited War," unpublished paper in author's possession; Susan L. Carruthers, "Not Just Washed but Dry Cleaned: Korea and the 'Brainwashing' Scare of the 1950s," in *Cold War Propaganda in the 1950s*, ed. Gary D. Rawnsley, 47–66; Ron Robin, *The Making of the Cold War Enemy: Culture and Politics in the Military-Intellectual Complex*, 162–81; Virginia Pasley, *21 Stayed: The Story of the American GIs Who Chose Communist China—Who They Were and Why They Stayed*; William E. Mayer, "Why Did Many GI Captives Cave In?" *U.S. News and World Report*, Feb. 24, 1956, 57–72.

31. Albert D. Biderman, "Dangers of Negative Patriotism," *Harvard Business Review* 40, no. 6 (Nov.–Dec., 1962): 93–99; idem., *March to Calumny*, 244; Dwight D. Eisenhower, Executive Order 10631, "The Code of Conduct," Aug. 17, 1955.

32. William Brinkley, "Valley Forge GIs Tell of Their Brainwashing Ordeal," *Life*, May 25, 1953, 108–24.

33. Thomas Alfred Palmer, "Why We Fight: A Study of Indoctrination Activities in the Armed Forces" (Ph.D. diss., University of South Carolina, 1971), 32–33.

34. H. S. Craig, memorandum for the record, "Returned POWs at Valley Forge General Hospital," May 12, 1953, "Prisoners of War, Korea Repatriations" file, PSB Central Files ser. 383.6, Eisenhower Library; "Ex-captives, Called Dupes of Reds, Flown Back to U.S. Amid Secrecy," *New York Times*, May 2, 1953; C. D. Jackson to Gen. Wilton B. Persons, memorandum, Nov. 5, 1953, box 7A, ibid.; Max Hastings, *The Korean War*, 321.

35. "Brain Washing at Valley Forge," *Nation*, May 23, 1953, 425–26; "Snafu at Valley Forge," *Newsweek*, May 18, 1953, 44–45.

36. Biderman, *March to Calumny*, 12.

37. "Ex-Captives Deny Disloyalty Taint," *New York Times*, May 4, 1953.

38. "Brain Washing at Valley Forge," 426.

39. Operations Coordinating Board, "National Operations Plan to Exploit Communist Bacteriological Warfare Hoax, Mistreatment of Prisoners of War, and Other Atrocities Perpetrated by Communist Forces During the Korean War," Oct. 9, 1953, box 26, PSB Central Files ser. 383.6, Eisenhower Library.

40. Norman Gary Horton, "Participation by the Military in the Anti-Communist Indoctrination of the Public" (M.A. thesis: University of Massachusetts, 1964), 49.

41. Christopher S. DeRosa, "A Million Thinking Bayonets: Political Indoctrination in the United States Army" (Ph.D. diss., Temple University, 2000), 181–82.

42. Eisenhower as quoted in Palmer, "Why We Fight," 32–33.

43. U.S. Department of Defense, *POW: The Fight Continues After the Battle: The Report of the Secretary of Defense's Advisory Committee on Prisoners of War*, 5–6; H. H. Wubben, "American Prisoners of War in Korea: A Second Look at the 'Something New in History' Theme," *American Quarterly* 22, no. 1 (spring, 1970): 4.

44. Peter Karsten, "American POWs in Korea and the Citizen Soldier: Triumph or Disaster?" in *The Military in America: From the Colonial Era to the Present*, ed. idem., 375.

45. Department of Defense, *POW*, 17.

46. Quoted in Young, "Name, Rank, and Serial Fiction," 25–62.

47. Special Preparedness Subcommittee, *Military Cold War Education,* 1250.

48. Ibid., 1166.

49. "Second Progress Report," 8–9; Mrozek, "Cult and Ritual," 182.

50. Of the 4,428 POWs repatriated, the army suspected only 565 of collaboration. The charges against 426 of those men were immediately dropped. The Defense Department dealt with ninety-two cases administratively and held fourteen courts-martial resulting in eleven convictions (Special Preparedness Subcommittee, *Military Cold War Education,* 562).

51. "Training Your Men in the Code of Conduct," *Navy Training Bulletin,* Feb., 1956, 11; Department of Defense, *POW,* 15; "Second Progress Report," 2–3.

52. Thomas, "Truth at USIA," 47.

53. Department of Defense, *POW,* vii.

54. Kenneth P. Landon to Elmer B. Staats, Feb. 11, 1955, OCB 091.4 "Ideological Programs" folder, file no. 2 (6) (Jan.–May 1955), box 71, Eisenhower Library; Palmer, "Why We Fight," 47–48; Loveland, *American Evangelicals,* 57.

55. Palmer, "Why We Fight," 52.

56. Ibid., 49.

57. Ibid., 50. See House of Representatives, *Investigation of Participation of Federal Officials of the War Department in Publicity and Propaganda, as it Relates to Universal Military Training,* H.R. 1073, 80th Cong., 1st sess., July 24, 1947, 24. For more on Militant Liberty, see Special Preparedness Subcommittee, *Military Cold War Education,* 1047; William Harlan Hale, "Militant Liberty and the Pentagon," *Reporter,* Feb. 9, 1956, 30–34; and U.S. Department of Defense, *Militant Liberty: A Program of Evaluation and Assessment of Freedom.*

58. Quotes are taken from Francis Stonor Saunders, *Who Paid the Piper: The CIA and the Cultural Cold War,* 284–85.

59. "First Progress Report," 5–6.

60. Ibid., 7; "Third Progress Report," 2–3.

61. "Second Progress Report," 2.

62. "Third Progress Report," 3.

63. As quoted in Kenneth Alan Osgood, "Total Cold War: United States Propaganda in the 'Free World,' 1953–1960" (Ph.D. diss., University of California–Santa Barbara, 2001), 309, 312; "Second Progress Report," 2.

64. Ibid., 59–60.

65. Ibid., 55.

66. John E. Juergensmeyer, *The President, the Foundations, and the People-to-People Program,* 58.

67. Loveland, *American Evangelicals,* 7, 25, 40, 64.

Chapter 5

1. "Cold War Conference Set for Today in SU," *Arkansas Traveler,* Apr. 14, 1961; "Roll Back the Shadow," folder 1, box 26, subser. 19, ser. 4, J. William Fulbright Papers, Special Collections Division, University of Arkansas Libraries, Fayetteville (hereafter JWF Papers); "Seminar Speakers Issue Call to Defend U.S. Principles," *Southwest*

Times Record, Apr. 15, 1961; Thomas B. Pryor to Jack Yingling, Aug. 9 and 10, 1961, folder 1, box 26, subser. 19, ser. 4, JWF Papers. Admiral Ward's quote at the beginning of the chapter is in: "Excerpts from Memorandum for the Deputy Secretary of Defense of July 27, 1961," Seminars "Cold War" secret file, box 82, Records of Robert S. McNamara, RG 200, National Archives Gift Collection, NARA, College Park, Md. (hereafter McNamara Papers).

2. Clifton Lloyd Ganus, interview by author, June, 1994, Harding College, Searcy, Ark.; William E. Drenner, president of City National Bank, to J. William Fulbright, Aug. 14, 1961, folder 5, box 28, subser. 19, ser. 4, JWF Papers; Thomas B. Pryor to Jack Yingling, Sept. 27, 1961, folder 1, box 26, ibid.; Mrs. Carl D. Corley to J. William Fulbright, Sept. 6, 1961, folder 4, box 28, ibid.

3. Brig. Gen. Wallace P. Campbell (Ret.), "Our Stake in the Far East," in *Report on Proceedings: Freedom Forum XXII, Panel, Speeches, Recommendations,* 81.

4. Sen. J. William Fulbright, "Memorandum Submitted to Department of Defense on Propaganda Activities of Military Personnel," Aug. 2, 1961, folder 1, box 26, subser. 19, ser. 4, JWF Papers.

5. Ibid.; "A Report on the Fulbright Memo," July 27, 1961, Seminars "Cold War" secret file, box 82, McNamara Papers.

6. Special Preparedness Subcommittee, Senate Armed Services Committee, *Report on Military Cold War Education and Speech Review Policies,* 28–29.

7. Cabell Phillips, "Rightwing Officers Worrying Pentagon," *New York Times,* June 18, 1961; George W. Brown, *Generals and the Public: Recent Policymaking in Civil-Military Relations,* 5; Miss Jean Scruggs to J. William Fulbright, Sept. 26, 1961, folder 2, box 28, subser. 19, ser. 4, JWF Papers.

8. "Statement of Senator J. W. Fulbright Relating to a Memorandum Submitted by Him to the Department of Defense," folder 4, box 25, subser. 19, ser. 4, JWF Papers.

9. Special Preparedness Subcommittee, *Report,* 7.

10. Phillips, "Rightwing Officers"; Congress, Senate, 87th Cong., 1st sess., *Congressional Record* 152 (1961), 1710.

11. Dwight D. Eisenhower to John Stennis, Jan. 15, 1962, "1962 Principals" file, "Stennis, John, Subcommittee" folder, box 44, Post-Presidential Papers, 1961–69, Eisenhower Library.

12. Thomas Alfred Palmer, "Why We Fight: A Study of Indoctrination Activities in the Armed Forces" (Ph.D. diss., University of South Carolina, 1971), 45.

13. Ibid., 46; Janowitz, *Professional Soldier,* 406.

14. "Memorandum for the Chairman JCS, OSO/OSD Proposal on DOD Role in the Cold War," Dec. 30, 1957, Central Decimal File 1958, CCS 385 (6-4-46) (2) sec. 43, box 77, RG 218, Records of the Joint Chiefs of Staff (hereafter RG 218), NARA, College Park, Md.

15. Memorandum for Colonel John, "Suggested Points of Cold War Conferences Speeches," June 10, 1960, military no. 28 (7) file, box 8, Records of the President's Committee on Information Activities Abroad (Sprague Committee), Eisenhower Library.

16. Chairman, Cold War Advisory Panel, to Chief of Naval Operations, Jan. 27, 1959, Department of Defense (4) Feb.–Sept., 1959 file, box 3, Subject subser., Special Assistant ser., Eisenhower Library.

17. "Evaluation Report on National Strategy Seminar Conducted at the National War College (July 12–13, 1959)," Tabs A through H, Aug. 27, 1959, sec. 1a folder, box 40, National War College Central Decimal File 1959, RG 218, NARA, College Park, Md.; Frank Rockwell Barnett, "Fourth Dimension in Defense," Dept. of Defense (3) Nov. 58–Jan. 59 file, box 3, Subject subser., Special Assistant ser., Eisenhower Library, 3.

18. Office of Naval Personnel, *Leadership Working Group Proceedings*, Feb., 1960–Jan., 1961, copy in University of Arkansas Libraries, Fayetteville, vi.

19. Ibid., 3-2, 3-3; Amos A. Jordan Jr., "Troop Information and Indoctrination," in *Social Research and Military Management: A Survey of Military Institutions*, ed. Roger W. Little, 365; Special Preparedness Subcommittee, *Report*, 174; Hubbell, "Moral Build-Up," 129; Marshall B. Jones, "Military Participation in the Rightist Revival: 1960–1964," in *The Radical Right*, 31.

20. Special Preparedness Subcommittee, *Military Cold War Education*, 989, 2505; idem., *Report*, 172–73.

21. NSC-5810/1, "Basic National Security Policy," May 5, 1958, White House Office/ Office of Special Assistant for National Security Affairs: Records, 1952–61, NSC ser., Policy Papers subser., box 25, Eisenhower Library. It is possible that an undiscovered directive gave specific authorization for Cold War seminars, but research thus far conducted indicates NSC-5810/1 is the directive in question.

22. House, *United States Defense Policies in 1961*, 87th Cong., 2nd sess., 1962, doc. no. 502, 76.

23. Special Preparedness Subcommittee, *Report*, 6–8.

24. "Introductory Remarks by Admiral Arleigh Burke, USN, Chief of Naval Operations Before the National Strategy Seminar for Reserve Officers—National War College—Washington, D.C., July 13, 1959," "Navy Line, 1959 (2)" folder, box 18, Evan Aurand Collection, Eisenhower Library; "Seminar on Current Affairs, Oct. 26–29, 1959," loose doc. in National War College Central Decimal File 1959, box 33, RG 218, NARA, College Park, Md., 10.

25. Office of the Commandant, "Defense Strategy Seminars, May 23, 1960," "3521 National War College (Aug. 27, 1959)" sec. 1 folder, National War College Central Decimal File 1959, box 40, RG 218, NARA, College Park, Md. This document apparently was misfiled. It was written in 1960, but filed in the 1959 files.

26. "Memorandum by Chief of Naval Operations for the Joint Chiefs of Staff on National War College Summer Seminars on National Cold War Strategy," Enclosure B, "3310 PSY Warfare 1959 May" folder, National War College Central Decimal File 1959, box 32, RG 218, NARA, College Park, Md.

27. Ibid. The closing speech at the graduation banquet was "National Will and the Reserve Officer."

28. In Myrtle Beach, South Carolina, physicians attending an air force weekend seminar agreed to buy five thousand copies of J. Edgar Hoover's *Master of Deceit* and place them in every hotel room in the city, no doubt alongside a copy of the Gideon Bible (Barnett, "Fourth Dimension in Defense" 12).

29. Special Preparedness Subcommittee, *Military Cold War Education*, 3008; idem., *Report*, 28,

30. "Report on the Fulbright Memo."

31. Rebecca A. Miller, "The Birchers, the Doctor, and the Wheeler Dealer: Super-patriotism Versus Corruption in a Small West Texas Town, Pecos, Texas, 1955–1963" (M.A. thesis, Texas Tech University, 1994), 2. For book-length scholarly treatments written during the post-McCarthy era, see Daniel Bell, ed., *The Radical Right*; R. Dudman, *Men of the Far Right*; Benjamin R. Epstein and Arnold Forster, *The Radical Right: Report on the John Birch Society and its Allies*; David Jansen and Bernard Eismann, *The Far Right*; and Harry and Bonaro Overstreet, *The Strange Tactics of Extremism*. For more recent interpretations of far-right political extremists, see Martin Seymour Lipset and Earl Raab, *The Politics of Unreason: Right Wing Extremism in America, 1790–1977*; Leo P. Ribuffo, *The Old Christian Right: The Protestant Far Right from the Great Depression to the Cold War*; David H. Bennett, *The Party of Fear: From Nativist Movements to the New Right in American History*; M. J. Heale, *American Anticommunism: Combating the Enemy Within, 1830–1970*; and Jerome L. Himmelstein, *To the Right: The Transformation of American Conservatism*.

32. As quoted in Reserve Noncommissioned Officer Course 45-0050 student text, vol. 7, Jan. 4, 1960, Continental Air Command, Mitchell Air Force Base, N.Y., copy in author's possession, 15-7.

33. Edwin A. Walker, interview by author, 1994; Fred J. Cook, *The Warfare State*, 265; Christopher S. DeRosa, "A Million Thinking Bayonets: Political Indoctrination in the United States Army" (Ph.D. diss., Temple University, 2000), 141. The elements of the Pro Blue program are in Edwin A. Walker's autobiography, *Pro Blue*, 17.

34. Special Preparedness Subcommittee, *Military Cold War Education*, 1389–1534; Walker interview.

35. Special Preparedness Subcommittee, *Military Cold War Education*, 2412, 2421, 2454.

36. Ibid., 2421.

37. Ibid., 1382.

38. Hubbell, "Moral Build-Up," 133.

39. Special Preparedness Subcommittee, *Military Cold War Education*, 1325.

40. Jones, "Military Participation," 35–37.

41. Special Preparedness Subcommittee, *Military Cold War Education*, 1042–43; Jerold Simmons, "The Origins of the Campaign to Abolish HUAC, 1956–1961, The California Connection," *Southern California Quarterly* 64, no. 2 (1982): 141–57.

42. National Council of Churches, *"Operation Abolition": Some Facts and Comments*; Special Preparedness Subcommittee, *Report*, 33.

43. "Station Airs Benson Film," *Arkansas Democrat*, Jan. 22, 1961; John L. Snell to Dr. George S. Benson, May 9, 1961, folder 6, box 25, subser. 19, ser. 4, JWF Papers.

44. Edward L. Hicks *"Sometimes in the Wrong, but Never in Doubt": George S. Benson and the Education of the New Religious Right*. See also Ted M. Altman, "The Contributions of George Benson to Christian Education" (Ph.D. diss., North Texas State University, 1971); James L. Atteberry, *The Story of Harding College*; and John C. Stevens, *Before Any Were Willing: The Story of George S. Benson*.

45. Quotes from the *Adventure Series* cartoons were transcribed from a copy in the author's possession.

46. Alan F. Westin, "Anti-Communism and the Corporations," *Commentary*, Dec.,

1963, 479–87; Peter H. Irons, "American Business and the Origins of McCarthyism: The Cold War Crusade of the United States Chamber of Commerce," in *The Specter: Original Essays on the Cold War and the Origins of McCarthyism,* by Robert Griffith, 74–89; Sam C. Sarkesian, ed., *The Military Industrial Complex: A Reassessment;* Cook, *Warfare State,* 286.

47. Mark Chesler and Richard Schmuck, "Participant Observation in a Super-Patriot Discussion Group," *Journal of Social Issues* 19, no. 2 (Apr., 1963): 18–31. See also Barbara B. Green, Kathryn Turner, and Dante Germino, "Responsible and Irresponsible Right-Wing Groups: A Problem in Analysis," ibid.

48. Billy James Hargis, "Communist America: Must It Be?" in *Protest from the Right,* ed. Robert A. Rosenstone, 29. See also John Harold Redekop, *The American Far Right: A Case Study of Billy James Hargis and Christian Crusade.*

49. Hargis as quoted in Bennett, *Party of Fear,* 329.

50. House, Committee on Un-American Activities, *Issues Presented by Air Reserve;* Fernando Penabaz, *Crusading Preacher from the West: The Story of Billy James Hargis,* 165–206; Billy James Hargis, *A Crusader's Auto-Biography,* 61–67.

51. Fred J. Cook, "Radio Right: Hate Clubs of the Air," *Nation,* May 25, 1964, 525; "Wild, Wooly Testimony of Anti-Red Was Nutty," *Charleston Gazette,* Sept. 2, 1961; idem., *The New Drive Against the Anti-Communist Program,* 87th Cong., 1st sess., 1961, 4–5, 20; Edward Hunter, "Your Peace of Mind: A Warm 'Cold War' Message for Christmas," *Counterattack,* Dec. 23, 1960, copy in the James D. Bales Papers, unprocessed collection, Special Collections Division, University of Arkansas Libraries, Fayetteville, 201–202.

52. William R. Kintner, "The Insidious Campaign to Silence Anti-Communists," *Reader's Digest,* May, 1962 (reprint), 1–5; Dan N. Jacobs, ed., *The New Communist Manifesto and Related Documents,* 42.

53. For more on fundamentalism, see Louis Gasper, *The Fundamentalist Movement;* George M. Marsden, *Fundamentalism and American Culture: The Shaping of Twentieth-Century Evangelicalism, 1870–1925;* David O. Beale, *In Pursuit of Purity: American Fundamentalism Since 1850.*

54. Norman Thomas, "The Ultra Right and the Military-Industrial Complex," as quoted in Special Preparedness Subcommittee, *Military Cold War Education,* 3034. Hampton's uniformed men aided the committee.

55. "Air Station to Hold Anti-Red School," *Chicago Daily News,* Aug. 8, 1960.

56. Press Release, ACLU, Illinois Division, Sept. 30, 1960, folder 2, box 33, subser. 19, ser. 4, JWF Papers.

57. Unnamed naval reserve aviator at Glenview to John L. McKnight, executive director of the Illinois ACLU, Mar. 9, 1961, folder 3, box 28, subser. 19, ser. 4, JWF Papers.

58. Morrison as quoted in Cook, *Warfare State,* 292–93.

59. Willie Morris, "Houston's Superpatriots," in *Protest from the Right,* ed. Robert A. Rosenstone, 42–58.

60. Quoted in Thomas, "Ultra Right," 3027.

61. Stan Twardy, "Carnival of Hate," in *Protest from the Right,* ed. Robert A. Rosenstone, 60.

62. Robert Goldthwaite, "Background of Naval Air Training Command/Civilian

Moral Leadership/Cold War Workshops," folder 1, box 34, subser. 19, ser. 4, JWF Papers.

63. Jones, "Military Participation," 26–27; Cook, *Warfare State,* 304.

64. Schwarz as quoted in Adm. Robert Goldthwaite, "Cold War Information Pact," folder 6, box 33, subser. 19, ser. 4, JWF Papers.

65. "The Story of Project Alert," ibid.; Paul B. Fay Jr. to James W. Fulbright, Oct. 12, 1961, folder 1, box 34, ibid.

66. Jones, "Military Participation," 28.

67. Adm. Robert Goldthwaite, "Project Alert Kit," folder 6, box 33, subser. 19, ser. 4, JWF Papers, 4.

68. "News Journal Reader's Forum: Varied Views Voiced on Senator, Project," *Pensacola News Journal,* Aug. 17, 1961; Jones, "Military Participation," 37.

69. Jones, "Military Participation," 38; Mrs. C. A. Patterson to the president, July 22, 1961, folder 2, box 34, subser. 19, ser. 4, JWF Papers.

70. Jones, "Military Participation," 42.

71. Ibid.

72. Ibid., 41.

73. "Report to the Joint Chiefs of Staff on Operations During FY 1961," 3523 Industrial College (July 25, 1961) sec. 1 folder, Industrial College of the Armed Forces Central Decimal File 1961, box 70, RG 218, NARA, College Park, Md.

74. Goldthwaite to Burke, Feb. 14, 1961, unprocessed collection, Arleigh Burke Papers, Operational Archives, U.S. Naval Historical Center, Washington Navy Yard, Washington, D.C.

75. Rickenbacker as quoted in Jones, "Military Participation," 44.

76. Ibid.

Epilogue

1. Treese, *Valley Forge,* 176.

2. Harlan D. Unrau, *Administrative History: Valley Forge National Park, Pennsylvania.*

3. Treese, *Valley Forge,* 175.

4. Vincent Nobile Jr., "Political Opposition in the Age of Mass Media: GI's and Veterans Against the War in Vietnam" (Ph.D. diss., University of California, Irvine, 1987), 239–40; Paul M. Mann, "'Lawyers, Guns, and Money': Government Power, Radical Politics, and the Vietnam Veterans Against the War" (M.A. thesis, Florida State University, 1994), 1–23.

5. Moser, *New Winter Soldiers,* 109.

6. Melvin Small and William D. Hoover, eds., *Give Peace a Chance: Exploring the Vietnam Antiwar Movement,* 145; Nancy Miller Saunders, "Through the Looking Glass," unpublished MS, copy in author's possession; Nancy Miller Saunders, interview by author, July 9, 1997; Don Donner, interview by author, July 10, 1997.

7. Moser, *New Winter Soldiers,* 108–109.

8. Nancy Miller Saunders, "Nancy Miller Saunders," *Durham Dispatch,* Mar., 1997.

9. Harry G. Summers Jr., *On Strategy: A Critical Analysis of the Vietnam War,* 1.

Bibliography

Manuscript Collections

Franklin D. Roosevelt Presidential Library. Hyde Park, N.Y.
    Civilian Conservation Corps Records.
National Archives and Records Administration. College Park, Md.
    Records of the Secretary of Defense's Advisory Committee on Prisoners of War.
    Robert S. McNamara Papers.
    Records of the Joint Chiefs of Staff.
    Civilian Military Training Camp Records.
    Records of the National Security Resources Board.
Harry S. Truman Presidential Library. Independence, Mo.
    President's Committee on Religion and Welfare in the Armed Forces.
    President's Secretary's Files.
    Psychological Strategy Board Records.
    Universal Military Training Records.
Dwight D. Eisenhower Presidential Library. Abilene, Kans.
    Lauris Norstad Papers.
    National Security Council Staff.
    Operations Coordinating Board Records.
    Post-Presidential Papers.
    Psychological Strategy Board Records.
    Records of the President's Committee on Information Activities Abroad
        (Sprague Committee).
    Special Assistant Series.
    Special Staff File Series.
U.S. Army Military History Institute. Carlisle Barracks, Pa.
    Lewis B. Hershey Papers.
U.S. Naval Historical Center. Washington Navy Yard. Washington, D.C.
    Arleigh Burke Papers.

Private Collections

Biblical Counseling Foundation. Palm Springs, Calif.
    John C. Broger Collection.
Freedoms Foundation. Valley Forge, Pa.
Harding University Archives. Searcy, Ark.
Moody Bible Institute. Chicago.
    Sermon from Science Records.
Seeley G. Mudd Library. Princeton University. Princeton, N.J.
    American Civil Liberties Union Papers.
Teachers College. Columbia University. New York.
    Citizen Education Project Records.
Union Theological Seminary. Chicago.
    Harry F. Ward Papers.
University of Arkansas Libraries. Fayetteville.
    Billy James Hargis Papers (unprocessed).
    J. W. Fulbright Papers.
    James D. Bales Papers (unprocessed).

Books and Articles

A Brief History of the United States Army Chaplain Corps. Department of the Army Pamphlet no. 165-12. Washington, D.C.: Department of the Army, September, 1974.

Ahlstrom, Sydney E. *A Religious History of the American People.* Garden City, N.Y.: Image Books, 1975.

"Air Force 'Pick-a-Faith' Drive Called Dictatorial." *Church and State,* September, 1955, 5.

Albanese, Catherine. *Sons of the Fathers: The Civil Religion of the American Revolution.* Philadelphia: Temple University Press, 1976.

"Alert America Convoys Visited by over 200,000." *Civil Defense Alert* 1, no. 10 (April, 1952): 1.

American Legion. *The Fort Knox Experiment.* Indianapolis: American Legion, January, 1948.

Atteberry, James L. *The Story of Harding College.* Searcy, Ark.: n.p., 1966.

Bacevich, Andrew J. *The Pentomic Era: The U.S. Army Between Korea and Vietnam.* Washington, D.C.: National Defense University Press, 1986.

Ballard, Jack Stokes. *The Shock of Peace: Military and Economic Demobilization after World War II.* Washington, D.C.: University Press of America, 1983.

Barlow, Jeffery G. *Revolt of the Admirals: The Fight for Naval Aviation, 1945–1950.* Washington. D.C.: Naval Historical Center, 1994.

Barnett, Frank, and Carnes Lord. *Political Warfare and Psychological Operations: Rethinking the US Approach.* Washington, D.C.: National Defense University Press, 1989.

Barrett, Edward W. *Truth Is Our Weapon.* New York: Funk and Wagnalls, 1953.

Beale, David O. *In Pursuit of Purity: American Fundamentalism Since 1850*. Greenville, S.C.: Unusual Publications, 1986.

Bederman, Gail, ed. *Manliness and Civilization: A Cultural History of Gender and Race in the United States, 1880–1917*. Chicago: University of Chicago Press, 1995.

Bell, Daniel, ed. *The Radical Right*. Garden City, N.Y.: Doubleday, 1963.

Bellah, Robert Neely. *Beyond Belief: Essays on Religion in a Post-Traditional World*. New York: Harper Collins, 1970.

———. *The Broken Covenant: American Civil Religion on Trial*. Chicago: University of Chicago Press, 1992.

Bennett, David H. *The Party of Fear: From Nativist Movements to the New Right in American History*. Chapel Hill: University of North Carolina Press, 1988.

Benson, Robert Louis, and Michael Warner, eds. *Venona: Soviet Espionage and the American Response, 1939–1957*. Washington, D.C.: National Security Agency, 1996.

Berube, Allan. *Coming Out Under Fire: The History of Gay Men and Women in World War II*. New York: Free Press, 1990.

Biderman, Albert D. *March to Calumny: The Story of American POWs in the Korean War*. New York: Macmillan, 1963.

———. "Dangers of Negative Patriotism." *Harvard Business Review* 40, no. 6 (November–December, 1962): 93–99.

Bodenheimer, Thomas, and Robert Gould. *Rollback! Right-Wing Power in U.S. Foreign Policy*. Boston: South End Press, 1989.

Bodnar, John, ed. *Bonds of Affection: Americans Define Their Patriotism*. Princeton, N.J.: Princeton University Press, 1996.

———. *Remaking America: Public Memory, Commemoration, and Patriotism in the Twentieth Century*. Princeton, N.J.: Princeton University Press, 1992.

Boller, Paul F., Jr. *George Washington and Religion*. Dallas: Southern Methodist University Press, 1963.

Boone, Joel T. "The Sexual Aspects of Military Personnel." *American Journal of Social Hygiene* 27, no. 3 (March, 1941): 113–24.

Borden, Penn. *Civilian Indoctrination of the Military: World War I and Future Implications for the Military-Industrial Complex*. New York: Greenwood Press, 1989.

Boyer, Paul. *By the Bombs Early Light: American Thought and Culture at the Dawn of the Atomic Age*. New York: Pantheon Books, 1985.

"Brain Washing at Valley Forge." *Nation*, May 23, 1953, 425–26.

Brands, H. W., Jr. *Cold Warriors: Eisenhower's Generation and American Foreign Policy*. New York: Columbia University Press, 1988.

Brinkley, William. "Valley Forge GIs Tell of Their Brainwashing Ordeal." *Life*, May 25, 1953, 108–24.

Bristow, Nancy K. *Making Men Moral: Social Engineering During the Great War*. New York: New York University Press, 1996.

Broadwater, Jeff. *Eisenhower and the Anti-Communist Crusade*. Chapel Hill: University of North Carolina Press, 1992.

Brown, George W. *Generals and the Public: Recent Policymaking in Civil-Military Relations*. Lawrence: Governmental Research Center, University of Kansas, 1964.

Burchard, Waldo W. "Role Conflicts of Military Chaplains." In *Religion, Society, and the*

Individual: an Introduction to Sociology of Religion, by J. Milton Yinger. New York: Macmillan, 1957.

Burk, W. Herbert. "The American Westminster." *Daughters of the American Revolution Magazine,* December, 1923, 704–707.

Campbell, Gen. W. P., (Ret.). "Our Stake in the Far East." In *Report on Proceedings: Freedom Forum XXII, Panel, Speeches, Recommendations.* Searcy, Ark.: National Education Program, 1962.

Carleton, Don E. *Red Scare! Right-wing Hysteria, Fifties Fanaticism and Their Legacy in Texas.* Austin: Texas Monthly Press, 1985.

Carpenter, Joel A. "Youth for Christ and the New Evangelicals." In *Reckoning with the Past: Historical Essays on American Evangelicalism from the Institute for the Study of American Evangelicals,* ed. D. G. Hart. Grand Rapids, Mich.: Baker Books, 1996.

———. "Fundamentalist Institutions and the Rise of Evangelical Protestantism, 1929–1942." *Church History* 49 (March, 1980): 62–75.

Carruthers, Susan L. "Not Just Washed but Dry Cleaned: Korea and the 'Brainwashing' Scare of the 1950s." In *Cold War Propaganda in the 1950s,* ed. Gary D. Rawnsley. New York: Palgrave Macmillan, 1999.

Carter, Paul Allen. *Another Part of the Fifties.* New York: Columbia University Press, 1983.

Caute, David. *The Great Fear: The Anti-Communist Purge Under Truman and Eisenhower.* New York: Simon and Schuster, 1978.

Chambers, John Whiteclay, II. *Draftees or Volunteers: A Documentary History of the Debate over Military Conscription in the United States, 1787–1973.* New York: Garland, 1975.

"Chaplains Condemn Army Entertainment." *United Evangelical Action,* March 15, 1946, 16.

Chapman, William E. *Roots of Character Education: An Exploration of the American Heritage from the Decade of the 1920s.* Schenectady, N.Y.: Character Research Press, 1977.

Cherry, Conrad. *God's New Israel: Religious Interpretations of American Destiny.* Englewood, N.J.: Prentice-Hall, 1971.

Chesler, Mark, and Richard Schmuck. "Participant Observation in a Super-Patriot Discussion Group." *Journal of Social Issues* 19, no. 2 (April, 1963): 18–30.

Choukas, Michael. *Propaganda Comes of Age.* Washington, D.C.: Public Affairs Press, 1965

Citizenship Training Manual 2000-25. Washington, D.C.: War Department, 1928.

Clabaugh, Gary K. *Thunder on the Right: The Protestant Fundamentalists.* Chicago: Nelson-Hall, 1974.

Clark, Keith C., and Laurence J. Legere, eds. *The President and the Management of National Security: A Report by the Institute for Defense Analysis.* New York: Frederick A. Praeger, 1969.

Clifford, John Garry. *The Citizen Soldiers: The Plattsburg Training Camp Movement, 1913–1920.* Lexington: University Press of Kentucky, 1972.

———, and Samuel R. Spencer Jr. *The First Peacetime Draft.* Lawrence: University Press of Kansas, 1986.

Coakley, Robert W., Paul J. Scheips, and Emma J. Portuondo. *Antiwar and Antimilitary Activities in the United States, 1846–1954.* Washington, D.C.: Office of the Chief of Military History, 1970.

Codevilla, Angelo M. "Political Warfare." In *Political Warfare and Psychological Operations: Rethinking the US Approach,* ed. Frank R. Barnett and Carnes Lord. Washington, D.C.: National Defense University Press, 1989.

Cohen, Elliot A. *Citizens & Soldiers: The Dilemmas of Military Service.* Ithaca, N.Y.: Cornell University Press, 1985.

Compton, Wilson. *Waging the Campaign of Truth.* Department of State pamphlet. Washington, D.C.: GPO, 1952.

Condit, Kenneth W. *The Joint Chiefs of Staff and National Policy: 1955–1956.* Washington, D.C.: GPO, 1992.

Cook, Blanche Wiesen. "First Comes the Lie: C. D. Jackson and Political Warfare." *Radical History Review,* December, 1984, 42–71.

Cook, Fred J. *The Warfare State.* New York: Macmillan, 1962.

———. "Juggernaut: The Warfare State." *Nation,* October 28, 1961, 76–337.

———. "Radio Right: Hate Clubs of the Air." *Nation,* May 25, 1964.

Corn, Joseph J. *The Winged Gospel: America's Romance with Aviation, 1900–1950.* New York: Oxford University Press, 1987.

Costello, John. *Virtue Under Fire: How World War II Changed Our Social and Sexual Attitudes.* Boston: Little, Brown, 1985.

Cox, Harvey Gallagher. *Military Chaplains: From Religious Military to a Military Religion.* New York: American Report Press, 1973.

Cremin, Lawrence A. *The Transformation of the School: Progressivism in American Education, 1876–1957.* New York: Alfred A. Knopf, 1961.

Crosby, Donald F., S. J. *Battlefield Chaplains: Catholic Priests in World War II.* Lawrence: University Press of Kansas, 1994.

Culbert, David. "*Why We Fight:* Social Engineering for a Democratic Society at War." In *Film and Radio Propaganda in World War II,* ed. K. R. M. Short. London: Croom Helm, 1983.

Daun Van EE. "From the New Look to Flexible Response, 1953–1964." In *Against All Enemies: Interpretations of American Military History from Colonial Times to the Present,* ed. Kenneth J. Hagan and William R. Roberts. Westport, Conn.: Greenwood Press, 1986.

"Denies Air Force Plan Violates Conscience." *Church and State,* October, 1955, p. 2.

Devine, Michael J. "The Diplomacy of Righteousness: The Legacy of John W. Foster." In *Traditions and Values: American Diplomacy, 1945–Present,* ed. Kenneth W. Thompson. Lanham, Md.: University Press of America, 1984.

Dick, Bernard F. *The Star-Spangled Screen: The American World War II Film.* Lexington: University Press of Kentucky, 1985.

Divine, Robert A. *The Sputnik Challenge.* New York: Oxford University Press, 1993.

The Doolittle Report: The Report of the Secretary of War's Board on Officer-Enlisted Man Relationships. Maxwell Air Force Base, Ala.: Air University Library, 1954.

Dorsen, Norman, and John G. Simon. "McCarthy and the Army: A Fight on the Wrong Front." In *Decisions and Revisions: Interpretations of Twentieth-Century American History,* ed. Jean Christie. New York: Praeger, 1975.

Dorwart, Jeffery M. *Eberstadt and Forrestal: A National Security Partnership, 1909–1949.* College Sation: Texas A&M University Press, 1991.

———. "Forrestal and the Navy Plan of 1945: Mahanian Doctrine of Corporatist

Blueprint." In *New Interpretations in Naval History,* ed., William B. Cogar. Annapolis, Md.: Naval Institute Press, 1989.

Doyle, Robert C. *Voices from Captivity: Interpreting the American POW Experience.* Lawrence: University Press of Kansas, 1994.

Dudman, R. *Men of the Far Right.* New York: Pyramid Books, 1962.

Drazin, Israel, and Cecil B. Currey. *For God and Country: The History of a Constitutional Challenge to the Army Chaplaincy.* Hoboken, N.J.: KTAV, 1995.

Drew, S. Nelson, ed. *NSC-68: Forging the Strategy of Containment.* Washington, D.C.: National Defense University Press, 1994.

Dubbert, Joe L. *A Man's Place: Masculinity in Transition.* Englewood Cliffs, N.J.: Prentice-Hall, 1979.

Dunn, Joe P. "UMT: A Historical Perspective." *Military Review* 61, no. 1 (January, 1981): 11–18.

Edwards, Jill. "The President, the Archbishop and the Envoy: Religion and Diplomacy in the Cold War." *Diplomacy and Statecraft* 6, no. 2 (July, 1995): 490–511.

Eisenhower, Dwight D. *At Ease: Stories I Tell to Friends.* Garden City, N.Y.: Doubleday, 1967.

Ekrich, Arthur Alphonse. *The Civilian and the Military: A History of the American Antimilitarist Tradition.* Colorado Springs: Ralph Myles, 1972.

Engelhardt, Tom. *The End of Victory Culture: Cold War America and the Disillusioning of a Generation.* New York: Basic Books, 1995.

Epstein, Benjamin R., and Arnold Forster. *The Radical Right: Report on the John Birch Society and Its Allies.* New York: Random House, 1967.

Everest, F. Alton. "The Moody Institute of Science." *Journal of the American Scientific Affiliation* 5, no. 3 (September, 1953): 10–11.

Fairbanks, James David. "The Priestly Functions of the Presidency: A Discussion of the Literature on Civil Religion and its Implications for the Study of Presidential Leadership." *Presidential Studies Quarterly* 11, no. 2 (spring, 1981): 214–32.

———. "Religious Dimensions of Presidential Leadership: The Case of Dwight Eisenhower." *Presidential Studies Quarterly* 12, no. 2 (spring, 1982): 260–67.

Falkner, Leonard. "We Relived the Miracle of Valley Forge." *American Magazine,* December, 1954, 98–103.

Ferrell, Robert H., ed. *Dear Bess: The Letters from Harry to Bess Truman, 1910–1959.* New York: W. W. Norton, 1983.

Fisher, Robert E. "The U.S. Navy's Search for a Strategy, 1945–1947." *Naval War College Review* 48, no. 3 (summer, 1995): 73–86.

Fitzpatrick, John C., ed. *The Writings of George Washington from the Original Manuscript Sources: 1745–1799.* Vol. 11. Washington, D.C.: GPO, 1932.

Flynn, George. *The Draft, 1940–1973.* Lawrence: University Press of Kansas, 1993.

Foner, Philip S. *Morale Education in the American Army.* New York: International Publishing, 1944.

Fones-Wolf, Elizabeth A. *Selling Free Enterprise: The Business Assault on Labor and Liberalism, 1945–1960.* Urbana: University of Illinois Press, 1994.

Ford, Nancy Gentile. *Americans All! Foreign-Born Soldiers in World War I.* College Station: Texas A&M University Press, 2001.

The Fort Knox Experiment, 1947. Fort Knox, Ky.: Public Information Office, UMT Experimental Unit, 1947.

Frady, Marshall. *Billy Graham: A Parable of American Righteousness.* Boston: Little, Brown, 1979.

Frankiel, Tamar. "Ritual Sites in the Narrative of American Religion." In *Retelling U.S. Religious History,* ed. Thomas A. Tweed. Berkeley and Los Angeles: University of California Press, 1997.

Franklin, Benjamin. "Proposals Relating to the Education of Youth in Pennsylvania." In *The Papers of Benjamin Franklin,* ed. Leonard W. Labaree. New Haven, Conn.: Yale University Press, 1961.

Fudge, Russell O. "Why? The Story of Information in the American Army." *Armored Cavalry Journal* 59, no. 2 (March-April, 1950): 16–20.

Fulbright, J. William. *The Pentagon Propaganda Machine.* New York: Liveright, 1970.

Gamoran, Adam. "Civil Religion in American Schools." *Sociological Analysis* 51, no. 3 (1990): 235–56.

Gasper, Louis. *The Fundamentalist Movement.* The Hague, Paris: Mouton, 1963.

Gatewood, Willard B., Jr. "From Scopes to Creation Science: The Decline and Revival of the Evolution Controversy." *South Atlantic Quarterly* 83, no. 4 (autumn, 1984): 363–83.

Gerhardt, James M. *The Draft and Public Policy.* Columbus: Ohio State University Press, 1971.

Gilbert, James Burkhart. *Redeeming Culture: American Religion in an Age of Science.* Chicago: University of Chicago Press, 1997.

Gilbert, Richard R. *The Nation with the Soul of a Church: A Critical Reflection.* Washington, D.C.: American Revolution Bicentennial Administration, 1976.

Gillis, John R., ed. *Commemorations: The Politics of National Identity.* Princeton, N.J.: Princeton University Press, 1996.

Ginzberg, Eli, James K. Anderson, Sol W. Ginsburg, and John L. Herma. *The Ineffective Soldier: Lessons for Management and the Nation.* Vol. 1, *The Lost Divisions.* New York: Columbia University Press, 1959.

Glendon, Mary Ann, and David Blankenhorn. *Seedbeds of Virtue: Sources of Competence, Character, and Citizenship in American Society.* New York: Madison Books, 1995.

Glick, Edward Bernard. *Soldiers, Scholars, and Society: The Social Impact of the American Military.* Pacific Palisades, Calif.: Goodyear, 1971.

Goffman, Erving. *Asylums: Essays on the Social Situation of Mental Patients and Other Inmates.* Chicago: Aldine, 1962.

Goldston, Robert. *The American Nightmare: Senator Joseph R. McCarthy and the Politics of Hate.* New York: Bobbs-Merrill, 1973.

Gorham, Eric B. *National Service, Citizenship, and Political Education.* Albany, N.Y.: State University Press, 1992.

Graebner, William. *The Engineering of Consent: Democracy and Authority in Twentieth-Century America.* Madison: University of Wisconsin Press, 1987.

Grandstaff, Mark R. "Making the Military American: Advertising, Reform, and the Demise of an Antistanding Military Tradition, 1945–1955." *Journal of Military History* 60, no. 2 (April, 1996): 299–323.

"Great Lakes Recruit Command: The Chaplain's Program." *The Chaplain: A Journal for Protestant Chaplains* 9, no. 2 (March–April, 1952): 34–35.

Green, Barbara B., Kathryn Turner, and Dante Germino. "Responsible and Irresponsible Right-Wing Groups: A Problem in Analysis." *Journal of Social Issues* 19 (April,
1963): 3–17.

Griffith, Robert K., Jr. *Men Wanted for the U.S. Army: America's Experience with an All-
Volunteer Army Between the World Wars.* Westport, Conn.: Greenwood Press, 1982.

———. *The Politics of Fear: Joseph McCarthy and the Senate.* Amherst: University of
Massachusetts Press, 1987.

Gushwa, Robert L. *The Best and Worst of Times: The United States Army Chaplaincy,
1920–1945.* Washington, D.C.: Office of the Chief of Chaplains, 1977.

Gustafson, Merlin. "The Church, the State, and the Military in the Truman Administration." *Rocky Mountain Social Science Journal* 2 (October, 1965): 2–10.

———. "The Religion of a President." *Journal of Church and State* 10, no. 3 (1968):
379–87.

———. "The Religious Role of the President." *Midwest Journal of Political Science* 14,
no. 4 (November, 1970): 708–22.

Haas, John W., Jr., Irwin A. Moon, F. Alton Everest, and Will H. Houghton. "Early Links
between the Moody Bible Institute and the American Scientific Affiliation."
Perspectives on Science and Christian Faith 43, no. 4 (December, 1991): 249–58.

Hagan, Kenneth J., and William R. Roberts, eds. *Against all Enemies: Interpretations of
American Military History from Colonial Times to the Present.* Westport, Conn.:
Greenwood Press, 1986.

Hale, William Harlan. "Militant Liberty and the Pentagon." *Reporter,* February 9, 1956,
30–34.

Haller, Mark H. *Eugenics: Hereditary Attitudes in American Thought.* New Brunswick,
N.J.: Rutgers University Press, 1963.

Hardman, Keith J. *Seasons of Refreshing: Evangelicalism and Revivals in America.* Grand
Rapids, Mich.: Baker Books, 1994.

Hargis, Billy James. *A Crusader's Auto-Biography.* Green Forest, Ark.: New Leaf Press, 1985.

———. "Communist America: Must It Be?" In *Protest from the Right,* ed. Robert A.
Rosenstone. Beverly Hills: Glencoe Press, 1968.

Hart, John Robbins. *Valley Forge during World War II.* New York: American Historical,
1944.

Hastings, Max. *The Korean War.* New York: Touchstone, 1988.

Haynes, Richard F. *The Awesome Power: Harry S. Truman as Commander in Chief.*
Baton Rouge: Louisiana State University Press, 1973.

Heale, M. J. *American Anticommunism: Combating the Enemy Within, 1830–1970.*
Baltimore: Johns Hopkins University Press, 1990.

———. "Red Scare Politics: California's Campaign Against Un-American Activities,
1940–1970." *Journal of American Studies* 20, no. 1 (April, 1986): 5–32.

Helgeland, John. "Civil Religion, Military Religion." *Foundations and Facets Forum* 5,
no. 1 (March, 1989): 22–44.

Henry, Patrick. "'And I Don't Care What It Is': The Tradition History of a Civil Religion
Proof-text." *Journal of the American Academy of Religion* 49, no. 1 (March, 1981): 35–47.

Hicks, Edward L. *"Sometimes in the Wrong, but Never in Doubt": George S. Benson and
the Education of the New Religious Right.* Knoxville: University of Tennessee Press,
1994.

Higgs, Robert J. *God in the Stadium: Sports and Religion in America.* Lexington: University of Kentucky Press, 1995.

High, Stanley. "The War Boom in Religion." In *The Army Reader,* ed. Karl Detzer. Indianapolis: Bobbs-Merrill, 1943.

Himmelstein, Jerome. *To the Right: The Transformation of American Conservatism.* Berkeley: University of California Press, 1990.

Hubbell, John G. "Moral Build-Up Gives New Strength to the Navy." In *The Navy Blue Book,* ed. Tom Compere. Indianapolis: Bobbs-Merrill, 1960.

Humphrey, Mary Ann. *My Country, My Right to Serve: Experiences of Gay Men and Women in the Military, World War II to the Present.* New York: Harper Collins, 1988.

Huntington, Samuel P. *The Common Defense: Strategic Programs in National Policy.* New York: Columbia University Press, 1961.

———. *The Soldier and the State: The Theory and Politics of Civil-Military Relations.* Cambridge, Mass.: Harvard University Press, 1957.

Hutcheson, Richard G. *The Churches and the Chaplaincy.* Atlanta: John Knox Press, 1975.

———. *God in the White House: How Religion Has Changed the Modern Presidency.* New York: Macmillan, 1989.

Inderfurth, Karl F., and Loch K. Johnson. *Decisions of the Highest Order: Perspectives on the National Security Council.* Pacific Grove, Calif.: Brooks and Cole, 1988.

Imrie, Matthew H. "The Fort Knox Experiment." *Army and Navy Chaplain,* April–May, 1947, 2–6, 32.

Information and Education in the Armed Services: A Report to the President by the President's Commission on Religion and Welfare in the Armed Forces. Washington, D.C.: GPO, 1949.

Irons, Peter H. "American Business and the Origins of McCarthyism: The Cold War Crusade of the United States Chamber of Commerce." In *The Specter: Original Essays on the Cold War and the Origins of McCarthyism,* by Robert Griffith. New York: New Viewpoints, 1974.

Jackall, Robert, ed. *Propaganda.* New York: New York University Press, 1995.

Jacobs, Dan N., ed. *The New Communist Manifesto and Related Documents.* New York: Harper Torchbooks, 1962.

Jacobs, Travis B. "Eisenhower, the American Assembly, and 1952." *Presidential Studies Quarterly* 22, no. 3 (summer, 1992): 455–68.

———. "Dwight D. Eisenhower's Presidency of Columbia University." *Presidential Studies Quarterly* 25, no. 3 (summer, 1995): 555–60.

Janowitz, Morris. *The Professional Soldier: A Social and Political Portrait.* New York: Free Press, 1960.

———. *Sociology and the Military Establishment.* New York: Russell Sage Foundation, 1965.

———. *The Reconstruction of Patriotism: Education for Civic Consciousness.* Chicago: University of Chicago Press, 1983.

———, and Stephen D. Westbrook, eds. *The Political Education of Soldiers.* Beverly Hills, Calif.: Sage Publications, 1983.

Jansen, David, and Bernard Eismann. *The Far Right.* New York: McGraw-Hill, 1963.

Jones, Marshall B. "Military Participation in the Rightist Revival: 1960–1964." In *The*

Radical Right: Proceedings of the 6th Intergroup Relations Conference. Houston: University of Houston, 1965.

Jordan, Amos A., Jr. "Troop Information and Indoctrination." In *Social Research and Military Management: A Survey of Military Institutions,* ed., Roger W. Little. Arlington, Va: Air Force Office of Scientific Research, 1969.

Jorstad, Erling. *Evangelicals in the White House: The Cultural Maturation of Born Again Christianity, 1960–1981.* New York: Edwin Mellen Press, 1982.

Juergensmeyer, John E. *The President, the Foundations, and the People-to-People Program.* New York: Bobbs-Merrill, 1965.

Jurika, Stephen, Jr., ed. *From Pearl Harbor to Vietnam: The Memoirs of Admiral Arthur W. Radford.* Stanford, Calif.: Hoover Institution Press, 1980.

Kammen, Michael. *From Liberty to Prosperity: Reflections upon the Role of Revolutionary Iconography in National Tradition.* Worcester, Mass.: American Antiquarian Society, 1977.

———. *Mystic Chords of Memory: The Transformation of Tradition in American Culture.* New York: Vintage Books, 1993.

———. *A Season of Youth: The American Revolution and the Historical Imagination.* Ithaca, N.Y.: Cornell University Press, 1988.

Karsten, Peter. *Soldiers and Society: The Effects of Military Service and War on American Life.* Westport, Conn.: Greenwood Press, 1978.

———. *Patriot-Heroes in England and America: Political Symbolism and Values over Three Centuries.* Madison: University of Wisconsin Press, 1978.

———, ed. *The Military in America: From the Colonial Era to the Present.* New York: Free Press, 1986.

Kaun, David E. *Super-Patriots in America: A Century of Growing Influence.* Durango, Colo.: Hollowbrook, 1995.

Kellor, Francis A. *Straight America: A Call to National Service.* New York: Macmillan, 1916.

Kennett, Lee. *G.I.: The American Soldier in World War II.* New York: Warner Books, 1987.

Kerry, John. *The New Soldier.* Ed. David Thorne. New York: Macmillan, 1971.

Key, Lawrence E. *Cultivating National Will: An Introduction to National Will.* Maxwell Paper no. 5. Maxwell Air Force Base, Ala.: Air War College, 1996.

Kington, Donald M. *Forgotten Summers: The Story of the Citizen Military Training Camps, 1921–1940.* San Francisco: Two Decades, 1998.

Kinkead, Eugene. *In Every War But One.* New York: W. W. Norton, 1959.

Kinnard, Douglas. *President Eisenhower and Strategy Management: A Study in Defense Politics.* Lexington: University Press of Kentucky, 1977.

Klitgaard, Robert E. "Onward Christian Soldiers: Dehumanization and the Military Chaplain." *Christian Century,* November 18, 1970, 1377–80.

Koppes, Clayton R., and Gregory D. Black. *Hollywood Goes to War: How Politics, Profits, and Propaganda Shaped World War II Movies.* New York: Free Press, 1987.

Kuhl, Stefan. *The Nazi Connection: Eugenics, American Racism, and German National Socialism.* New York: Oxford University Press, 1944.

Kutler, Stanley I. *The American Inquisition: Justice and Injustice in the Cold War.* New York: Hill and Wang, 1983.

Laurie, Clayton D. *The Propaganda Warriors: America's Crusade Against Nazi Germany.* Lawrence: University Press of Kansas, 1996.

Lee, Alton. "Army Mutiny of 1946." *Journal of American History* 53, no. 3 (December, 1966): 555–71.

Leffler, Melvyn P. *A Preponderance of Power: National Security, the Truman Administration, and the Cold War.* Stanford, Calif.: Stanford University Press, 1992.

Linder, Robert D. "Civil Religion and Baptist Responsibility." *Southwestern Journal of Theology* 18, no. 2 (spring, 1976): 25–39.

————, and Richard V. Pierard. *Twilight of the Saints: Biblical Christianity and Civil Religion in America.* Downes Grove, Ill; Intervarsity Press, 1978.

Lipset, Martin Seymour, and Earl Raab. *The Politics of Unreason: Right Wing Extremism in America, 1790–1977.* New York: Harper Torchbook, 1970.

Littell, Marcia S. "Interfaith Rituals, Symbols and Experience: Working Reports on Their Promise and Problems." *Dialogue and Alliance: Journal of the International Religious Foundation* 3, no. 1 (spring, 1989): 76–80.

Little, Stuart J. "The Freedom Train: Citizenship and Postwar Political Culture, 1946–1949." *American Studies* 34, no. 1 (spring, 1993): 35–67.

Litto, Fredric M. "Addison's Cato in the Colonies." *William and Mary Quarterly* 23, no. 3 (July, 1966): 431–49.

Love, William Robert, Jr. *The Chiefs of Naval Operations.* Annapolis, Md.: Naval Institute Press, 1980.

Loveland, Anne C. *American Evangelicals and the U.S. Military, 1942–1993.* Baton Rouge: Louisiana State University Press, 1996.

Lucas, W. Scott. *Freedom's War: The American Crusade against the Soviet Union.* New York: New York University Press, 1999.

————. "Beyond Diplomacy: Propaganda and the History of the Cold War." In *Cold War Propaganda in the 1950s,* ed., Gary D. Rawnsley. New York: Palgrave Macmillan, 1999.

————. "Campaigns of Truth: The Psychological Strategy Board and American Ideology, 1951–1953." *International History Review* 18, no. 2 (May, 1996): 279–302.

Ludmerer, Kenneth M. *Genetics and American Society: A Historical Appraisal.* Baltimore: Johns Hopkins University Press, 1972.

Luedtke, Luther S., ed. *Making America: The Society and Culture of the United States.* Chapel Hill: University of North Carolina Press, 1992.

Lowenthal, David. "Identity, Heritage, and History." In *Commemorations: The Politics of National Identity,* ed. John R. Gillis. Princeton, N.J.: Princeton University Press, 1996.

Lynn, Robert Wood. "Civil Catechetics in Mid-Victorian America: Some Notes About American Civil Religion, Past and Present." *Religious Education* 68, no. 1 (January-February, 1973): 5–27.

Lyons, Gene M., and Louis Morton. *Schools for Strategy: Education and Research in National Security Affairs.* New York: Praeger, 1965.

Macleod, David I. *Building Character in the American Boy: The Boy Scouts, YMCA, and Their Forerunners, 1870–1920.* Madison: University of Wisconsin Press, 1983.

Mallery, Lawrence R., Jr., comp. *Sourcebook: Peacetime Compulsory Military Training.* Philadelphia: American Friends Service Committee, 1948.

Marling, Karal Ann. *George Washington Slept Here: Colonial Revivals and American Culture, 1876–1986.* Cambridge, Mass.: Harvard University Press, 1988.

Marsden, George M. *Fundamentalism and American Culture: The Shaping of Twentieth-Century Evangelicalism: 1870–1925.* New York: Oxford University Press, 1980.

Martin, James Kirby, and Mark Edward Lender. *A Respectable Army: The Military Origins of the Republic, 1763–1789.* Arlington Heights, Ill.: Harlan Davidson, 1982.

Marty, Martin E. *A Nation of Behavers.* Chicago: University of Chicago Press, 1976.

———. *Religion and Republic: The American Circumstance.* Boston: Beacon Press, 1987.

———. *Modern American Religion.* Vol. 3, *Under God Indivisible, 1941–1960.* Chicago: University of Chicago Press, 1996.

May, Ernest R., ed. *American Cold War Strategy: Interpreting NSC 68.* New York: Bedford Books, 1993.

Mayer, William E. "Why Did Many GI Captives Cave In?" *U.S. News and World Report,* February 24, 1956, 57–72.

McBride, Joseph. *Frank Capra: The Catastrophe of Success.* New York: Simon and Schuster, 1992.

McClellan, B. Edward. *Schools and the Shaping of Character: Moral Education in America, 1607–Present.* Bloomington: Eric Clearing House for Social Studies, Indiana University, 1992.

McClelland, David C. *Education for Values.* New York: Irvington, 1982.

McLoughlin, William G., Jr. *Billy Graham: Revivalist in a Secular Age.* New York: Ronald Press, 1960.

Melanson, Richard A. "Paul H. Nitze to Norman Podhoretz: The Tradition of Anti-Communist Containment." In *Traditions and Values: American Diplomacy, 1945–Present,* ed. Kenneth W. Thompson. Lanham, Md.: University Press of America, 1984.

Menninger, William C., M.D. *Psychiatry in a Troubled World: Yesterday's War and Today's Challenge.* New York: Macmillan, 1948.

Miller, Richard Lawrence. *Truman: The Rise to Power.* New York: McGraw-Hill, 1986.

Millett, Allan R., and Peter Maslowski. *For the Common Defense: A Military History of the United States of America.* New York: Free Press, 1994.

Millis, Walter. *Arms and Men: A Study in American Military History.* New York: G. P. Putnam's Sons, 1956.

Moral Leadership Program in the Air Force. Gunter Air Force Base, Ala.: Air Force Extension Course Institute, 1967.

Morgenthau, Hans. *Politics Among Nations.* New York: Knopf, 1985.

Morris, Willie. "Houston's Superpatriots." In *Protest from the Right,* ed. Robert A. Rosenstone. Beverly Hills: Glencoe Press, 1968.

Moser, Richard R. *The New Winter Soldiers: GI and Veteran Dissent during the Vietnam Era.* New Brunswick, N.J.: Rutgers University Press, 1996.

Moskin, J. Robert. "Why do Women Dominate Him?" In *The Decline of the American Male,* by George Leonard et al. New York: Random House, 1958.

Moskos, Charles C. *A Call to Civic Service: National Service for Country and Community.* New York: Free Press, 1988.

Mrozek, Donald J. *Sport and American Mentality, 1880–1910.* Knoxville: University of Tennessee Press, 1983.

———. "The Cult and Ritual of Toughness in Cold War America." In *Rituals and Ceremonies in Popular Culture,* ed. Ray B. Browne. Bowling Green, Ohio: Popular Press, 1980.

Munson, Edward Lyman. *The Management of Men: A Handbook on the Systematic Development of Morale and the Control of Human Behavior.* New York: Henry Holt, 1921.

Napoli, Donald S. "The Mobilization of American Psychologists, 1938–1941." *Military Affairs* 42, no. 1 (February, 1978): 32–36.

National Council Against Conscription. *The Militarization of America: Report Issued by Albert Eisenhower, Dorothy Canfield Fisher, Reuben Gustavson, William J. Millor, S.J., Arthur Morgan, Ray Lyman Wilbur and Fifteen Others.* Washington, D.C.: National Council Against Conscription, 1948.

National Council of Churches. *"Operation Abolition": Some Facts and Comments.* New York: Office of Publication and Distribution, n.d.

"The Navy: Storm Over the Pentagon." *Newsweek,* October 17, 1949, p. 23.

Neal, Steve. *The Eisenhowers.* Rev. ed. Lawrence: University Press of Kansas, 1984.

"Needed Chaplaincy Reforms." *Christian Century,* February 28, 1951, 261–63.

Neuhaus, Richard John, and Michael Cromartie, eds. *Piety and Politics: Evangelicals and Fundamentalists Confront the World.* Washington, D.C.: Ethics and Public Policy Center, 1987.

Oakes, Guy. *The Imaginary War: Civil Defense and American Cold War Culture.* New York: Oxford University Press, 1994.

Ohl, Bob. "Navymen: Characters with Character." *All Hands,* September, 1954, 14–17.

O'Neill, William L. *American High: The Years of Confidence, 1945–1960.* New York: Free Press, 1989.

"Orphaned Chaplains." *Christian Century,* November 22, 1944, 1342–43.

Oshinsky, David M. *A Conspiracy So Immense: The World of Joe McCarthy.* New York: Free Press, 1983.

Overstreet, Harry, and Bonaro Overstreet. *The Strange Tactics of Extremism.* New York: McGraw-Hill, 1963.

Pach, Chester J. *Arming the Free World: The Origins of the United States Military Assistance Program, 1945–1950.* Chapel Hill: University of North Carolina Press, 1991.

Paine, Thomas. "The American Crisis." In *Thomas Paine: Collected Writings,* ed. Eric Foner. New York: Library of America, 1995.

Parry-Giles, Shawn J. *The Rhetorical Presidency: Propaganda and the Cold War, 1945–1955.* Westport, Conn: Praeger, 2002.

———. "Rhetorical Experimentation and the Cold War, 1947–1953: The Development of an Internationalist Approach to Propaganda." *Quarterly Journal of Speech* 80, no. 4 (November, 1994): 452–63.

Parvin, Earl. *Missions USA.* Chicago: Moody Press, 1985.

Pasley, Virginia. *21 Stayed: The Story of the American GIs Who Chose Communist China—Who They Were and Why They Stayed.* New York: Farrar, Straus, and Cudahy, 1955.

Pearlman, Michael. *To Make Democracy Safe for America: Patricians and Preparedness in the Progressive Era.* Chicago: University of Illinois Press, 1984.

Penabaz, Fernando. *Crusading Preacher from the West: The Story of Billy James Hargis.* Tulsa, Okla.: Christian Crusade, 1965.

Perko, F. Michael. *Schooling and the American Civil Religion.* New York: United Ministries in Education, 1986.

Pierard, Richard V. "Billy Graham and the U.S. Presidency." *Journal of Church and State* 22, no. 1 (winter, 1980): 107–28.

———, and Robert D. Linder. *Civil Religion and the Presidency*. Grand Rapids, Mich.: Academie Books, 1988.

Pleck, Elizabeth H., and Joseph H., eds. *The American Man*. Englewood Cliffs, N.J.: Prentice-Hall, 1980.

Pleiffer, David A. "Riding the Rails up Paper Mountain: Researching Railroad Records at NARA." *The Record: News from the National Archives and Records Administration* 29, no. 1 (spring, 1997): 27–28.

Pogue, Forrest C. *George C. Marshall: Ordeal and Hope, 1939–1943*. London: MacGibbon and Kee, 1968.

———. *George C. Marshall: Organizer of Victory, 1943–1945*. New York: Viking Press, 1973.

———. *George C. Marshall: Statesman, 1945–1959*. New York: Viking Press, 1987.

Pope, Steven Wayne. *Patriotic Games: Sporting Traditions in the American Imagination, 1876–1926*. New York: Oxford University Press, 1997.

Powers, Richard Gid. *Not Without Honor: The History of American Anticommunism*. New York: Free Press, 1995.

Prados, John. *Keepers of the Keys: A History of the National Security Council from Truman to Bush*. New York: William Morrow, 1992.

Preer, Jean. "The American Heritage Project: Librarians and the Democratic Tradition in the Early Cold War." *Libraries and Culture* 28, no. 2 (spring, 1993): 165–88.

President's Advisory Commission on Universal Training. *A Program for National Security*. Washington, D.C.: GPO, 1947.

Public Papers of the Presidents of the United States: Herbert Hoover. Vol. 3, *1931*. Washington, D.C.: GPO, 1976.

Public Papers of the Presidents of the United States: Harry S. Truman. Vol. 1, *1945*. Washington, D.C.: GPO, 1961.

———. Vol. 2, *1946*. Washington, D.C.: GPO, 1962.

———. Vol. 4, *1948*. Washington, D.C.: GPO, 1964.

———. Vol. 6, *1950*. Washington, D.C.: GPO, 1965.

Putney, Clifford Wallace. *Muscular Christianity: Manhood and Sports in Protestant America, 1880–1920*. Cambridge, Mass.: Harvard University Press, 2001.

Qualter, Terence H. *Propaganda and Psychological Warfare*. New York: Random House, 1965.

Rawnsley, Gary D. *Cold War Propaganda in the 1950s*. New York: Palgrave Macmillan, 1999.

Redekop, John Harold. *The American Far Right: A Case Study of Billy James Hargis and Christian Crusade*. Grand Rapids, Mich.: William B. Eerdmans, 1968.

Ries, John C. *The Management of Defense: Organization and Control of the U.S. Armed Forces*. Baltimore: Johns Hopkins University Press, 1963.

Ribuffo, Leo P. *The Old Christian Right: The Protestant Far Right from the Great Depression to the Cold War*. Philadelphia: Temple University Press, 1983.

Robin, Ron. *The Making of the Cold War Enemy: Culture and Politics in the Military-Industrial Complex*. Princeton, N.J.: Princeton University Press, 2001.

Roosevelt, Theodore. *The Valley Forge Speech*. Boston: Independent, 1904.

Rosamond, Robert. *Crusade for Peace: Eisenhower's Presidential Legacy with the Program for Action.* New York: Lexington, 1962.

Rosenthal, Michael. *The Character Factory: Baden-Powell and the Origins of the Boy Scout Movement.* London: Collins, 1986.

Rosenstone, Robert A., ed. *Protest From the Right.* Beverly Hills, Calif.: Glencoe Press, 1968.

Rotundo, Anthony E. *American Manhood: Transformations in Masculinity from the Revolution to the Modern Era.* New York: Basic Books, 1993.

Royster, Charles. *A Revolutionary People at War: The Continental Army and American Character, 1775–1783.* New York: W. W. Norton, 1979.

Salmond, John A. *The Civilian Conservation Corps, 1933–1942: A New Deal Case Study.* Durham, N.C.: Duke University Press, 1967.

Sarkesian, Sam C., ed. *The Military Industrial Complex: A Reassessment.* Beverly Hills: Sage, 1972.

Saunders, Francis Stonor. *Who Paid the Piper: The CIA and the Cultural Cold War.* London: Granta Books, 1999.

Schaffer, Ronald. *America in the Great War: The Rise of the War Welfare State.* New York: Oxford University Press, 1991

Schrecker, Ellen. *The Age of McCarthyism: A Brief History with Documents.* New York: Bedford Books, 1994.

Schwartz, Barry. *George Washington: The Making of an American Symbol.* New York: Free Press, 1987.

Senate Armed Services Committee. *Authorizing Military Support to the Sixth National Jamboree of the Boy Scouts of America, Valley Forge State Park, Pa.* Washington D.C.: GPO, 1963.

Seymour, Martin Lipset, and Earl Raab. *The Politics of Unreason: Right-Wing Extremism in America, 1790–1970.* New York: Harper Torchbooks, 1973.

Sherraden, Michael W. "Military Participation in a Youth Employment Program: The Civilian Conservation Corps." *Armed Forces and Society* 7, no. 2 (winter, 1981): 227–45.

Sherry, Michael S. *In the Shadow of War: The United States Since the 1930s.* New Haven, Conn.: Yale University Press, 1995.

Shoemaker, Christopher C. *The NSC Staff: Counseling the Council.* Boulder, Colo.: Westview Press, 1991.

Shulman, Holly Cowan. *The Voice of America: Propaganda and Democracy, 1941–1945.* Madison: University of Wisconsin Press, 1990.

Shy, John. *A People Numerous and Armed: Reflections on the Military Struggle for American Independence.* Ann Arbor: University of Michigan Press, 1993.

Simmons, Jerold. "The Origins of the Campaign to Abolish HUAC, 1956–1961: The California Connection." *Southern California Quarterly* 64, no. 2 (1982): 141–57.

Small, Melvin, and William D. Hoover, eds. *Give Peace a Chance: Exploring the Vietnam Antiwar Movement.* Syracuse, N.Y.: Syracuse University Press, 1992.

Smith, Geoffrey S. "National Security and Personal Isolation: Sex, Gender, and Disease in the Cold War United States." *International History Review* 14, no. 2 (May, 1992): 307–37.

Smith, Wilbur M. *Will H. Houghton: A Watchman on the Wall.* Grand Rapids, Mich.: William B. Eerdmans, 1951.

Smylie, James H. "The President as Republican Prophet and King: Clerical Reflections on the Death of Washington." *Journal of Church and State* 18, no. 2 (spring, 1976): 233–52.

"Snafu at Valley Forge." *Newsweek,* May 18, 1953, 44–46.

Spalding, Matthew, and Patrick J. Garrity. *A Sacred Union of Citizens: George Washington's Farewell Address and the American Character.* New York: Rowman and Littlefield, 1996.

Sparrow, John C. *History of Personnel Demobilization in the U.S. Army.* Washington, D.C.: GPO, July, 1952.

Spillman, Lynette P. *Nation and Commemoration: Creating National Identities in the United States and Australia.* New York: Cambridge University Press, 1997.

Sproule, J. Michael. *Propaganda and Democracy: The American Experience of Media and Mass Persuasion.* New York: Cambridge University Press, 1997.

Stevens, John C. *Before Any Were Willing: The Story of George S. Benson.* Searcy, Ark.: Harding University, 1991.

Summers, Harry G., Jr. *On Strategy: A Critical Analysis of the Vietnam War.* Novato, Calif.: Presidio Press, 1982.

Swanson, Edward. *Ministry to the Armed Forces.* Washington, D.C.: General Commission on Chaplains and Armed Forces Personnel, 1968.

Swomley, John M., Jr. *The Growing Power of the Military.* Washington, D.C.: National Council Against Conscription, 1959.

———. *The Military Establishment.* Boston: Beacon Press, 1964.

Tansill, William R. *The Concept of Civil Supremacy Over the Military in the United States.* Public Affairs Bulletin no. 9. Washington, D.C.: Library of Congress Legislative Reference Service, 1951.

Taylor, Alfred R., Kenneth D. McCracken, and C. E. Beatty, eds. *Song Book of the United States Naval Academy.* Annapolis, Md.: Log of the U.S. Naval Academy, 1922.

Taylor, Maxwell. *The Uncertain Trumpet.* New York: Harper, 1959.

Thayer, George. *The Farther Shore of Politics: The American Political Fringe Today.* New York: Simon and Schuster, 1967.

"Training Your Men in the Code of Conduct." *Navy Training Bulletin,* February, 1956, 11.

Treese, Lorett. *Valley Forge: Making and Remaking a National Symbol.* University Park: Pennsylvania State University Press, 1995.

Truman, Harry S. *Memoirs of Harry S. Truman.* 2 vols. Garden City, N.Y.: Doubleday, 1955–56.

Trussell, John B. B., Jr. *Birthplace of an Army: A Study of the Valley Forge Encampment.* Harrisburg: Pennsylvania Historical and Museum Commission, 1990.

Tuch, Hans N., and G. Lewis Schmidt, eds. *Ike and USIA: A Commemorative Symposium.* Washington, D.C.: U.S. Information Agency Alumni Association and Public Diplomacy Foundation of Washington, D.C., 1991.

Twardy, Stan. "Carnival of Hate." In *Protest from the Right,* ed. Robert A. Rosenstone. Beverly Hills: Glencoe Press, 1968.

U.S. Congress. House. Committee on Un-American Activities. *Issues Presented by Air Reserve Center Training Manual.* Washington, D.C.: GPO, 1960.

———. Senate. Committee on the Judiciary. Subcommittee to Investigate the Administration of the Internal Security Act and other Internal Security Laws.

Communist and Workers' Parties' Manifesto Adopted November-December 1960, Interpretation and Analysis. 87th Cong., 1st sess., 1961.

———. *The New Drive Against the Anti-Communist Program.* 87th Cong., 1st sess., 1961.

———. Senate. Committee on Armed Services. Subcommittee on Special Preparedness. *Military Cold War Education and Speech Review Policies.* Washington, D.C.: GPO, 1962.

———. *Report on Military Cold War Education and Speech Review Policies.* Washington, D.C.: GPO, 1962.

U.S. Department of Defense. *POW: The Fight Continues After the Battle: The Report of the Secretary of Defense's Advisory Committee on Prisoners of War.* Washington, D.C.: GPO, 1955.

———. *Militant Liberty: A Program of Evaluation and Assessment of Freedom.* Washington, D.C.: GPO, 1955.

U.S. Department of State. *Foreign Relations of the United States, 1946.* Vol. 6, *Eastern Europe and the Soviet Union.* Washington, D.C.: GPO, 1969.

———. *The Campaign of Truth: The International Information and Education Exchange Program, 1951.* Washington, D.C.: GPO, 1951.

Unrau, Harlan D. *Administrative History: Valley Forge National Park, Pennsylvania.* Denver: National Park Service, 1985.

Valley Forge Park Commission. *Report of the Valley Forge Park Commission, Commonwealth of Pennsylvania, January, 1947, to January, 1951.* Philadelphia: James Hogan, 1951.

Venzke, Rodger R. *Confidence in Battle, Inspiration in Peace: The United States Army Chaplaincy, 1945–1975.* Washington, D.C.: Office of the Chief of Chaplains, Department of the Army, 1977.

Vincitorio, Gaetano, ed. *Studies in Modern History.* New York: St. John's University Press, 1968.

Walker, Edwin A. *Pro Blue.* Dallas: American Eagle, 1965.

Walker, Howell. "Washington Lives Again at Valley Forge." *National Geographic,* February, 1954, 187–202.

Wamsley, Gary L. *Selective Service and a Changing America: A Study of Organizational Environmental Relationships.* Columbus, Ohio: C. E. Merrill, 1969.

Watts, Steven. *The Republic Reborn: War and the Making of Liberal America, 1790–1820.* Baltimore: Johns Hopkins University Press, 1987.

Watson, Mark S. "Two Years of Unification." *Military Affairs* 13 (winter, 1949): 193–97.

Watson, Robert J. *The Joint Chiefs of Staff and National Policy: 1953–1954.* Washington, D.C.: Historical Division, Joint Chiefs of Staff, GPO, 1986.

Weaver, Clyde E., and Chalmer E. Faw. "A Day with the Navy." *Christian Century,* July 2, 1952, 777–78.

Webb, Willard J., and Ronald H. Cole. *The Chairmen of the Joint Chiefs of Staff.* Washington, D.C.: Historical Division, Joint Chiefs of Staff, 1989.

Weems, Mason. *A History of the Life and Death, Virtues & Exploits of General George Washington,* ed. Mark Van Doren. New York: Macy-Masius, 1927.

Weigley, Russell Frank, comp. *The American Military: Readings in the History of the Military in American Society.* Reading, Mass.: Addison-Wesley, 1969.

Wesbrook, Stephen D. *Political Training in the United States Army: A Reconsideration.* Columbus: Mershon Center, Ohio State University, 1979.

Westin, Alan F. "Anti-Communism and the Corporations." *Commentary,* December, 1963, 479–87.

"What Happens When Protestants Are Caught Napping." *Christian Century,* July 5, 1944, 797–98.

Whillock, Rita Kirk. "Dream Believers: The Unifying Visions and Competing Values of Adherents to American Civil Religion." *Presidential Studies Quarterly* 24, no. 2 (spring, 1994): 375–88.

Whitfield, Stephen J. *The Culture of the Cold War.* Baltimore: Johns Hopkins University Press, 1990.

Wilcox, Clyde. *God's Warriors: The Christian Right in Twentieth-Century America.* Baltimore: Johns Hopkins University Press, 1992.

Wilkins, John R. "Three days in the Pentagon." *Christian Century,* March 12, 1952, 308–309.

Wilson, John F. *Public Religion in American Culture.* Philadelphia: Temple University Press, 1979.

Wohig, Dorothy T., ed. *The Papers of George Washington.* Revolutionary War Series, vol. 6. Charlottesville and London: University Press of Virginia, 1994.

Wolk, Herman S. "The Battle of the B-36." *Air Force,* July, 1996, 60–65.

Woods, Randall B. *Fulbright: A Biography.* New York: Cambridge University Press, 1995.

Wubben, H. H. "American Prisoners of War in Korea: A Second Look at the 'Something New in History' Theme." *American Quarterly* 22, no. 1 (spring, 1970): 3–19.

Yarmolinsky, Adam. *The Military Establishment.* New York: Harper and Row, 1971.

Index

Committee for Free Europe, 92
Committee on Public Information, 33
Common Council of American Unity,
    91–92
Communism on the Map, 151, 156, 158
Compton Commission, 68–69, 70
congressional committees, topics: Cold
    War seminars, 137–38, 141, 143, 148,
    151; communist activity, 150–51, 153;
    hippies at Valley Forge, 165; Korean
    POWs, 123–27; TI&E spiritual needs,
    70–71; UMT/Fort Knox experiment,
    69
congressional legislation: civil defense,
    87; military manpower, 40, 69–70;
    religious symbols, 105–106; space
    program, 113; UMT programs, 35, 65,
    66, 69; unification movement, 56, 57;
    USIS creation, 89
Continental Army, 4–6
Craig, Harold, 78
Creel Committee, 33
CTCA (Commission on Training Camp
    Activities), 31–32

D'Ascenzo, Nicola, 48
Davis, Elmer, 44, 102
"Dear Uncle," 151–52
Defense Strategy Seminars, 143–46
demobilization, World War II, 50–51, 55
democratization approach, Marshall's,
    39, 41–42, 51
Denfeld, Louis, 57
"The Devil and John Q.," 151
Devine, John M., 66–68, 69
Dewey Canyon III, 167
Divine, Robert, 113
Docherty, George M., 105
Doolittle Board, 51
Douglas, William O., 103
draft system, 30–31
Dulles, John Foster, 98, 104–105

education. *See* public schools
Eisenhower, Dwight D. (and administra-
    tion), 77; at Boy Scout Jamboree, 108;
    Cold War seminars, 136, 138;
    Columbia University presidency, 95–

96; Dulles' attitudes, 104–105; and
    Freedoms Foundation, 78–80;
    Graham's role, 99, 100–103; JCS role,
    139; and McCarthy, 116–18; Militant
    Liberty program, 127–31;
    neoevangelical movement, 55; New
    Look policy, 110–13, 139; Pledge of
    Allegiance, 105; and POW myth, 119–
    26; psychological warfare policies,
    113–15; public opinion, 115–16;
    summarized, 106
Elson, Edward L. R., 103
eugenics movement, 44
evangelicalism: military, 58, 59–64, 72–74,
    127–31; national, 53–55, 97–103. *See also*
    Cold War seminars

Fayetteville, Arkansas, 133–34
FCDA (Federal Civil Defense Adminis-
    tration), 87–89
Federal Civil Defense Act, 87
Federal Civil Defense Administration
    (FCDA), 87–89
Federal Council of Churches (FCC), 63,
    104
films/movies, 44–45, 72–73, 126, 129, 150–
    52
Fine, Benjamin, 75
Finnegan, John, 28
Fisher Body Corporation, 73
Ford, John, 129
Foreign Policy Research Institute (FRPI),
    143–44, 154–55
Forrestal, James V., 56, 57, 110
Fort Knox experiment, 66–70, 71
Fort Smith, 134–35
Fosdick, Raymond B., 29–30, 32–33
Freedom Forums, 152, 153
Freedoms Foundation, 77–80, 88–89, 133,
    152
Freedom Train, 86–87
"Fresh Laid Plans," 151
FRPI (Foreign Policy Research Institute),
    143–44, 154–55
Fulbright, James W., 135, 136–37, 160

gadget evangelism, 72–73
Ganus, Clifton Lloyd, Jr., 133–34, 157

Gates, Thomas, 140–41
General Electric, 152
General Order No. *21,* 140–41
Geneva Conventions, 124
Glenview Naval Air Station, 155–56, 157
Goffman, Erving, 63–64
Goldthwaite, Robert L., 137, 149–50, 157, 159, 160
Graham, Billy, 97–103, 118
Gray, Gordon, 92
Greene, Glenn A., 157
Guerilla Theater, 166–67
Gulf Power, 158

Hammer, Mike, 118
Hampton, Isaiah, 155–56
Hannah, James H., 121
Harding College, 148, 151–52, 157
Hargis, Billy James, 79, 146, 147, 153, *154*
Harness subcommittee, 69
Harrison, William K., 103
"Hate America" campaign, 90
Hearst, William Randolph, 97
Henry, Carl F. H., 53
Herndon, Rogers, 122
homosexuality, 117–18
Hoover, Herbert, 22, 38, 78
Hopley, Russell, 87
"Hours of Freedom," 96
Houston, Texas, 156
HUAC (House Un-American Activities Committee), 150–51
Hundley, Maury, 67
Hunter, Edward, 153
Hutton, Edward D., 78

ICAF (Industrial College of the Armed Forces), 138, 143, 145, 160
ICL (International Christian Leadership), 131
ideological programs: Militant Liberty, 127–31; and POW myth, 119–26; Truman's approach, 81–86. *See also* character education programs; Cold War seminars; psychological warfare policies
I&E (Information and Education Division), 45

immigrants, 11, 26, 32
Industrial College of the Armed Forces (ICAF), 138, 143, 145, 160
In Every War but One (Kinkead), 119
Information and Education Division (I&E), 45
Interallied Games, 33
International Christian Leadership (ICL), 131

Jackson, Charles Douglas "C.D.", 113–14
Jacobson, Louise, 159
Jam Handy Agency, 127
Johnson, Louis A., 57, 84
Joint Chief of Staffs: Cold War seminars, 139–40, 142, 143, 160; Eisenhower/Truman administrations contrasted, 139; Militant Liberty program, 127–29, 130–31; New Look policy, 112–13; unification movement, 56–58

Kellor, Frances, 26
Kennan, George F., 81, 84, 89
Kennedy, John F., 138
Kinkead, Eugene, 119, 123
Kinter, William R., 144
Kintner, William, 154–55
Knox, Henry, 12
Korean War, 86, 91, 108, 119–27
lavender scare, 117–18
"Letters from America," 91–92
Life magazine, 41
Little Orphan Annie, 78
Little Switch Operation, 121–22
"Long Telegram," 81
Loveland, Anne, 131
Lubbock, Texas, 157
Luce, Henry, 97

MacArthur, Douglas, 38, 48, 83
March to Calumny (Biderman), 119–20
Marine Corps, U.S., 130, 140–41
Marshall, George C.: Character Guidance Program, 71; citizenship programs, 95, 96; demobilization problems, 51; motivational approach, 39, 40–42, 46, 117; on spiritual morale, 52

ISBN 1-58544-378-6

9 781585 443789   90000